Life in 1940s
LONDON

About the Author

Mike Hutton is a London social historian. His previous books include *The Story of Soho* and *Life in 1950s London*. He lives on the border of Leicestershire and Northamptonshire.

Life in 1940s LONDON

MIKE HUTTON

AMBERLEY

For Tony Weber
A true Londoner and proud of it

First published 2013
This edition first published 2014

Amberley Publishing
The Hill, Stroud
Gloucestershire, GL5 4EP

www.amberley-books.com

British Library Cataloguing in Publication Data.
A catalogue record for this book is available from the British Library.

ISBN 978 1 4456 4378 6 (paperback)
ISBN 978 1 4456 3537 8 (ebook)

Typeset in 10pt on 12pt Sabon.
Typesetting and Origination by Amberley Publishing.
Printed in the UK.

Contents

Part 2: Peace

PART 1

War

1

The Day War Broke Out

She held the pearl-handled pistol to her head and pulled the trigger. Surely a girl familiar with guns on the grouse moors of Britain should have made a better job of her attempted suicide. Poor Unity Mitford made a terrible hash of it. She only succeeded in reducing her mental age to that of a twelve-year-old child. This became apparent when she was finally reunited with her family back in England. Earlier that afternoon Unity, the sister-in-law of Britain's own would-be fascist leader, Oswald Mosley, had gone to the Englisher Garten in Munich, distraught at the prospect of war between the country of her birth and her beloved Germany. She was seeking what she thought was an honourable release from an intolerable situation. The date was 3 September 1939. 'The day war broke out' became a popular catchphrase associated with the lugubrious comedian Rob Wilton; it was a day to be remembered by all those who were around at the time.

Throughout the country people crowded close to their wireless sets to hear the reedy voice of Prime Minister Neville Chamberlain conclude his broadcast: 'Now may God bless you and may he defend the right, for it is evil things that we will be fighting, brute force, bad faith, injustice, oppression and persecution, and against them I am certain right will prevail.'

Most of those listening were not so sure. The cast of the *Cherry Orchard* had gathered for final rehearsals at the Queen's Theatre. As the radio was switched off the first air-raid siren wailed its way down Shaftesbury Avenue. It was all too much for Edith

Evans who, losing any semblance of a stiff upper lip, screeched in alarm, 'I'm an actress. I can't do anything but act.' With tears flowing, she added, 'What am I to do? What's to become of me?' It was as if she expected to be sent off to the front line at any moment. Alec Guinness guided her out into the late summer sunshine to regain her composure.

Several miles away in East Ham, Jean Picton, a five-year-old child, witnessed a more measured, but no less profound, response to the news. She was too young to understand the full implications of the broadcast, but her grandmother's horrified reaction remained with her. Head in hands and rocking backwards and forwards in her armchair, the old lady kept repeating, 'Oh God, not again.' The horrors of the Great War remained, with few families left unscarred.

For Stan Willis, it was his wedding day. Not for him a sleek limousine to whisk him to the church. He walked all the way from Fulham to Putney, only to find that the bridge over the Thames had been shut due to the emergency. He arrived at the church just in time to meet his bride, May Hahn, hot and bothered after a lengthy detour. She was the daughter of a wealthy West End art dealer and her parents took a very dim view of her marrying a wood machinist with seemingly few prospects. The bride, however, was delighted to be marrying the man she loved and, doubtless, to be losing her Germanic surname. Despite her family having lived in London for several generations the strained atmosphere at the modest reception served to highlight the two chasms that existed in British society at the outbreak of war – class division and suspicion of all things foreign. Snobbishness and xenophobia formed a constant backdrop to everyday life.

London in 1939 was the greatest city in the world, both in size and influence. It was growing greedily as it pushed its borders ever deeper with the creation of new, leafy suburbs. Its population was in excess of 8 million, dwarfing all other British cities, of which only Glasgow exceeded 1 million. Its sprawling docks handled roughly a quarter of the country's imports and London was also a major hub for the distribution of goods throughout the regions. Still a major manufacturing centre, its output remained greater than any other British industrial city.

The Square Mile in the City of London dominated the world of banking and insurance, giving employment to thousands who commuted in each day. London was rich, its citizens earning more than their provincial cousins. Unfortunately, it was also a more expensive place in which to live. London was a centre of academic excellence – London University, Imperial College and the London School of Economics all enjoying international reputations, as did its leading public schools. London had a thriving cultural life with many West End theatres clustered around Shaftesbury Avenue (London's answer to Broadway). There was ballet and opera, art galleries and museums, housing many of the world's greatest treasures. It was also a royal capital. Despite the shock abdication of Edward VIII, the royal family retained a popularity that for once crossed the class divide.

So, on the surface London presented itself with a certain swagger, but another far less appealing version was never far away. This was a dirty, smelly, chaotic London, a direct counterpoint to the grandeur and pomp it liked to project. Its roads were often choked with traffic. Most of its thoroughfares had not been designed to take the volume of modern-day traffic. Horse-drawn wagons and hand carts were still common, inching their way forward wedged between towering red buses and cursing cab drivers. Away from the fashionable squares of Mayfair and Kensington, much of London remained almost Dickensian in its poverty. Across the capital, particularly in the East End, ancient alleys and courtyards survived with little sanitation and no electricity. Dwellings were damp with mildew and people lived huddled together in homes where the sun never penetrated. This London was grubby and soot stained. It was a city of smells. There was belching smoke, not only from coal fires favoured by most households, but also factories and backstreet workshops. It formed a backdrop to London life which often developed into a wall of fog in the winter. While nannies pushed heavy prams across Hyde Park and those living in suburbia mowed their lawns and clipped their privet hedges, elsewhere slaughterhouses and tanneries existed alongside humble terraced houses and tenements. Even taking a trip on a bus or the tube offered little comfort in an age when few paid much attention to personal hygiene.

Londoners were viewed with suspicion by those living in other parts of the country. In those days dress generally defined the wearer's social background. The working-class man wore his cloth cap almost as a badge of honour throughout the country, but few denied that the typical Londoner was different from his provincial cousin. He tended to be short in stature but quick in wit and never lost for a word. H. J. Massingham described how his 'astuteness, nonchalance, easy insufficient fellowship, bonhomie, casual endurance, grumbling gusto, shallowness, unconcern for anything but the passing moment, jackdaw love of glitter, picaresque adaptability and jesting spirit make up a unique individual'. In other words, a bit of a geezer! His female counterpart provided a perfect match.

Most men wore hats at the end of the 1930s, and these helped underscore their class stereotype. Bowlers and a dark suit indicated respectability and authority, as to a lesser extent did the homburg. Top hats were still common, particularly in the City, and proclaimed the wearer's status. It was left to the trilby to cross the class divide. Favoured by callow young men trying to ape the stars of the silver screen, it was also donned by many of the aspiring middle-class citizens. Separate again were the wide-boys, the spivs – all pencilled moustaches and loud suits. A woman's background was more difficult to pinpoint, but normally the quality of her shoes, handbag and makeup did the trick. The social divide permeated every corner of British life. It was complex and confusing, with each sector having subtle sub-divisions.

While snobbery was divisive, the population joined as one in their suspicion of foreigners. The pink of British influence spewed its way over the world map. Generations had been brought up to believe in British superiority. Teaching in schools endorsed this false assertion. There were few black or Asian faces to be seen. Large groups of foreigners were only found in clusters in areas like Clerkenwell and Soho. Anti-Semitism was common, particularly among the upper classes, many of whose beliefs differed little from those of Hitler. The *Daily Mirror* called them 'treacherous, upper crust riff-raff' who had championed the 'pale grey Ribbentrop'.

Even before war was declared, detailed plans had been drawn up for the evacuation of London's children. By September 1939 the exercise to get youngsters to the relative safety of the countryside was well underway. Main-line stations were clogged up with hordes of children, duly labelled, clutching their gas masks and a small bundle of essential belongings. While many were plucked away from their parents, five-year-old Brian Abbott, whose family lived in Penge, travelled with his mother, who lodged with him throughout a six-month stay in Theale, Berkshire. Others more fortunate, like twelve-year-old Pat Desbruslais, went from Finchley to stay with relatives in rural Yorkshire. Although not compulsory, the take-up of the scheme was far less than the authorities anticipated. Legions of scruffy kids, many from deprived backgrounds, arrived in a suspicious rural England, which led to much unhappiness. Many of the East End kids had never seen a field, let alone sheep and cattle. While a proportion found loving and caring homes, tales of abuse and cruelty filtered back. Some Jewish children were even forced to eat pork and attend church services. Within weeks there was a steady drift back to London, with parents opting to keep their children in a familiar environment and risk the consequences.

Protection from the expected air raids came with the installation of rudimentary air-raid shelters and the issuing of gas masks. Children under four years old were issued with a 'Mickey Mouse' version. Older children and adults were recommended to wear their masks for fifteen minutes a day in order to get used to them. My sister remembers how unpleasant they were to wear. It was difficult to breathe easily and rather frightening in appearance for a child. While not compulsory, everyone was encouraged to carry their mask. The John Lewis organisation warned their partners that failure to do so could lead to dismissal. Similar warnings were issued to those employed by Unilever. It was a fag having to carry the cumbersome mask cases everywhere and it didn't take long before doing so encouraged ribald comments from passers-by.

Despite there continuing to be no hint of air raids, the installation of Anderson shelters was in full swing. The shelters were supplied free for those on a small income, while a nominal charge was made for those better off. They were constructed of sheets of corrugated steel which were bolted together and sunk about 3 feet below ground. The entrance was protected by a steel roof and the shelter could accommodate up to half a dozen adults. Other than taking a direct hit, it was reckoned that the occupants would survive even the heaviest raid – that was providing you could endure the claustrophobic atmosphere and the damp. Many shelters flooded even after a brief shower. As a five-year-old, Jean Picton loved the shelter in her parents' garden in East Ham, which she called her 'fairy house'.

The face of London was changing, particularly at night, as it was forced into a prolonged period of darkness that was to last for the duration of the war. Familiar streets merged into a blackened maze. The blackout, stringently enforced by ARP wardens, was particularly welcomed by lines of prostitutes and small-time crooks, whose activities were helpfully masked. Initially, all theatres and places of entertainment were closed. The cast of the Windmill Theatre continued to rehearse, allowing the manager Vivian Van Damm famously to claim, 'We never closed.' Grumpy old George Bernard Shaw referred to the closures as 'a master stroke of unimaginative stupidity'. Sports that relied on outside floodlighting were doomed for the length of the war. Kew Gardens was mysteriously closed for the first few days of the war. What danger rare plants and specimen trees could unleash was unclear. Certainly, there were real dangers. A direct hit on London Zoo could have caused mayhem, so the elephants and pandas were despatched to Whipsnade, while the large cats and carnivores were retained in Regent's Park, but an armed keeper patrolled the cages in case of a direct hit. Poisonous snakes and spiders were destroyed, while the aquarium was drained and the fish either eaten or bottled for the benefit of future students. In truth, all over London a massive cull was taking place. Thousands of pet dogs and cats were put down, causing a plague of rats to engulf the capital. It is uncertain if the pet owners were trying to save their furry friends from the dreaded Hun or, more likely, to save on feeding costs.

Service uniforms became increasingly common as the year progressed. Even the sentries outside Buckingham Palace cast off their traditional uniforms in favour of drab khaki. Conscription was falteringly introduced in April 1939 and the prospect of war encouraged many volunteers. Ostensibly, those called up could choose which service they preferred. In reality, too many young men opted for the RAF or the Navy and were disappointed to be assigned to 'square bashing' in an Army unit. Food rationing was not introduced until January 1940, but in September 1939 each householder was required to fill in details of everyone living with them, after which identity cards were issued. These details were eventually used for the distribution of ration books. The effect of the war was gradually gaining pace. The Chancellor of the Exchequer, Sir John Simon, didn't help the national mood by increasing income tax from 5s to 7s 6d in the pound in September. He urged citizens to spend less at Christmas. Since when did Britain listen to politicians? Who knew what the future would bring? Londoners went on a spending spree, leaving most stores bare. My own father laid in a store of tinned fruit. Each Sunday for much of the war we enjoyed a treat of peaches or pineapple. As a net importer of food, it was essential for Britain that every available plot of land was used for cultivation. In October the Minister of Agriculture championed the spread of allotments, even in urban areas. A service was broadcast from St Martin-in-the-Fields publicising the project. Allotments started to appear all over London like acne on a teenager's face. Eventually, even London's leading parks succumbed to a tide of enthusiastic vegetable growers.

Meanwhile, while thousands of children were returning to London after a brief encounter with an unfamiliar countryside, many of the well-to-do were travelling in the opposite direction. Dust sheets were in short supply as numerous grand houses were mothballed. Others were put up for sale but found few buyers. Petrol rationing, introduced in September, had the effect of reducing road congestion as people squirreled away their allowance for emergencies. Numbers of London taxis were acquired by the auxiliary fire services, ensuring public transportation was constantly crowded.

In times of stress we all tend to seek entertainment to take our minds off what has been worrying us. So it was throughout the first weeks of the war. Happily, the government allowed theatres and cinemas to re-open after a few days in what they described as 'safe areas'. Golders Green was the unlikely setting for the reopening of *The Importance Of Being Ernest* on 14 September to a blaze of publicity. John Gielgud declared they were all thrilled to be back, although he intimated that he expected to be called up at any time. He wasn't, as, together with many other actors, he was granted exemption. This choice was not extended to ballet dancers, who were generally considered to be 'queer' by the authorities, and the existing prejudice of the day required them to toughen up and serve their country. While the West End theatre and music hall remained popular, it was to the cinema that most flocked to seek their escapism. Massive picture houses dominated Leicester Square, while others clustered around Regent Street and the Haymarket. The suburbs also hosted some of the country's most extravagant cinemas. In Tooting, the extraordinary Granada was based on the Alhambra palace in Spain. Many suburbs supported three or four choices and still queues snaked their way outside as patient customers waited for the second house. News cinemas were also popular – although footage of German tanks advancing across Poland gave cause for concern, but for the time being London was strangely normal. True, the West End was crowded and somehow more vibrant. There was an air of expectation, even excitement, particularly among the young.

An outlet was needed for this sense of expectation, and many found it in the huge variety of dance halls. Even the fashionable Café de Paris lowered its social guard somewhat. Where previously men in tailed suits had danced with jewel-bedecked socialites, now even lounge suits and uniforms (preferably officers') were admitted. The middle classes had stormed the barricades of privilege; the clientele as much Kingsbury as Kensington. Across the river in Streatham, over a thousand people crushed together at the Locarno. Not to be outdone, the Paramount in Tottenham Court Road promoted a jitterbug marathon, attended by 1,400 gyrating youngsters. The dance craze had been imported from America and the parents of Middle England lamented seeing their daughters losing all sense of decorum.

Dancing at London's luxury hotels tended to be jolly rather than abandoned. Geraldo played at the Savoy, while Ambrose alternated between the Thameside Venue and the Mayfair Hotel. Vera Lynn, who had spent several years with Charlie Kunz and his Casani Club orchestra, recorded 'Two Sleepy People' with Denny Dennis together with Ambrose and his orchestra in 1938. In June the following year, she again featured with Bert Ambrose on 'If I Didn't Care' on Decca. The soon-to-be-anointed 'forces' sweetheart' was waiting to take her place in Britain's popular music hierarchy. She was to be the star now, not the bandleader as had previously been the case. It is strange that although the war threw up other leading female singing sensations, few British male singers obtained star status. The one who became popular after his death was Al Bowlly, who was killed by a German bomb in 1941. The other was not British either. Leslie Hutchinson (Hutch) did make it. Born in Grenada, he arrived in London in 1927 and acquired the accent and bearing of an English gentleman. As his popularity spread, he was able to buy his suits in Savile Row, shirts in Jermyn Street and he rode in Rotten Row. A superb pianist with a rather thin, affected voice, he became a sought-after attraction. A long line of society women, including Edwina Mountbatten, also sought him out, as did Princess Marina of Greece. Extremely attractive as a young man, his list of lovers was not confined to women and included Ivor Novello and Cole Porter. By 1939 he was already a recording star of many years standing. That year his releases included 'You Go To My Head', 'Begin The Beguine' and 'I Get Along Without You Very Well'.

As the year drew to a close, people were becoming accustomed to evenings living in a darkened world. Restaurants and clubs, which had been deserted, began to attract custom again. It had been strange to have a Guy Fawkes Night without a single firework being let off. Neither had a single bomb exploded in London – not a German one, that is. In June 1939 on a Saturday evening six bombs did explode around Regent Street, planted by members of the IRA. One was near the Monico Restaurant on Piccadilly Circus, another close behind the Quadrant and more in Sackville Street. Although there were injuries to passers-by, miraculously no-one was killed.

The Times reported that the police hoped crowds heading for Trafalgar Square to see in the new year would be smaller than normal. In the event, only an intrepid few turned up. The fact that New Year's Eve fell on a Sunday guaranteed this. Hotels were granted an extension until 2.00 a.m. on the Monday. A few weeks' purdah had proved quite enough for London's brave band of socialites, and the capital's swankiest hotels enjoyed a bumper evening. Previously unconsidered underground spaces were spruced up to welcome fashionable guests. Celebrations were hectic and more poignant than usual in the knowledge that many of the young men dancing the night away would shortly have far more onerous challenges to face. Pubs were also granted an extension to 12.15 a.m., a rarity for a Sunday night. Many in London stayed out to see in the new year – a new decade. Beneath the bonhomie, even the least sensitive must have pondered their future. Few could have foreseen the length of the conflict, hardship and terror to come. Yet many were to claim that the war years were the happiest of their lives. Unfortunately, five years later, thousands of Londoners were unable to voice their opinion.

2

The Lull Before the Storm

Londoners can be a bolshie lot. By the beginning of 1940 they were in top gear. They had been warned to expect a firestorm unleashed by the Luftwaffe, and what happened? Nothing. It was impossible to believe anything the politicians said. Many considered that their children had been evacuated without good cause. The general mood among Londoners was sour. Moaning had become a national pastime. By contrast, the government was worried by what they judged to be the complacency that was widespread across the capital. They knew that the 'phoney war', as it was to become known, was unlikely to last long. A persistent view had spread that somehow London was impervious to attack. This was underlined by the royal family still living in Buckingham Palace. That, without doubt, would be a prime target, and if there was any real danger surely the king and his family would be shipped abroad or at least to the country?

Still, there was plenty for Londoners to feel unhappy about. It was the coldest winter in years and coal was in short supply. The roads and pavements were like skating rinks, while water pipes froze, adding to the general sense of gloom. Food rationing was introduced on 8 January – Happy New Year, everyone! Britain had long shifted from being a largely agricultural society and was now dependant on food imports. Matters were made worse by lurking German U-Boats, which were to terrorise the merchant fleet. At first, rationing was targeted on basic foodstuffs, including sugar, butter and bacon. By March the net had been extended to include meat, milk, tea, cheese, eggs and cereals. Even jam and tinned fruit were brought under the increasing rationing umbrella. Fish was not rationed, but expensive because of restricted supplies. News of a delivery to a fishmonger spread quickly and in no time a queue formed. Queuing became the norm and was a constant source of irritation. Life was humdrum and time-consuming. Every household had to register with a shop (or shops if they preferred different suppliers) to guarantee their sparse supplies. The beige-coloured ration books became as important to a housewife as the money in her purse. Initially the shopkeepers were required to snip out the appropriate coupons and return them to their local food office. It soon became obvious that this scheme was an administrative nightmare and by the beginning of 1941 a more sensible stamping of the appropriate coupon was introduced. The theory was that supplies to shops should equate to the number of customers registered, hardly an exact science. As supplies became limited, so prices rose. This led to heated arguments, scuffles and minor outbreaks of violence as some traders even attempted to raise prices above those stated on the packaging. Clothes rationing was not introduced until June 1941. Although fashion shopping was no longer enjoyable with the eking out of coupons, by 1941 the population had more pressing problems to contend with. But not just yet.

During the early part of the war, Albert Knight (known as Rocky) lived in Dame Street, Islington. As an eight-year-old he remembers the area being largely working class, unlike the gentrified status Islington enjoys today. True, the same Georgian and Victorian houses dominated, but they were yet to be inhabited by bankers and hedge-fund managers. His parents occupied the ground floor of a terraced house. His father was a compositor on the *Daily Mail*. Their living was basic by today's standards, but fairly typical of many Londoners. The kitchen was in the basement and contained a solid fuel brick copper. The dining room had a wrought-iron range, which had to be cleaned daily with blacking. There was also a small sitting room and the three bedrooms were on the ground floor. There was a small toilet but no bathroom. Linoleum rather than carpets lined the floors and lighting was supplied by wall-mounted gas lights.

Without regular deliveries of coal they were unable to cook or keep warm, and welcome supplies were made by a horse-drawn cart. The coalman wore a kind of leather hood that extended to his shoulders for protection. The huge sacks were emptied through a grill directly into the coal shed situated in their small back garden.

By today's standards many would have been considered to be living in poverty, and yet the Knights would certainly not have thought of themselves as in that category. They were relatively well-to-do. How perceptions change! Life was hard and austere. Food for most was basic, but on the whole healthy. It was rare to see anyone much overweight, and certainly not obese.

While for the moment London was being spared from attack, elsewhere on the battlefront the news was bleak. The members of Britain's cabinet were at odds with one another as the outlook worsened. On 4 April Prime Minister Chamberlain was again too optimistic in his assertion that 'Hitler had missed the boat'. Within a week Germany had invaded Denmark, which was overrun in a day. Our own troops were forced to retreat in Norway. It seemed the German tide was irresistible and it appeared only a matter of time before it would be our turn. On 8 May, in a charged atmosphere in the House of Commons, Tory MP Leo Amery addressed Chamberlain, invoking the words of Oliver Cromwell: 'I say let us have done with you. In the name of God, go.' He went. A good man whom history has treated badly. Perhaps it was a case of being the wrong man in power at the wrong time. He stood back for the right man, albeit one with many stains and flaws. His time had come.

The following week the new Prime Minister, Winston Churchill, also addressed the House with the first of a series of stirring wartime speeches. Did it stiffen the resolve of the British people for what lay ahead? Probably. Here was an elderly, yet somehow reassuring, figure. Pugnacious, bloody-minded, a showman, a natural communicator and orator. His seemingly easy flow of words would, however, have been rehearsed in front of a mirror to accentuate every phrase and movement to achieve maximum effect. This information was relayed to my father by Sir Timothy Bligh, a close associate of Churchill. With his stance hunched like that of a prize fighter and his voice growling with emotion, he told the country he offered them nothing 'but blood, toil and sweat'. This was language the man in the street understood. No more appeasement, rather a scrap, a real punch-up. He continued that now the country was out to 'wage war by sea, by land and air, with all the strength God can give us … against a monstrous tyranny never surpassed in the dark, lamentable catalogue of human crime'. We were to seek victory, 'victory, victory at all costs, victory in spite of all the terror, victory however long and hard the road may be, for without victory there is no survival…'

Britain had found a man to follow and pin their hopes to. Most were buoyed and enthused, except his wife Clementine, who, writing from Downing Street in June following his stirring 'We shall fight them on the beaches' speech, brought him down to earth with a bump. A mutual friend had told her that Winston was in danger of being disliked by his colleagues and staff by his 'rough, sarcastic and overbearing manner'. She went on to chide him for his contemptuousness to colleagues, 'that is so bad that no ideas are offered either good or bad for fear of a put down.' Underlining her thoughts further, she tells him he needs to 'combine urbanity, kindness and, if possible, Olympic calm … besides you won't get the best results by irascibility and rudeness'. She was probably the only person in the country able to give such good advice.

Churchill had every reason to feel grumpy. A month earlier the retreat from Dunkirk had been portrayed as a miracle. Indeed it was, with over 300,000 British and French troops being rescued by an extraordinary improvised fleet of small boats from under the gaze of the Germans. Churchill, quite rightly, noted that 'wars are not won by evacuations'. However, by the middle of the year the mood in London had changed. Sure, life was still grim and the outlook uncertain, but it was as if the weather reflected a more upbeat public mood. The cold, bitter winter had given way to a summer of long, sunlit days. Although understandably worried about their prospects, many now exhibited an outward sense of bravado. Maybe it was the sight of so many servicemen thronging the streets. Not just British troops either. There were Australian soldiers with their distinctive slouch hats and other Commonwealth troops from New Zealand and Canada.

There were tough-looking Polish airmen and Czechs mingling with French sailors, Dutch and even a few Norwegians who had managed to escape the advancing Germans. This was a heady brew to add to the already crowded streets. An array of uniforms, a gabble of foreign languages. It was almost as if London had become a frontier town overnight. With so many allies the possibility of defeat seemed inconceivable. To the young office workers and shop girls, the West End now offered a sense of romance. These were exciting times. Not all extended a warm welcome to the newcomers. The free French were much in evidence. They tended to congregate around the York Minster pub in Dean Street. It became known (and still is today) as 'the French pub', or just 'the French'. It was from a small room above the bar that General Charles de Gaulle called on the free French to fight on against the Germans and the Vichy Government of Marshall Pétain. Although the speech was not heard by many in France, its message was and served as a rallying cry to carry on the fight. While Londoners generally admired de Gaulle, this admiration did not extend to most of his compatriots. Too easily defeated in the eyes of many, they had left Britain vulnerable. They strutted like peacocks, gossiped and intrigued and were not generally trusted. This dislike was not shared by many young women, who found them dashing and exciting. They were resented by British troops, in a forerunner to the problems encountered with the Americans, who tended to nab all the best-looking girls. The Australians and other Commonwealth troops were generally welcomed and any trouble surrounding them tended to centre on drunkenness and fighting. The Dutch congregated around 'De Hems' in Macclesfield Street in Soho, and it was left to the Poles to get the overall stamp of approval from the Londoners. This reputation was reinforced later when stories of their fearless escapades during the Battle of Britain surfaced.

The relative warmth shown towards foreign and Commonwealth troops did not extend to foreigners and refugees generally. This was underlined when on 10 June Benito Mussolini announced to cheering crowds in Rome that Italy was at war with Britain and France. There was an immediate backlash against Italians and the businesses they ran. The whole

Italian community was targeted, not helped by Churchill's exhortation to the authorities to 'collar the lot'. Italians of both sexes from seventeen to seventy who had lived in the country for less than twenty years were rounded up. Throughout London gangs targeted Italian shops, ice-cream parlours and restaurants, smashing their windows and trashing their stock. German businesses had suffered a similar fate the year before, but many Italians were shocked by the virulence and spitefulness of the attacks. Placards were put up in shop windows claiming to be Swiss, but to no avail. In Soho a group of women marched down Old Compton Street intent on harming neighbours with whom previously they had enjoyed good relations. This, in a community drawn from across the globe which prided itself on co-existence. The women were confronted by Rosie Blau, a Jewish woman who shamed them into dispersing. Jews, though, were also being constantly criticised. Jealousy and resentment of Jews bubbled away across all sections of society.

Italians made up a large part of London's catering and hotel trade. Many owned their own businesses, while a huge number worked as waiters or in the kitchens of London's top hotels and restaurants. The police used Churchill's instructions to nab many from the Italian underworld that they had been longing to lay their hands on. Darby Sabini, the leader of London's most notorious pre-war gang, was interned, during which time his son was killed while on active service with the RAF. More respectable, established figures from the Italian community were also rounded up, including the Quaglino brothers and Peppino Leoni, owner of the famous Quo Vadis restaurant. These were respected men who had lived in Britain for many years. It cut no ice, they were packed off to Lingfield Racecourse, before being herded to a disused cotton mill in Bury. Denials of Italian nationality were ignored by the authorities. Bertorelli's in Charlotte Street displayed a notice stating that the owners were British, whose sons (like Darby Sabini's) were serving in the British Forces. It made no difference. Life in the Bury camp was foul. Most slept on straw palliasses, while others had to endure bare boards. Sanitation was primitive, with less than twenty cold water taps for some 2,000 inmates. The food was disgusting, all the more so for famous restaurateurs, and to cap it all the roof leaked. Internment was all-encompassing and in many cases unfair, but it served to satisfy the public's distrust of foreigners. Perhaps those in Bury and other internment camps were the lucky ones. A deal was done with the Canadian government for them to take a large consignment of Italian internees. Some 1,500 of them, together with 400 British troops, set sail in the former Blue Star cruiser SS *Arandora Star*. This was to be no luxury cruise. As well as appallingly cramped conditions, news filtered back to Britain of guards stealing and using physical violence on the Italian passengers; hardly the picture fed to us as wartime children of British fair play that set us apart from other nations. It has never been explained why the ship did not carry the Red Cross emblem, but it was torpedoed by a German U-Boat off the coast of Ireland, with the loss of 700 men.

Not only foreigners were interned. On 13 April, six weeks after the birth of their fourth child, Max, the Mosleys drove to their flat in Dolphin Square to be confronted by the police with a warrant for Sir Oswald's arrest. He was shipped off to Brixton prison, despite not being charged or sent for trial. Although by now he was perhaps the most hated man in Britain he had never done anything illegal and he was certain the matter would be swiftly resolved. Many of Mosley's old British Union of Fascists chums were also detained in Brixton. Without her knowledge, his wife Diana was put under surveillance. On 29 June she was also taken into custody and sent to Holloway. Diana declined the offer to take her baby with her, opting to leave him in the safety of the country with his nurse. She had a rough reception in Holloway, being given a dirty basement cell with no window. She slept on a thin mattress placed directly onto a damp floor. Eventually, she was given a better cell which, although tiny, was at least dry. It was acknowledged that although she had met Hitler as recently as 1939, Diana's only crime was being married to Sir Oswald. Despite numerous enquiries and appeals, the Mosleys remained in their separate jails for eighteen months. It was thought that their release would enrage public opinion. The late summer of 1940 was particularly stressful for Diana. Writing to Violet Hammersley, she recalled,

Ten hours is too long of concentrated noise and terror. The screaming bombs ... simply make your flesh creep ... The great fires everywhere, the awful din that never stops and wave after wave of aeroplanes, ambulances tearing up the street and the horrible unnatural blaze of searchlights ... In every street you can see a sinister little piece roped off with red lights round it or roofs blown off, or every window out of a house ...

That is surely as good a description as any of what Londoners were having to endure at the height of the Blitz.

Eventually, following a supper with Diana's brother Tom, it was Churchill who came up with a solution. Oswald was transferred to Holloway and the couple were granted a small apartment in the grounds of the prison. It was a strange arrangement that entitled them to cook their own meals and tend a small plot of vegetable garden. They were finally released in 1943 but kept under house arrest. It was reckoned that Mosley had spent £100,000 (a huge sum then) of his own money championing the British Union of Fascists. Even into old age, the couple clung unashamedly to their far-right-wing views.

The fall of much of Europe led to an influx of refugees. They too were viewed with suspicion. Distress at their misfortune tended to be short-lived as perceived defects were soon found. Belgians were considered dirty (hardly surprising following their ordeal in reaching London). Cricklewood was one of the areas designated for their re-housing. The locals were hardly welcoming. The Belgian children were denied access to local play groups and there were reports of refugees being booed in London streets. Despite its reputation for warmth and harmonious living alongside a host of nationalities, the East End was no more welcoming. Again, newcomers from France and Holland were accused of being dirty and smelly. Memories appeared to be short. There was a distinct lack of charity being extended across the capital, no more so than in Kensington. Here, well-to-do citizens were appalled to find two blocks of luxury flats had been assigned to families from Malta. Locals sniffed their displeasure at these people's strange personal habits. Worse still, they infested the shops and snapped up the few delicacies still on offer; this was too much to bear with one's servants having gone AWOL to join the forces or work in some wretched factory. There were, of course, those who did their best to welcome the unfortunate refugees and extend a charitable spirit to those interned, but a sense of distrust in foreigners was planted deep in the British psyche. It was, of course, a time of stress for most Londoners too, with many men-folk away on service duty. Constant shortages and a fear of the future all served to promote self-interest. Few of us like change when it is forced upon us. The stress of war was to bring out the very best and the worst in Londoners.

It was still possible to have a stab at normality; to try and ignore the constant reminder of war. Cinemas and theatres played to full houses. What better way to escape everyday worries. Radio also became an important part in most people's lives, with the BBC offering a mixture of news, music and comedy. An inter-services cricket match at Lords drew a near-capacity crowd, while the summer exhibition at the Royal Academy was deemed a great success, with the number of exhibits well up on 1939. Augustus John, who had resigned as a Royal Academician in 1938, was re-elected in 1940. From his studio in Pelham Street SW7, four portraits and a painting of *Blue Cineraria* (which was purchased for the nation by the Chantrey Trust) were selected. L. S. Lowry also had two works chosen, including his famous offering of *The Mill Gates*. Music continued to play an important part in Londoners' lives. The season of Henry Wood Promenade Concerts started on 10 August at the Queen's Hall. Ann Shelton recorded 'A Nightingale Sang in Berkeley Square' with Bert Ambrose and his orchestra. These diversions could not hide the increasing preparations for war, which were visible all over London. Anti-aircraft guns vied for space with mounted searchlights, while above barrage balloons swayed gently in the summer breeze.

Any doubts that the war was about to arrive in London were dispelled by the third of Churchill's speeches to the House of Commons since the outbreak of hostilities. On 18 June he stated, 'I expect the Battle of Britain is about to begin.' In an appeal to the British people he concluded, 'Let us therefore brace ourselves in our duties and so bear ourselves that if the British Empire and Commonwealth last for a thousand years men will say this was their finest hour.' Words no more win wars than military evacuations, but throughout the country young men were preparing to honour his prediction. There remains disagreement regarding the starting date for the Battle of Britain. 10 July saw the first raids on the British mainland. A systematic bombing of southern British ports and airports was put into effect. Terry Norton, a young boy then living in Wallington in Surrey, remembers being fascinated by seeing the sky filled with sinister German bombers. Like others living in the suburbs, watching deadly dogfights against a bright summer sky became something of a bizarre spectator sport. The first bomb to land in the London area had been dropped earlier in June when a goat was killed in a field near Colney. What prompted real alarm in London came with the bombing of Croydon Airport on 15 August, just two days after Hitler's Day of the Eagle, the codename for the German operation to destroy the RAF. This was to be a prelude to the invasion of Britain known as Operation *Sea Lion*. The bombing at Croydon destroyed the terminal building where only a few months previously well-heeled travellers had sat reading and drinking cocktails prior to their flights to fashionable European resorts. Hangars and stores were also wrecked, together with factories situated close to the airport. In all, sixty-eight people were killed in a foretaste of what London would shortly have to endure. A single Luftwaffe pilot who lost his bearing during a raid may well have affected the eventual outcome of the war. Thinking he was despatching his incendiaries over the Short Brothers factory in Rochester, he inadvertently dropped the first incendiary bombs over a part of residential London. Churchill was incensed. The next day over eighty British aircraft headed for Berlin. Although many lost their way en route, they dropped their bombs in and around Berlin. Little damage was done, except to Hitler's pride. He had vowed that no enemy planes would ever bomb Berlin. Crucially, and disastrously from a German perspective, he was to switch the attention of the Luftwaffe away from bombing British ports and his vowed destruction of RAF fighter command. Instead, he ordered the Blitzkrieg of London. It is possible that this single decision saved Britain from defeat – a case of an inflated ego triumphing over hard facts and common sense.

Although it was a week after the onset of the Blitz, 15 September is the day celebrated as Battle of Britain Day. Goering arranged two major daylight raids in an attempt to finally crush the RAF. Over 200 Luftwaffe bombers and fighter escorts were routed. As the retreating Germans were pursued it was realised in Berlin that Luftwaffe losses were unsustainable. Two days later, Hitler shelved Operation *Sea Lion* indefinitely. The young airmen of the RAF had bought Britain time. It was now the turn of Londoners to have their spirit and resolve tested to the limit.

3

The Blitz

> It is not the walls that make the city, but the people who live
> within them. The walls of London may be battered, but the
> spirit of the Londoner stands resolute and undismayed.
>
> King George VI

'Look, London's burning.' My mother had plucked me from my
bed and parted the blackout curtains. Seen through bleary eyes,
this was perhaps my earliest memory; a crimson sky to the east
as far as the eye could see. I was far too young to understand the
full implications of the inferno but my mother, in common with
many others at that time, realised she was witnessing a historic
event; the start of the Blitz on London. For those living in the
East End it was to be a time of terror. A time which would test
the strongest nerves and, for those who survived, a time they
would never forget.

Earlier on that glorious summer afternoon of 7 September
1940, young Terry Norton was again attracted by a strange
humming noise. Glancing skywards he saw a swarm of German
bombers and fighter planes heading towards the docks lining the
Thames. It was just before five o'clock in the afternoon when
the airborne armada reached its target. An hour later they had
gone, leaving behind a trail of chaos, death and destruction. The
Thames, the very source of London's growth and prosperity, now
acted as a magnet for its intended destruction. As the next wave
of bombers arrived at just gone eight o'clock, the reflections

from the moon acted as a silent seductress, leading and guiding the hundreds of enemy planes. The Surrey commercial docks were ablaze. A timber warehouse helped spread the fire. Rows of modest terraced houses surrounding the docks were destroyed. For those on the ground trying to cope, it was as if the whole world was on fire. The blaze spread to the London docks and a paint factory. The air was acrid and foul. At least one German plane lost its bearings and dropped its load on fashionable Pont Street in the West End. It was West Ham, though, and Bermondsey that were taking the brunt of the assault, which spread out to include Bow, Whitechapel, Poplar, Stepney and Shoreditch. These were areas of extremely high-density population, and which endured crowded slum conditions. This was an indignity that old London had never experienced before. Fires raged out of control, with the fire brigade unable to cope. A dreadful stench hung over the area. Burning rubber, tar and paint combined to form a lung-rasping cocktail. The night left over 400 dead, and with roads blocked it was difficult for ambulances to gain access. Soon the sweet, sickly smell of sugar was added to the mix as a moored Tate & Lyle barge was hit. Flames leapt hundreds of feet skyward, creating an eerie, hellish light. The fire was so intense that the old Thames itself was alight. In the West End, miles away, it was possible to read a newspaper (despite the blackout) from the frightening glow.

Three days earlier, Hitler, enraged at the killings caused by the RAF raid on Berlin, had promised revenge. To rapturous applause he had boasted, 'We will raze their cities to the ground.' It was no idle boast – for months Londoners endured a relentless bombardment. In a sense it underlined the failure of the Luftwaffe to win the aerial battle that became known as the Battle of Britain.

The day following the initial assault, Winston Churchill visited the worst-affected areas. Worries had been expressed about the effect of the devastation on civilian morale. He was met with a chorus of 'Good old Winston' and 'We can take it!' There was the odd dissenting voice, but overall the visit was a propaganda success. That night the bombers returned, inflicting another 400 fatalities and a further still 300 on 9 September. St Katherine's

Dock was completely gutted in one of the heaviest raids of the war. Once more flames rose 200 feet skywards and a cocktail of burning produce deepened the stinking air, attacking the eyes and throat. And still the daily carnage continued.

Schoolchildren were practising fire drill and being trained on how to cope during an attack. Some guidance was truly bizarre. Jean Picton, who lived with her parents in East Ham (one of the worst-affected areas), was instructed by her form teacher that 'on the word "go" all of us children were to run as fast as we could to our neighbouring homes, touch our Anderson shelter and then run back to school'. She still remembers the look on her mother's face as, flushed and breathless, having banged on the front door she pushed past, running hell for leather into the back garden. She then touched the shelter before running back through her house shouting 'can't stop' to her mother, who shouted after her, 'What on earth is going on?' The teacher timed all the children as they staggered back, but Jean still has no idea what the weird exercise was supposed to achieve. Her memories of the Blitz are of being carried downstairs and into the Anderson shelter; 'It was cold, damp and musty, even in the summer.' She remembers hearing thuds and bangs that woke her up. One morning they emerged to the smell of burning and dust hanging in the air. The row of houses backing onto their garden had completely disappeared, leaving just a pile of smouldering rubble. Shortly afterwards, the houses opposite were hit and she was fascinated by the way that half a house was left gaping open to the elements with furniture from an upstairs bedroom hanging at a crazy angle, teetering on the edge. This became a common sight. It was an unwelcome intrusion of privacy as a curious public looked on.

Across London, to the north in Islington, Rocky Knight remembers being prevented from going home because an entire row of shops just 100 yards from his house had been destroyed. Rescue workers could hear a ticking which they assumed was a bomb. After careful investigation an alarm clock was discovered. Both Rocky and Jean, in common with most youngsters, can remember collecting shrapnel which was often still hot following a raid. Jean thought them 'quite beautiful, very jagged with sharp bits'. They were silver, blue or pink and girls looked upon them as jewels. Children swapped examples among themselves to improve their collection. My own prized piece was a brass cone from an incendiary bomb.

Rocky Knight's father worried about the continual bombardment and thought he was lucky when he was drafted up to Coventry to work in an engineering factory. He found lodgings in a house near his work and on 10 November the family moved up to join him. Four days later, the Luftwaffe turned their attention to Coventry with a twelve-hour blitz that flattened much of the city. It seemed for some there was no escaping the war.

The Luftwaffe had already extended their bombing of London to the financial centre of the city. Night after night the bombs were unleashed, injuring thousands and causing hundreds of fatalities. London's infrastructure was creaking under the endless attacks. Road and rail travel were severely disrupted. Gas mains were fractured and electricity supplies affected, with leading hospitals also sustaining damage. Walking was usually accompanied by the sound of crunching glass that festooned the streets. On 13 September Buckingham Palace was bombed. That afternoon the king and queen visited the East End. They received an enthusiastic reception. There was now a sense that bombs held no respect for position or privilege. The visit was again a huge propaganda plus.

As the bombing continued the public mood worsened considerably. People were very unhappy about the lack of public shelters and anti-aircraft fire. The skies were being left open so that our intercepting fighter planes could operate without the danger of attracting friendly fire. This had not been made clear to the public and resentment quickly deepened. What anti-aircraft fire there was proved ineffective until the introduction of radar. It was estimated that some 30,000 shells were being fired to secure a direct hit that would bring an enemy aircraft down. They were more likely to cause damage to factories and houses, but the sound of defensive gunfire did help the flagging morale. For a period, our own gunfire killed more civilians than enemy pilots. Exposed to endless nights of bombing, Londoners were desperate to seek safe shelters and underground tube stations seemed the obvious choice. This had been discouraged by the previous Home Secretary, the austere Sir John Anderson. As early as 8 September a huge crowd congregated outside Liverpool Street station and demanded entrance. Troops were called to reinforce beleaguered officials but eventually the doors were opened. Then it was every man for himself. There were unseemly scuffles as everyone sought what they thought was a favoured spot. Overnight it became London's largest air-raid shelter. By the beginning of October the former Mayor of Hackney and now Home Secretary, Herbert Morrison, succumbed, with the support of Churchill, and got many underground stations opened as night-time shelters. No-one was allowed to stake a claim before 4.00 p.m. and the platforms had to be totally cleared to allow the smooth running of the trains the following morning.

The clamour for public shelters had intensified following a huge raid on central London in the early hours of 17/18 September. The whole of Oxford Street from Tottenham Court Road along its entire length to Marble Arch was affected. Fires raged out of control, acting as a guide for the next wave of bombers. By the morning the John Lewis store was a gutted wreck. The journalist Kingsley Martin, getting rather carried away, referred to it as being 'like the ruins of a Greek temple'.

Both Peter Robinson and Selfridges were also hit. Three floors of the Peter Robinson store, built in 1924, had been destroyed and yet four days later it was trading again, despite its boarded-up frontage. Bourne & Hollingsworth also showed resourcefulness, for despite being badly hit they traded through a massive gap in their frontage, passing purchases to customers waiting on the pavement outside. The extent of damage to the building was partly camouflaged by rows of bunting. It was the John Lewis store that really caught the public imagination. Defying the massive damage to their building, they sold the little stock that was not ruined on the pavement alongside piles of dress models that looked uncannily like corpses. Waring and Gillow remained closed until an unexploded bomb was defused. It was reckoned that about 10 per cent of bombs failed to explode on impact. This caused constant disruption, with roads often having to be closed off for days.

October initially saw a lessening of the raids, but all this changed on the night of 15 October. A night of the full moon, some 400 bombers droned their way over London, killing hundreds and leaving over 1,000 people seriously injured. Within six months of his resignation Neville Chamberlain was struck down by cancer. Even in death, the war continued to intrude. A memorial service was held in November 1940 at Westminster Abbey. It was un-heated and freezing cold; the wind whipped through windows blasted by bombs. Members of the Cabinet, headed by Churchill, huddled in their overcoats to pay their last respects. In the background an air-raid siren wailed, not even allowing Chamberlain to make a peaceful exit.

Along with Westminster Abbey, St Paul's Cathedral was one of the most iconic sites in London and, as such, a constant target for the Luftwaffe. Christopher Wren was supposedly responsible for the design of over fifty churches, Temple Bar, the Custom House and numerous company halls, but his masterpiece was surely St Paul's. For all the work he created during his long lifetime, he remained content to be paid a salary of £200 a year. He was guided by a sense of public duty rather than the greed now synonymous with the City of London. He was forty-three when the first stone of the cathedral was laid. He was still around thirty-four years later when the last stone was placed to complete the building that is so associated with London across the world.

The cathedral lived a charmed life during the Blitz, while all around ancient buildings and alleyways were smashed and incinerated. In September 1940 a delayed action bomb fell close to the clock tower. It caused a huge, 20-foot crater and the device was transported to Hackney Marsh where it was detonated. This time a hideous hole over 100 feet in diameter was created. On 10 October a bomb fell through the roof and destroyed the high altar. Then the cathedral received another direct hit in April 1941, but the nearest the building came to destruction happened on the frightening night of 29 December 1940. The area was peppered with incendiary bombs, causing a hellish inferno. Paternoster Row was razed to the ground and with it some 4 million priceless books. The iconic photograph taken from the roof of the *Daily Mail* office in Tudor Street shows the cathedral standing proud and unbowed amid the mayhem.

Jean Clarke was an eight-year-old in 1940 and lived in Barking. At her local school they had to assemble in a corridor with a reinforced roof during a raid. Bombing was now a daily event. At night she was sent to bed wearing warm clothes. When the air-raid siren wailed its warning she ran down to the Anderson shelter in the back garden. There was no need to carry a torch as most nights the sky was crimson from the fires burning over the East End. Doubts have subsequently been championed about poor morale, but Jean can only remember a sense of neighbourliness and 'all being in the same boat'. The local girls were encouraged to knit socks for serving soldiers, and playtime included whip-and-top games, skipping and doing handstands. Children are so adaptable, and in bombed-out streets, with people they knew being killed, they still managed to enjoy that desperate summer.

A more cynical John Betjeman, writing to Gerard Irvine in October 1940, summed up his feelings with a variation on a well-known nursery rhyme:

Ding dong bell
Pussy's in the well
Who put him in?
The Lord Jesus.

When the Blitz started in earnest, thirteen-year-old Pat Desbruslais was packed off to boarding school to the relative safety of Potters Bar. Obviously, teachers thought corridors gave some kind of divine protection, for the pupils here had to sleep cheek-by-jowl in long, draughty passageways. They were brought back early from summer holidays to dig potatoes and tend the vegetable gardens in their version of 'dig for victory'. The campaign had been introduced by the government, encouraging every household to start an allotment to help overcome food shortages. Lawns, borders and public spaces were turned into vegetable gardens. People were encouraged to keep chickens, rabbits and goats. The campaign was a huge success with almost 1,500,000 allotments growing staple vegetables and even some more exotic varieties.

Robin Burns lived in Cricklewood and his bedroom overlooked the playing fields of Haberdashers' Aske's Hampstead School, where ack-ack guns were sited. His father was an ARP warden, seconded to the heavy rescue unit. Each borough was required to supply these units and they were routinely manned by those who had been employed in the building trade. The men were issued with heavy overalls, a steel helmet and a respirator, together with an oilskin cape to be used in case of a gas attack. They had to complete a first aid course, which was vital as they were often the first to reach the injured. They were also issued with a van with a trailer for carrying lamps, ropes and heavy-lifting equipment. The bravery of these men has been largely ignored. They were often confronted with horribly gruesome sights, which continued to haunt many. A colleague of Robin's father was deeply traumatised and eventually committed suicide. Robin's father was still visibly upset into old age by a recurring memory of a young girl he dug from the wreckage of her house. Covered in dust, but seemingly unmarked, she asked in a whisper, 'Am I going to die?' 'Course not, darling,' he told her. Smiling, she closed her eyes and never opened them again.

Amid the mayhem of war, a strange tradition continued. Welsh dairies had run their own shops in London for generations. The late Jack Pleasant, living in Rye after the war, recalled 'Hughie Thomas, who owned a dairy in our street in Bow. His family had a farm in Carmarthen and batches of cows were brought from there to town and housed in a byre as a source of fresh milk. Every three months they were taken back to the farm and replaced by another batch for a stint of London life. There was a lovely statue of a milkmaid in the dairy's window.' There were many such dairies across London. 'By contrast with today, instead of expecting tips, our dairyman used to give us a Christmas gift of a small parcel of goodies for our loyalty. It usually included a pot of cream, which was a real treat.'

Like many youngsters, Ivy Robinson returned from being evacuated just before the onset of the Blitz. Her parents decided to move away from the East End to Edmonton in North London. There she shared a bedroom with her three siblings, while her parents squeezed into the small box room. Bombing led to the closure for some time of the local school and education was spasmodic, usually undertaken in a neighbour's house. There were constant air-raid warnings known as 'moaning minnies', which howled away in the continuing summer sunshine. There was a daylight raid as the mother and the four children set off for home. People darted for cover, but two women refused to let them use their shelters even though German planes were flying directly above. Eventually, an elderly man, showing rather more neighbourly solidarity, invited them in. As they made a dash for the shelter several Spitfires appeared, hunting down the bombers. This was live theatre and despite the danger, they stood outside cheering, suddenly feeling quite invincible. As their rented house didn't have its own shelter, the children slept with their beds hard against a window (as I did) so if a bomb fell nearby the broken glass shot across the room without causing any injury.

Sleeping in the underground stations was throwing up all sorts of problems, the most pressing being the unsanitary conditions. The stench was unbearable. By mid-October chemical toilets were introduced. This alone improved the mood, and sing-songs and even solo performances by 'resting' professionals were organised. The securing of favoured spots in the stations continued to be a source of friction. Here again the underlying antagonism towards Jews surfaced. They were accused of aggressively seeking the best spaces on the platform and panicking during raids. This is disputed by Raymond Cooney who, as a teenager, lived with Sylvia, his younger sister, and their parents on Ogle Street close to Goodge Street underground station. The area had a fairly large Jewish community and the Cooneys had many Jewish friends. They can recall no tension or anti-Jewish feelings. Raymond was only jealous that he was not allowed time off school to celebrate their religious holidays. Their Jewish neighbours worshipped at a synagogue in Grotrian Hall in Wigmore Street, which was destroyed by enemy action in 1943 (one of thirteen London synagogues during the war). The Cooneys were in a minority. The thinly-disguised anti-Semitism had deepened since the onset of war. There was a widespread feeling that the Jewish community were not 'doing their bit' for the country. A common complaint was: how many did you see in uniform? They also seemed to have access to scarce luxury foods and they were additionally suspected of being involved in the black market. Dr Tony Kushner, a research fellow at the Department of History at the University of Southampton, presents a different perspective on anti-Semitism in his paper 'The Heymishe Front'. He quotes the case of Welshman Ernest Jones who had a Jewish mother working at an engineering company in central London. He spoke of a vehement anti-Semitism. It was impossible to shake their conviction that Jews ran the country, owned the wealth and, in particular, monopolised the wartime black market. Kushner goes on to explain that 'Jewish involvement in the black market, while relatively large, only in fact reflected Anglo-Jewish over-representation in the food, clothing, furniture, wholesale and retail trades where illicit trading was concentrated'.

Anti-Semitism was particularly entrenched in the East End where there was a large Jewish community. When times are tough people need someone to blame. The Jews were different and easily identifiable. Again, it was claimed that they panicked during raids, monopolised shelters and even demanded full rents for damaged properties they owned. They were accused of flaunting their wealth and not volunteering to work as wardens or firewatchers. Dr Kushner insists this is disproved by events. He states 'the bravery revealed by East End Jews also defied popular stereotypes. Jews were awarded thirteen George Cross medals for bravery during the course of the war.' A citation for Jewish Harry Errington states that

during the Blitz he was blown across the basement and injured. Simultaneously, the building was wrecked by high explosives. Dazed and injured, he found that two of his colleagues were missing. They were pinned down by the debris with raging fires all around. Though the heat was almost too great to be endured, Errington, putting on a wet blanket, worked his way through the debris with his bare hands. At any moment the remainder of the building threatened to collapse. He found one of his comrades and dragged him up a stone staircase, almost choked with fallen debris, into the street and then, in spite of the heat, went back into the inferno and saved the life of the second man.

In common with the Italians, thousands of foreign Jews were interned during the war. Many Germans and Austrians were deported to Canada and Australia. Once more, it appears that they were often disgracefully treated. Heino Alexander wrote of his journey, 'Having suffered in a German concentration camp, it seems terrible to receive the same treatment at the hands of the British ... cooped up like cattle in a cage of barbed wire, the deported internees were forcibly robbed, kicked and struck by their ruffianly escort.' Those interned from London and other centres throughout the country enjoyed far more sympathetic treatment in camps on the Isle of Man, where a talented collection of musicians and artists made life more bearable for other inmates with concerts, recitals and exhibitions.

Meanwhile, with the Blitz still raging, Jean Picton was taken to the cinema in East Ham by her gran. It was the night the local celluloid factory went up in flames. She recalled,

> The cinema was about twenty minutes walk from home. If there was an air-raid warning during the film a notice would come up on the screen telling the audience that the alert had sounded and you should take shelter. My Gran and I left halfway through the film to hurry home before the planes came overhead. We always seemed to have a gap before the first bombs fell, but we were a bit too far away to make it home before we heard the awful sound of the German planes above. We children had been told in the event of hearing a bomb whistling down we were to drop to the ground and put our hands over our ears. So upon hearing the high pitched whistle I did just that and hit the ground in a second, but my Gran thought it would be better if we dived into the nearest doorway, the end result being me being dragged along the pavement on my tummy by Gran and just getting in to the doorway as the bomb went off! It was a big one.

She can remember the whole street being lit up. She continued, 'I can remember looking down at the front of my new coat and seeing all my covered buttons had been scratched down to the bare metal. I began to cry and my Gran said don't worry, darling, the bomb missed us.' But Jean replied she wasn't worried about the bomb, rather that her mother would be cross because she had spoilt her new coat. Of course, her mother was just relieved that she was safe and sound. All their windows at home had been blown out and the fire at the celluloid factory burned on for days.

Within a week there was another heavy raid. Her mother pushed all three of her children into the cupboard under the stairs and lay prostrate across them for protection. Jean remembers a loud bang and then complete darkness. Again, all the windows were blown out. Her father lit candles and asked if everyone was alright. 'Yes,' they shouted and then someone asked, 'Where's Grandad?' Although he was a big man, they couldn't find him. Shouting was no good as he had been deafened in the Great War. It was Jean who spotted his legs sticking out from beneath the sideboard. With difficulty they lifted the heavy sideboard and the old man was found to be fine despite the devastation all around him. Another raid followed soon after and Jean remembers her father taking her into the garden. 'Look, this is history in the making,' he said, and while her mother begged them to take cover, the pair stood arm in arm and stared skywards. 'It was a like a wonderland of lights and flashes. I could see and hear the planes diving and swerving like giant black eagles, weaving in and out of the searchlight beams. There were puffs of smoke and small explosions like a firework display … to the sound of engines revving. Now and again a very big burst and whine in between the loud bang of the ack-ack guns set up in the recreation ground nearby.' She says, even now in her autumn years, she owes so much to those brave young airmen of the RAF. Despite the revisionist views of mainly young historians, she, like all those I interviewed for this book, remembers the feeling of closeness and friendliness of Londoners, of laughter, joking and sing songs. Rose-tinted glasses syndrome? Possibly, but they were there, unlike many of the historians. Of course there were crooks and dishonest and selfish behaviour, but overall the evidence remains that the wartime population was stoic and brave.

The bombs continued through December, well into 1941. There was a customary lull over Christmas, when Londoners pushed the thought of war to the back of their minds and celebrated as much as restrictions would allow. The feeling of goodwill was short lived. The nearest to a firestorm that London was to witness came on 29 December 1940, and yet the raid was not particularly heavy. As it was the first Sunday after Christmas, many of the offices and warehouses of the city lay deserted and unattended. To make matters worse the Thames was at a low ebb and fireboats were unable to get close to the fast-spreading inferno. The incendiaries started over 1,200 separate fires, which merged into two mighty conflagrations centred on the old City of London. From Moorgate to Old Street, and Aldersgate to Cannon Street, little was spared. Strangely, many iconic buildings survived, including the Bank of England and perhaps London's greatest landmark, St Paul's. One device did lodge on the outside of the dome. Stirrup pumps eventually managed to dislodge it and while all the surrounding streets and ancient alleyways fell victim to the fire, Wren's masterpiece remained solid and unmoving. It served as a graphic symbol of London's defiance. Others of Wren's churches were destroyed in the flames that were a precursor of the terror experienced later in the war by Dresden. The Port of London's docks were reduced to a fraction of their capacity, and yet fewer than 200 people perished in what could have developed into London's greatest wartime tragedy.

London enjoyed a brief respite, but on 11 January eighteen children were among the forty killed in an attack on Liverpool Street station. Worse was to follow when a direct hit on Bank tube station killed 111 people. The docks were again the target two days later, with Victoria and Albert Docks and Woolwich Arsenal badly damaged. The same day saw tragedy come to Hendon. A single plane dropped its load and for once no warning siren sounded. The result was devastating, with some hundred houses destroyed. Sixty people were killed, with over 200 seriously injured. Public outrage was louder than at any time during the heavier bombing of the previous year. Why had there been no warning?

Between March and May 1941 there were a further six major raids on London. In the first of these Buckingham Palace again sustained damage, as did St Bartholomew's hospital, but it was the destruction of the fashionable Café de Paris nightclub near Leicester Square that received the most publicity. No more tragic than hundreds of other scenes of destruction, its reputation for luxury and exclusiveness continued to grab our attention.

Ironically, it was also advertised as being the safest venue in town. The Rialto cinema had been built in 1912 and subsequently the basement was opened as a nightclub in 1924. It soon attracted the custom of the Prince of Wales. Where the Prince went others followed. Although wartime conditions dictated that formal evening dress was no longer compulsory, it still retained its air of grandeur. It was an exact replica of the Palm Court aboard the doomed liner *Lusitania*. Entering 'the bridge', there was a central lobby with a view of the restaurant. Twin staircases, each of twenty-nine steps, swooped down to the dance floor. Diners instinctively looked up to view every entrance. That fateful night uniforms dominated rather than tailed coats. The ladies, though dressed for the occasion, still created a whiff of glamour and romance. West Indian 'Snakehips' Johnson was the resident bandleader. He had been appearing earlier in the evening at the Embassy Club. He rushed back to the Café de Paris to a background of ack-ack fire and falling bombs. Slim and standing over 6 feet tall, he was his normal exuberant self as he led the band into the opening number of 'Oh Johnny' right on time at 9.30 p.m. As the band started up a bomb freakishly fell directly down an airshaft and exploded on the dance floor. There was pandemonium. Survivors, torn and tattered, staggered out onto the street. 'Snakehips', like several other victims, died totally unmarked. The nearby Honeydew restaurant was used as a mortuary as the injured were taken off to Charing Cross hospital. Some thirty bodies were recovered with another fifty revellers who were seriously injured. Eventually the death toll increased to eighty. The shadow of the doomed liner had spread to the heart of London's West End.

'The Big Blitz back again,' screamed the newspaper headlines, but the worst was still to come. It was South London's turn on 15 March, although the worst single incident was recorded further north in Southgate, where over forty people were killed. Four days later, hundreds of parachute bombs missed their target of the docks and fell onto residential areas in West Ham, Poplar and Stepney. It seemed nowhere in the capital was safe.

A month later and April saw the heaviest raids yet. Wednesday 16 April gained an unwelcome notoriety. It saw the introduction by the Luftwaffe of the Junkers Ju 88 dive bombers, which screamed their way into London's consciousness and had citizens covering their ears in terror. Over a thousand people were now being killed each night, with tens of thousands of homes being damaged in a week. Great London landmarks were hit, including the Houses of Parliament, the Admiralty and the Law Courts. Fashionable Jermyn Street and Eaton Square were smashed. How much more could London take? Britain's favourite crooner, Al Bowlly, was killed at his flat in Duke Street just off Oxford Street. He was only forty-two and, like his showbiz colleague 'Snakehips' Johnson, he died without a mark on him. Doubtless because he was one of many who died that night, he was buried in a mass grave at Hanwell cemetery.

Londoners' fears that the Wednesday raid was a forerunner of another period of sustained attack seemed to be accurate when the Luftwaffe struck again on the Saturday. This time they targeted an area further west. Many felt that if the same level of raids was sustained for much longer the public's resistance would crack. The city was pockmarked with great gaps in most streets, like missing teeth in a smiling face, but London wasn't smiling. Homelessness was now an urgent and growing problem. Supplies of food were scarce, worse than at any time since the outbreak of war. Life was as miserable as it was dangerous. Surely things had to improve? They did for a time.

For weeks there were very few raids. The mood was calmer. A sense bordering on normality started to take root. On 10 May, 60,000 turned up at Wembley to watch the Cup final. The guard was down and London was being set up to take a sucker punch. Why did so few spot the portents? Saturday 10 May offered the Luftwaffe their perfect conditions. There was a full moon and once more the Thames was at a low ebb. By daybreak on the Sunday more than 3,000 were either dead or seriously injured. This was to be the single heaviest and most devastating attack of the entire war. Marylebone was the only mainline station to remain open. Roads were blocked, as were all the bridges from the Tower to Lambeth. The Tower itself was hit, while the House of Commons was gutted and Westminster Hall set ablaze. The War Office was damaged, as was the Royal Naval College at Greenwich. Nowhere was sacrosanct.

The Law Courts, the Palace of St James, Westminster Abbey, the Mansion House – none were spared. Over 2,000 fires raged, with one near the Elephant and Castle fanning into the worst conflagration since the raid of 29 December. More than 5,000 houses were destroyed that ghastly night, and yet it was to be the last of the Blitz. London had taken everything the Luftwaffe could throw at it and was still standing. Just. Like an old bare-fist fighter, it stared at the world through bruised, blood-shot eyes and could hardly believe that its rival had walked away. They still didn't know that yet and, of course, there were still many dark days to come. But, the Blitz was over. Over 300,000 houses had been destroyed and over 20,000 lay dead. But it was over. It would be months before there was another raid. Thousands of landmarks, including over a dozen Wren churches, had been destroyed; much of ancient London was gone or badly damaged, but the German strategy had failed. The anticipated destruction of London and the breakdown of civilian morale had not transpired. During the Battle of Britain and the Blitz, the Luftwaffe had lost 2,400 aircraft without achieving any of its objectives. It was the introduction of radar that so strengthened London's defence capability and accounted for a huge increase in Luftwaffe losses. But it was greater events elsewhere that were finally going to relieve the pressure on London. In June, Germany invaded Russia.

Watch out though, it's time to lock up your daughters – the Yanks are coming!

4

A US Invasion

February 1942 witnessed an invasion of London. Happily, not the one that had been feared. There were no jack-booted Germans goose-stepping their way down Whitehall. It did, however, feature another foreign army whose presence was to profoundly affect Londoners' lives for the next three years.

Back on 7 December 1941, Japan attacked the American fleet at Pearl Harbour. Four days later, Germany declared war on the United States. This was guaranteed to extend American involvement in the war, beyond the existing Lend-Lease agreement with the Allies. Now Britain could expect direct military assistance rather than just the supply of weapons, food and raw materials. The government needed some good news as reports had just come through of the destruction of two important British ships by the Japanese. The sinking of *The Repulse* and her consort *The Prince of Wales* was a shock for the British public and foretold the unexpected weakness of the Allied position in the Far East.

The previous Christmas had been particularly bleak for Londoners. The stores' shelves were virtually empty of goods normally available for presents and what there was was reckoned to be overpriced. Most children's Christmas stockings were confined to homemade or second-hand toys; perhaps a Rupert Bear or *Beano* annual and, for the lucky ones, an orange and a few nuts. The new year brought fresh disasters in the Far East and North Africa. Both the Japanese and Rommel were on the march. In February the unthinkable happened: the surrender of Singapore.

Despite the welcome arrival of the first American troops, the seemingly endless tide of bad news continued when in August 1942 the death of the Duke of Kent was announced. The younger brother of the king was popular with the public, who liked his informal style. The Duke had been aboard a flying boat bound for Iceland, before it was due to continue onto Newfoundland. In fact, it only made it to a misty hillside in Caithness where it crashed. There was a memorial service held in Westminster Abbey, which was conducted with considerable pomp. The Duke's dissolute lifestyle was not generally known by the British public. Despite being married to the beautiful Princess Marina of Greece and Denmark, who bore him three children, he was involved in numerous affairs, which were not confined to women, including Ivor Novello and Noel Coward. Outwardly sophisticated, he had a love of the arts and was a talented sportsman. He had a particular interest in jazz and, unfortunately, the drug habit that was often associated with the music. While initially tolerant of his indiscretions, Princess Marina eventually fell under the spell of the West Indian musician 'Hutch'. Five years after her marriage in 1933 she had a fling with the entertainer and serial seducer. She was elegant, charming and yet, somehow, vaguely tragic. He was said to have been attracted by her slight, but noticeable, limp which underlined her vulnerability. After their romance faded they remained friends until her death in 1968.

As ever, looking to save money, the authorities decided to close down London's underground shelters, except those in central London where Covent Garden, Green Park, Bond Street and Trafalgar Square were spared. Apart from a few incendiaries, there had been no attacks on London for over six months. Once more, the government worried that complacency would set in and Churchill warned that the danger was certainly not over. Ernest Gowers, the public official in charge of civil defence for London, was more graphic, warning that future raids would make those experienced as recently as May 1941 seem as 'though they were mere picnics'.

By the end of 1942, there were close on 250,000 US troops stationed in Britain. They were largely service staff and airmen. The mass of ground forces didn't arrive in large numbers until the autumn of 1943. Even before Pearl Harbour, there had been some 2,000 personnel attached to the US Embassy. The GIs were now transported across the Atlantic in purpose-built liberty ships and others arrived aboard requisitioned luxury liners, including the *Queen Mary* and the *Queen Elizabeth*. There was not much luxury left for the troops to enjoy as up to 15,000 men were squeezed aboard. Many of the airmen and crew were despatched on arrival to the flatlands of East Anglia, where airfields peppered the countryside, many no more than 10 miles apart. London was also to be home to many and soon the area around Grosvenor Square became known as 'little America', The first arrivals were billeted in the former Hotel Splendide on Piccadilly, which was the former home of the National Sporting Club. Others were packed off to the Badminton Club in Shepherds Market, while the Washington Hotel in Curzon Street became a favourite haunt for US servicemen on leave from units across Britain.

It was, perhaps, a natural consequence of US wealth, as well as military power, that they set about taking over swathes of London's most fashionable neighbourhoods. In 1943 the War Office requisitioned the Great Room in the Grosvenor House Hotel on Park Lane as the mess room for US officers. The great mansions of Park Lane had largely been demolished to make way for some of London's swankiest hotels. In the late 1920s, Grosvenor House had boasted the world's largest skating rink. As the skating fad diminished, the rink was converted to become the country's largest ballroom and host to many of London's smartest 'knees ups'. The Ministry of Works removed all the hotel's equipment and the Americans installed their own kitchen and stores. Run exclusively by the US Army authorities, it could accommodate over 1,000 officers at each sitting. This was only made possible by a self-service system, which still required a staff of almost 400 to keep it functioning. In keeping with the austerity elsewhere in London, the servicemen were encouraged to 'eat all you take on your plate, or explain why'. The long line of customers became known as 'the willow run' after the assembly line at Ford's factory outside Detroit.

Further down the road General Dwight Eisenhower dossed down in two rooms on the first floor of the Dorchester Hotel.

Reckoned to be one of the safest buildings in London, its roots were secured by 3 feet of reinforced concrete supporting the eight floors of bedrooms. Luckily, this flimsy claim was never put to the test. The hotel remained shaken but not stirred by several near misses. By 1944, over twenty hotels were serving as US billets and hundreds of other buildings in the neighbourhood were being used for accommodation.

For the non-commissioned ranks, their first introduction to London centred on a club. Not a sophisticated nightclub or even one of the many seedy joints that sprouted up all around Piccadilly and Leicester Square. Rainbow Corner was a huge Red Cross club situated on the corner of Denman Street and Shaftesbury Avenue. An area of temptation for those with a love of the theatre or, more likely, for those in search of love. At a price, that is! The five-storey building had previously been home to Café Monico, part of the giant Joe Lyons organisation. After months of reconstruction work, it was ready to act as the focal point for the thousands of US troops visiting London during the remainder of the war. Here was a slice of America right in the heart of this vast, crowded, strange city. There was a selection of cafes and restaurants serving food not available elsewhere in London. Waffles, dunking doughnuts and, glory be, fresh coffee (not that Scottish imposter Camp coffee that contained just 4 per cent of coffee essence). Accommodation was also available with hot showers (another rarity in London). The club also offered valet and laundry services plus a barber to keep hair shorn to military requirements. Once freshly bathed and relaxed, the GI may fancy a trip out to explore old London town. In the lobby were three arrows, one pointing to Leicester Square – 100 yards; then Berlin – 600 miles, and New York – 3,271 miles. If he chose to stay in he could settle down to read the US national newspapers and even a selection of the US regional press. There were pinball machines to play and a chance to write home. Help was available for those who struggled with writing from good-hearted London-based US residents. Adele Astaire was among those volunteering. The GIs she assisted probably were unaware that the sister and former dance partner of Fred Astaire was now a Lady, in name, at least. In 1932 she had married Lord Charles Cavendish.

Dancing was, perhaps, the greatest attraction at Rainbow Corner. The live music on offer was often world class. The club rocked at various times to Glenn Miller, who broadcast direct from the club, as did the great Artie Shaw and his Naval Band. Petula Clark remembers making an early appearance before a typically boisterous and rowdy audience. The jitterbug was all the rage. It suited the sentiment of the times, and was wild, exuberant and unrestrained – live for today, don't worry about tomorrow. For the carefully selected 'nice' English girls given entry for these dances, the jitterbug was a total revelation. They were quite literally swept off their feet.

Most Britons knew very little about Americans except what they had seen on the silver screen. Surely they couldn't all be cocktail-swigging millionaires or gun-toting gangsters? The Londoners' usual doubts about foreigners were reflected in a survey that ranked Americans no higher in the pecking order than the newly reviled Italians. The feeling existed that without the attack on Pearl Harbour the Yanks would never have entered the war. So, while obviously welcomed for their military might, the arrival of thousands of Americans proved to be something of a culture shock. For a start, they looked different. They were generally taller, smarter and rarely lacking in self-confidence. Or, put another way, dead cocky. Their uniforms were well cut, so much so that British squaddies often mistook American private soldiers as officers and saluted them.

By contrast, the British troops attracted some waspish comments from Evelyn Waugh. In his diary for 15 May 1943, he describes them as 'horrible groups of soldiers in shabby battledress with necks open, their caps off or at extravagant angles, hands in pockets, cigarettes in sides of their mouths, lounging about with girls in trousers and high heels and film star coiffures!' He continues that he has never seen so many ugly girls making themselves so conspicuous. Presumably, all the good lookers were hanging around the GIs.

Although, ostensibly, speaking the same language, there were many areas of potential misunderstanding between the two major allies. To help alleviate these problems, the GIs were issued with a *Short Guide to Britain*. Golden rules included never to criticise the royal family or to discuss religion. British food (or the lack of it) was also dangerous territory, apparently. They were warned about warm beer which, over half a century later, still encourages ribald comments from old veterans. There was also the language barrier to overcome. Guys were blokes or chaps, very confusing. A movie house was a cinema, while a sidewalk became a pavement. The list was endless, best illustrated by a receptionist at a leading hotel asking at the top of her voice if 'anyone had a rubber?' The line of servicemen waiting to check in really thought their luck had changed. When they finally explained to the red-faced flower of British innocence that a rubber to an American was a condom, they regretfully realised she was looking for an eraser. Similar mirth was expressed when an attractive waitress being distracted from her work by admiring GIs was told, 'Sorry, I really must get on laying the table.'

The British class system was another area of misunderstanding between the allies. Most Americans were baffled. It was at its most obvious in the distinction between officers and other ranks. The easy-going relationship running through the US military concerning differing ranks had the British senior military spluttering into their pink gins. Discipline above all else was vital. What on earth were these chaps going to be like under fire? For their part, the Americans thought the British attitude crazy and counterproductive. The pinnacle of British military snobbishness was to be found in the exclusive cavalry regiments, described by an American officer as 'the most mentally inert, unprofessional and reactionary group in the British Army'. He went on to suggest that under the British system few of the serving American officers would have been allowed to rise above the rank of NCO. Some of his contemporaries were so offended that they felt that Britain didn't deserve to be rescued by 'Uncle Sam'.

For their part, the British officer class tended to view their American cousins as a shade too boisterous and a touch uncouth. Differences also appeared in attitudes towards black GIs, who represented about 10 per cent of the US troops in Britain. With only about 8,000 black people living in Britain at the outbreak of war, many Londoners had never seen a black face before. While having no particular liking for them, they were shocked at the way they were treated by many of the white US troops. Perhaps it was an inherent dislike of bullying and sympathy for those unable to properly defend themselves. A general feeling developed that the black GIs were friendly, polite and fun to be around. Certainly that was true as far as many English girls were concerned. This frequently led to trouble, particularly when troops from the southern states took objection. There were frequent flare-ups on the streets of London with the US military police, known as 'Snowdrops' (because of their white helmets), wading in with their long batons. Blacks were frequently turned away from dance halls and restaurants for fear of their owners losing the lucrative business of the white American troops. The problem was highlighted when legendary West Indian cricketer, Learie Constantine, was asked to leave a West End restaurant at the insistence of American customers. The case ended up in court and the hotel's management was fined a derisory £5 10s. Justice Birkett regretted that the law, as it stood, gave him no opportunity to increase the fine. The British government was concerned at the number of black GIs arriving. The establishment, in the form of Foreign Secretary Anthony Eden, voiced its concern, albeit in a tongue-in-cheek manner. 'Our climate is badly suited to negroes,' he suggested to the US Ambassador. Nothing changed and a form of military apartheid continued in the US until late 1947.

As unpleasant incidents increased, so Londoners generally took the side of the minority blacks. Quentin Crisp, who was later to become something of a gay icon, had no colour prejudice. He was just overwhelmed at the opportunities offered to him by the GIs, 'like cream on strawberries' he enthused, delighting in their tight-fitting uniforms. While the famous, particularly those connected to the arts, were able to indulge themselves without too much trouble from the police, homosexuality was still an offence for which one could be imprisoned. Crisp and his friends had to operate in a twilight world, living in constant danger of violence or arrest.

Another source of trouble didn't take long to surface after the arrival of the Americans. British servicemen felt hard done by. There were no comfortable Red Cross clubs for them to enjoy while on leave. Worse still was the pay differential, which was an area for deep resentment. All ranks were paid far less than their American counterparts. A US private soldier was paid more than a flight lieutenant serving in the RAF. According to the Brits, the Yanks were 'overpaid, oversexed and over here'. So what, replied the GIs, rather bitingly; the Brits were 'undersexed, underpaid and under Eisenhower'. Violence erupted regularly as the English girls developed a real taste for Americans, often sidelining British squaddies.

Evelyn Waugh bemoaned what he saw as the social contamination of central London full of American soldiers. Warming to his subject, he continued, 'For their comfort there swarmed out of the slums and across the bridges multitudes of drab, ill-favoured, adolescent girls and their aunts and mothers, never before seen in the squares of Mayfair and Belgravia. There they passionately and publicly embraced in the blackout and at high noon and were rewarded with chewing gum, razor blades and other trade goods.'

Admiral Sir Edward Evans lamented that 'Leicester Square is the resort of the worst type of women and girls consorting with both British and American troops'. It was difficult to tell which were prostitutes and which were girls just looking for fun. The whole area surrounding Piccadilly was being sustained by a tidal wave of lust. Middle England was shocked. The *Sunday Pictorial* started a campaign to clean up Piccadilly and the surrounding area in August 1942.

Love, rather than lust, was a particular worry for the US authorities. Marriage tended to be frowned upon. The feeling was that it distracted and weakened the servicemen's resolve. Marriage to a foreign national was particularly unwelcome. Bigamy and illegitimate children were also causes of concern. But young couples do fall in love. The Poles had shown a considerable liking to Scottish girls, with thousands of them taking Celtic brides. Many Canadian forces also married British sweethearts, and in September 1942 General Eisenhower decreed that US forces could marry providing they had the permission of their commanding officer. Ignoring this instruction would make them liable to a court martial. However, the groom was not allowed any additional perks or allowances above those of his single colleagues. No medical help for his bride or free travel to the States. Nor was automatic US citizenship to be granted. Getting a girl pregnant was officially thought to 'bring discredit on the service'. Occasionally, a marriage was sanctioned. A more usual tactic was to get the GI transferred to another unit far away and hope the problem would resolve itself in time, leaving many a British father to fume. The one request category always to be refused was that between a white English girl and a black GI. Mixed-colour marriages were still illegal in most US southern states.

The Americans began to win over public opinion when thousands of them were set to work helping repair the huge number of damaged houses throughout London. Children were particularly drawn to them by their overall friendliness and, of course, the prized gift of chewing gum. Increasingly, the GIs were welcomed into Londoners' homes and the initial mutual reserve was lowered. Iris Chapple spent her childhood in Brixton with her mother. She can remember trips with her mum and her friends to the Dorset Arms on Clapham Road, which was a favourite haunt of American servicemen. She remembers being fascinated by them. She loved their accents and being called 'honey'. They would bring the kids lemonade and sweets as they waited for their mothers to reappear, usually red faced and giggling, sometimes holding the ultimate prize – a couple of pairs of nylons. Iris's mum worked as a cleaner in the Chancellor's office at 11 Downing Street. Although physically close to the seat of power, life for the mother and daughter was really tough. They were desperately poor by today's standards, but Iris never felt she went without. Bombed out during the Blitz, when she was too young to remember, they were to suffer again later in the war.

There was another group of Americans stationed in London whose effect was, perhaps, as profound as the thousands representing the military. There were over 100 US journalists reporting regularly from London. The best-known of these was Ed Murrow, whose radio broadcasts were to achieve something of a cult status. He did much to highlight Britain's struggle prior to American military involvement, particularly during the

Blitz. He was a pioneer in radio news reporting and achieved celebrity status, both in London and the US. American reporting from London has subsequently been criticised as thinly veiled propaganda. Perhaps some of the journalists were the forerunners of the modern-day spin doctor, but they reported with great skill and London has much to thank them for.

As the years progressed, so Londoners and their American visitors began to understand and accept each other's national characteristics and peculiarities. British reserve dropped as some of the Americans' openness rubbed off. People began speaking to strangers; even some class barriers were beginning to be cast aside or at least tempered. Londoners had become used to seeing GIs filling the best restaurants, the dance halls and cinemas, chatting up girls, crowding the pubs and moaning about the beer, hailing taxis and shouting, 'Shake it, lady, shake it' as the Windmill girls went through their routine.

And then they were gone. Well, most of them. Everyone in the country was aware that something momentous was about to take place as American and Allied troops were moved south to take place in the D-Day landings. Suddenly, London seemed deserted. Restaurant owners stood anxiously in their entrances looking for customers, but few came. Working girls patrolled the streets around Piccadilly, but business for them was slack also. Londoners reverted to type, quietly going about their business as usual. Ed Murrow said that he wanted to shout, 'Don't you know history is being made this day?' Most people did indeed understand the significance of the disappearance of the troops from the streets. Many Londoners had husbands, lovers, brothers, friends about to be involved in the landings. This was an anxious time, there were bound to be many deaths and serious injuries. It was a time for quiet contemplation.

Outside Rainbow Corner, the girls had gone, the spivs vanished. Many Americans never returned to London. Thousands died on the Normandy beaches and the bloody road to final victory. They left behind broken hearts, broken dreams, babies and memories. Happy memories. They had brought a vibrancy and hope to a wide-eyed London, never to be forgotten.

5

Crime and Treason

The poor are always with us, and in London so are the criminals. Not just the professional gangsters, but the thieves, con-men, ponces and violent thugs. Chuck in a few murderers and a couple of traitors, and this is the murky brew of London's sordid underbelly. The war provided a perfect backdrop for criminal activity. Shortages brought on by rationing created a ready market for a deprived population willing to pay over the odds for almost anything that was not generally available. The career criminals, spivs, wide-boys and chancers were aided by the darkness provided by the black-out. With many younger policemen having volunteered for military service, the crooks settled down to enjoy a golden age.

The National Service Act of September 1939 imposed conscription on all men aged eighteen to forty-one. A hard core of career criminals just ignored their call-up papers. Despite the government's pledge of relentlessly pursuing draft dodgers, the villains knew better. They simply didn't turn up to register, guessing correctly that the authorities would have more pressing priorities. Forgers were much in demand. Copies were available (at a price) of medical discharge papers. Men who had a genuine medical condition were coerced or paid to present themselves again for a medical, posing as the person trying to avoid call-up. There were even cases of doctors issuing fake certificates for patients. At least one doctor was struck off. Reserved occupations provided the gold standard for exemption. These were people employed in areas essential to the war effort and many tried to bend the rules in order to avoid conscription.

For the first couple of years of the war, crime in London fell. It didn't last. Late in 1941 the *Evening Standard* was reporting a surge in street violence. The arrival of thousands of fit, young servicemen from around the world was a recipe for trouble. Fresh legislation also created many new offences, which had the effect of increasing the crime figures. Even to speak out of turn could, theoretically, lead to a hefty fine or even imprisonment. It was an offence to 'spread despondency or alarm' by criticising the war effort.

Leading London gangster Billy Hill thought those joining up were mugs. He had no intention of registering. His war was going to be spent in dedicated fighting to make money, rather than against the Germans. In his late twenties at the outbreak of war, Hill was born into one of London's most notorious crime families. Eventually, he became known as 'the boss of the underworld'. He was a resourceful and intelligent man who was actively involved in the black market and supplying forged documents, but his speciality was organising smash-and-grab raids. He was unusual in the criminal community by combining the use of extreme violence with a capability for detailed planning. He and his side-kicks were responsible for a number of daring raids on West End jewellers, including the Goldsmiths and Silversmiths Association in Piccadilly, and he also targeted the Ciro Pearls organisation. When police activity became too hot in the West End for a time, Hill diverted his attention to plundering suburban jewellers. Always seeking new methods of operation, Hill switched to daylight raids. In these he stood on the passenger's car seat with his head and shoulders thrust through the open sunroof. As the driver pulled up on the pavement outside the jeweller's window, Hill smashed away with a sledge hammer, scooping up the rings, watches and other jewellery, before making a swift getaway with tyres screeching. The method worked very well, with an £11,000 heist on New Bond Street, but his luck was just about to run out. This type of raid required two cars, the second blocking the road to delay any possible chase. On 26 June 1940, Hill and his associates targeted

Hemmings, the upmarket jewellers in Conduit Street. Swinging rapidly round the corner from Bond Street, the first car mounted the pavement but the driver lost control, knocking a uniformed policeman to the ground. Not a great start. Then, as Hill was poised to smash the window, the driver had more bad news. The bumper on the car had become caught and the car was stuck. 'Run for it,' Hill shouted and the men from the two cars made off in different directions. Police whistles sounded and spirited members of the public gave chase. Hill sprinted to Bruton Street and entered an office building. Charging to the upper floors he came down a different staircase and told a waiting policeman that the culprit was still inside the building. The constable was never going to fall for that old trick. Hill was sentenced to two years in jail. A time for him to take stock, scheme and to plan the next phase of his burgeoning career.

Like Billy Hill, the Messina brothers, who were to control London's vice trade for the next decade, ignored orders to present themselves to recruiting offices. The Messina boys were of impeccable pedigree for running the vice industry. Their father, a Sicilian, moved to Malta as a young man, helping to run a brothel in Valetta. He married a Maltese girl who gave birth to Salvatore and Alfredo, before the family moved to Egypt. There, over time, the couple built up a chain of brothels. Their family also increased with the birth of Attilio and Eugenio. Eugenio was the first to arrive in London during the 1930s. It was a time in London when most street girls worked freelance, or under the control of their ponce. Many were French or Belgian who had married British men to enable them to work in London. They were known affectionately as 'Fifis'. Eugenio was able to claim British citizenship as his father was a Maltese national. He married Colette, a French girl, and wasted no time in getting her to work the streets. He was shortly joined by his brothers and they set about recruiting more girls from the Continent. English girls were then added to the team. Tempted with promises of marriage and expensive gifts, once on board they were ruthlessly exploited.

In the spring of 1941, single women were required to register for war service. The girls were instructed to inform the authorities that they were working as prostitutes. Honesty, for once, paid off as the authorities thought it unwise to let the women contaminate those recruited to work in government offices and factories. The Messinas ruled their empire by intimidation and a fear of violence. Some of the rules imposed on the girls were bizarre. Swearing was discouraged and the wearing of low-cut dresses banned. They were not allowed to mix socially and usually had to be escorted, even when shopping, by their maid. An almost monastic life, where any breaking of the Messina code was likely to be punished by a beating or the slash of a razor. During these early years there was competition on almost every street corner from a host of other women, both professional and part-timers, Messina girls secured the most lucrative pitches. These became no-go areas. Anyone trespassing was violently attacked. So the Messinas extended their kingdom, raking in thousands of pounds each week. They were responsible for introducing the ten-minute rule. Few clothes were removed and the punter and the girl were expected to be back on the street within ten minutes. Failure led to money being deducted from her earnings and, again, violence for repeated failures. The brothers toured the streets at night, driving their expensive cars, to ensure their rigid rules were adhered to. Time and motion study had entered the sex industry. As the money rolled in they invested in property throughout the West End, particularly in Soho when prices were at rock bottom. It was only in the 1950s that the brothers were finally hounded out of the country.

While the Blitz brought out the very best in most Londoners, for others it was an ideal opportunity for personal gain. Looting in Germany was punishable by death, yet the courts in Britain tended to take a relatively lenient attitude, treating the offence as theft. This encouraged organised gangs who patrolled the streets during raids, aiming to be first on the scene of devastation which normally allowed them easy access to a building. Some refined their art by driving a vehicle purporting to be an ambulance and wearing stolen uniforms. Neighbours watched in silence as covered stretchers were brought out. But it wasn't mutilated bodies being concealed, it was loot. ARPs and bomb disposal units were also rumoured to be involved. People already distraught returned home to find that not only had their house been wrecked, but that anything of value had been stolen. Worse ghoulish tales emerged. Bodies were being stripped of watches and jewellery. Could it really be true that in the mayhem surrounding the bombing of the Café de Paris even fingers were cut off to secure valuable rings? War has the power to create both unlikely heroes and bestial behaviour that defies the imagination.

By comparison, the black market seems inconsequential, but it led to much bitter resentment. Unless, of course, it was you who could lay your hands on some item in really short supply. It was then that the high moral ground was abandoned – for a time at least. The imposition of rationing and general shortages led to a massive trade in black market goods. Bogus ration books were produced by dodgy printers and were often distributed in clubs and pubs. In 1944, 14,000 newly issued ration books were stolen and were soon fetching up to £5 each. It was clothes coupons that attracted the biggest premium. Although thousands flooded the market, the forgeries were normally relatively easy to detect and frequent arrests were made. Petrol rationing was also stringently monitored, with regular roadside checks organised by the police.

The government became concerned that a belief had developed that only the poor were being charged with minor coupon breaches. To help redress the balance, a number of high-profile arrests were made. Ivor Novello was sent to prison for the misuse of petrol, much to the distress of his army of fans. The band leader Victor Sylvester was convicted of smuggling goods into the country with the connivance of a US serviceman, while Noel Coward was added to the star-studded cast of miscreants. He was convicted for failure to offer his holdings of US dollars to the Treasury. He pleaded ignorance, no better defence than the average spiv. It cut no ice. He was found guilty. Perhaps the most high-profile case went straight to the heart of the establishment. Sir Peter Laurie was Provost Marshall of the military police, no less. He was convicted at the Old Bailey of rationing irregularities. Leading companies and hotels were also sanctioned, including Joe Lyons, Swan and Edgar, Sainsbury and Woolworths. Both the Savoy and Grosvenor House also fell foul of the authorities, but still the sense of unfairness persisted.

It didn't take long for crowds to congregate outside Rainbow Corner after the arrival of the Americans. It became a clearing house for nylons, perfume, watches and even items of food. Spivs and barrow boys jostled with lines of girls trying to attract the GIs' attention. Deals were struck and hours later the goods would appear on Berwick Street market. Herman Schultz was convicted in 1943 for selling underwear and stockings on his stall in the market. He was found to have an astonishing stash of £3,000 in notes hidden away in his flat. He was sentenced to three months' hard labour and fined a massive £500. The US authorities had created an Office of Prices administration in order to try and restrict illegal activity. Despite the jailing of GIs for being involved, the trade continued unabated throughout the war. Other suppliers of valuable black market goods were dockers and railway employees. Here, petty pilfering was reckoned to be a perk of the job, considered no worse than a businessman fiddling his expenses.

By the latter part of the war, it was deserters who were reckoned to be responsible for as much as 10 per cent of crime. With 1 in 100 reckoned to have deserted, most made their way to what they hoped would be the anonymity of a crowded London. The death penalty for desertion had been abolished, but any British serviceman detained could expect up to ten years in a military prison. In May 1944 British and US military police conducted a massive swoop on the West End. They targeted hotels, bars, restaurants, clubs and amusement arcades. The Corner House in Coventry Street was raided and every customer was required to prove their identity. At the Astoria dance hall in Charing Cross Road the band was forced to stop playing mid-number as identity and leave papers were checked. Fixed bayonets were even used when raiding particularly dubious premises. Despite these wide-ranging raids, only about 100 arrests were made. Swoops on London dog tracks also netted a few more deserters, but overall the results were disappointing. The increase in crime continued. By 1943 matters had deteriorated further with a spate of kidnapping and armed robberies attributed to deserters. Some 2,000 police flooded Soho, checking all premises. This time seventy-five were detained. The availability of guns was being attributed to the surge in crime and weapons bought from GIs were still being used in London long after the end of the war.

For a week in February 1943, the headlines were dominated not by news of the war, but of the 'Blackout Ripper'. On 9 February the body of forty-year-old Margaret Hamilton was found strangled in a surface shelter in Montague Place, Marylebone. It was thought that the motive was theft. The following morning the mutilated body of Evelyn Oatley was found in her flat in Wardour Street. Claims have been made that she had once been a Windmill girl, a fact refuted by her family. Maybe she had been a dancer, but latterly had turned to prostitution. She had also been strangled, as well as being defiled with a tin opener. The police deduced that the mutilation had been perpetrated by a left-handed assailant. The marks on Margaret Hamilton's throat also indicated they were made by a left hand. Three days later, another prostitute, Margaret Lowe, was discovered in Gosfield Street, also strangled and savagely mutilated. While the pathologist Sir Bernard Spilsbury was still making his initial examination in Gosfield Street, news came of the discovery of a fourth body. Doris Jonannet, a part-time prostitute, was discovered in Sussex Gardens. Once again she had been defiled. The killer had been reckless; the police found clear fingerprints at each crime scene, although they did not match any held in police records.

By Saturday 14 February, the papers were in full cry, with headlines such as 'West End search for mad killer'. By now the killer appeared to be out of control. Two days previously, Greta Hayward had a very lucky escape. She had been picked up by a young officer cadet and taken for a drink at the Trocadero on Piccadilly. Later they sauntered down the Haymarket and the cadet offered her money to have sex with him. She declined but as they turned off the main road he suggested 'at least let me kiss you goodnight'. Placing his gas mask on the ground, he put his arms around her, grabbing her by the throat and began to choke her. He was disturbed by a delivery boy and he ran off leaving Greta unconscious, but also his gas mask, which contained his service number. Undeterred, the killer now picked up Katherine King, another street walker, in Regent Street. Back at her flat, he gave her £5, which was way over the normal asking price.

At that moment there was a power cut. At once he attempted to strangle her but she was a feisty girl and fought him off. He was losing his touch. Alarmed by her screams for help, he gave her another fiver (about £200 at today's values) and fled, this time leaving his service belt.

With the evidence of the gas mask and the service belt, the police expected a confession. No chance. It appeared from the billet passbook that the cadet, Gordon Cummins, had been back every night before the time of the murders. A perfect alibi? Not quite. His fingerprints were found at the scene of each crime. He also had cigarette cases belonging to two of the murdered women and a fountain pen with Doris Jonannet's initials on it. It seemed that Cummins was a larger-than-life character and a fantasist. He claimed to be the illegitimate son of a member of the House of Lords. He had a lofty, superior manner and was known to his fellow cadets as 'the duke'. He claimed his belt had been inadvertently picked up by someone else and insisted gas masks were always being mislaid. Following his arrest, another girl reported she had been attacked after being picked up outside Oddentino's in Regent Street. Cummins attempted to strangle her with a row of beads she was wearing. Luckily for her, she had kept her high-heeled boots on. As they struggled, she gave him a hefty kick, knocking him off the bed. Suddenly he appeared embarrassed and, apologising, gave her £10 before making a speedy exit.

Despite the weight of evidence against him, including being picked out at an identity parade, Cummins pleaded not guilty. The jury took less than an hour to find him guilty. On 25 June 1941 Cummins was hanged at Wandsworth prison, the only murderer recorded as having been despatched during an air raid.

Worries about less sensational murders nagged away long after the conviction of Harry Dobkin. How many killings had gone unnoticed under the cover of constant bombing and the confusion that followed? Harry and Rachel Dobkin had entered into an 'arranged' marriage at Bethnal Green synagogue way back in 1920. Within days it became obvious that this was no love match and the couple separated. Maintenance of £1 per week became a constant source of friction. Payments were spasmodic as Harry drifted, sometimes finding jobs in the clothing trade. By the outbreak of war he had secured employment as a fire watcher for solicitors in Kennington Lane. On 12 April 1941 Rachel was reported missing. While obviously distressing for her family, her disappearance raised no alarms with the authorities. Rachel was added to the huge list of people unaccounted for in London.

Two days after Rachel was reported missing, there was an unexplained fire that flared through a bomb site at the back of the offices where Harry worked. Once again it raised no suspicion as fires in wartime London were commonplace. Harry's undoing came with the further demolition by the local authorities of a former Baptist chapel. They found a partially preserved body under a pile of rubble. The pathologist's examination revealed that it was the body of a woman who had been strangled. Dental records revealed that the deceased was Rachel Dobkin. The jury took only twenty minutes to find Harry guilty. His mistake had been to cover her body in builders' lime (which helped preserve it) rather than quick lime. He reckoned Rachel had constantly nagged and pestered him about money. The price Harry paid was high indeed. On 7 January 1943 Dobkin was hanged, one of thirty-seven despatched at Wandsworth prison during the war.

While, during much of 1941, London was being attacked from the skies, down on the streets another battle was being fought. There had been a shift in the power of West End gangland. With so many Italians interned, the White gang from Islington, with the help of a large Jewish element, was pushing for control of Soho. One of the few Italian strongholds were three clubs situated at 17 Wardour Street. There had been previous trouble when Eddie Fleischer had been beaten up and banned from the premises by 'Babe' Mancini, the club's nominal manager. Trouble broke out again at the rather grand-sounding West End Bridge and Billiard Club. Wanting to avoid further confrontation, 'Babe' slipped away and went home to change out of his evening dress. Later, assuming the trouble had passed, he went upstairs to assess any damage. As he climbed the stairs he heard someone say, 'There's Babe, let's knife him!' Mancini was convinced it was Fleischer. Turning, he saw he was being followed by Harry 'Scarface' Distleman. Fighting broke out and in the confused melee Distleman staggered back, crying out, 'I am terribly hurt, Babe done it.'

At his trial for murder, Mancini's defence was not helped by the fact he had chased Fleischer and inflicted a dreadful wound that almost severed Eddie's arm. Claiming he had arrived unarmed, Mancini insisted he had found the knife lying on the floor. Mancini pleaded guilty to manslaughter, encouraged by a similar case earlier in the year that resulted in a prison sentence. His hopes were raised by a seemingly favourable summing up by the judge, but the jury had other ideas. It is quite possible that his Italian background weighed against him in the prevailing hostile climate. 'Babe' Mancini was hanged at Pentonville prison on 17 October 1941. He was the first client of Albert Pierrepoint since he was appointed chief executioner by the Home Office. As the hood was placed over his head, Mancini bid the attending officials an upbeat 'cheerio'. 'Babe' was the first Soho gang member to be executed for twenty-three years. It served as a poignant reminder to career criminals to be extremely careful not to inflict fatal wounds.

GIs also featured in a number of murders, but it was an inept couple trying to ape the antics of 'Bonnie and Clyde' that captured the headlines. Karl Hulton was a deserter, who was posing as Lieutenant Ricky Allen. Born in Sweden, he had grown up in Massachusetts. A fantasist, he met his unlikely partner in crime in a Hammersmith café in October 1944. Elizabeth Jones had a troubled background, having run away from school at thirteen. More recently she had been a dancer at various dubious West End clubs. While impressionable, she still retained a certain prudishness from her strict Welsh upbringing, insisting that she was never sexually intimate with Hulton. They were an odd couple, but he persuaded her to go on a pathetic, violent and doomed crime spree. She believed he had been a Chicago gang leader and she fancied herself as a gangster's moll. Driving in a stolen Army truck, their first target was a woman riding a bike. They knocked her to the ground and stole her handbag. Flushed with success, they then attempted to rob a taxi driver in the Edgware Road. Pointing a gun at the driver, Hulton had not noticed a passenger in the back, an American officer who also drew his gun. Hulton beat a hasty retreat and, jumping into the truck, the hapless couple sped off.

They next gave a girl they saw carrying two suitcases towards Paddington station the promise of a lift to Reading. Once outside London, Hulton stopped the truck and attacked the stranger with an iron bar before dumping her behind a hedge on a river bank. The following night they hailed a taxi. Driving out of London again, they reached a deserted stretch of the Great West Road, where they asked the driver to stop. Unsuspecting, he was shot by Hulton at point blank range and his body dumped in a roadside ditch. Jones then went through his pockets, taking the little cash he possessed and a few personal belongings, including a cigarette lighter and a fountain pen. Oblivious to the fact that the body had been found and the car registration circulated, they spent the following afternoon at the White City dog track, losing the nineteen shillings they had stolen from the cab driver. On 10 October the car was spotted in the Fulham Palace Road and Karl Hulton was arrested with his gun still in his pocket. Jones was picked up soon after, having confessed to a friend, 'If you had seen someone do what I have seen, you wouldn't be able to sleep at night.'

Unusually, the Americans agreed that Hulton would not face a court martial but be tried by a British court. Both were found guilty, but Jones was subsequently reprieved. Hulton was hanged at Pentonville on 7 March 1945. Elizabeth Jones was released into the community in 1954. All these killers had proved to be inadequate, rather pathetic individuals, seedy 'bit' players in London's dramatic war.

As the war drew to its conclusion, those who had betrayed the country were spotlighted. Vengeance was not unleashed to the extent witnessed across the rest of Europe, but the government felt the need to make an example of high-profile offenders, to add to those who had been convicted earlier. Four men were tried for treason and one for treachery. All were sentenced to death, but two were reprieved. Theodore Schurch, a British soldier of Swiss descent, had deserted at Tobruk and volunteered to help German intelligence. He had been a member of the British National Party before the war. He was arrested in Rome in March 1945 and was the only British serviceman to be executed for treachery during the war. He was hanged at Pentonville prison in January 1946.

What bad blood had entered the veins of John Amery was evident from an early age. Born into a leading Tory family, with all the advantages of wealth and position, he must have been a cause of constant distress to his family. Both his father, Leo, and subsequently his brother, Julian, achieved high political office. Perhaps it was living in his father's shadow, but even at Harrow school he was identified as rebellious. His headmaster suggested he was 'morally an imbecile'. And so it proved. He married a prostitute, had over seventy motoring convictions and was bankrupt by the age of twenty-four. He fought for Franco in the Spanish Civil War before going to live in France in 1941, where he met French fascist leader Jacques Doriot. Convinced that communism was undermining European society, he was recruited by the Nazis to make pro-German broadcasts to Britain. His family must have squirmed in disbelief and shame, but his disastrous lack of judgement continued with his forming of the Legion of St George in the spring of 1943. This was a largely futile attempt to recruit Allied prisoners of war to fight for Germany against the Red Army. After making further broadcasts and writing propaganda for the Germans, Amery moved to Northern Italy in a last-ditch attempt to support Mussolini. During the last weeks of the war, he was captured by Italian partisans who handed him over to the British. He was taken into custody by Captain Alan Whicker, who was attached to the British Army's film and photographic unit. Amery seemed unwilling to accept the gravity of his situation. He told detectives from Scotland Yard who had been flown out to question him that he didn't expect to be charged and if he was his father would sort things out. Back in England he was charged with high treason at Bow Street Magistrates' Court on 9 May 1945. He was remanded in Brixton Prison to await trial. There were gasps of disbelief at the Old Bailey when on 8 November he pleaded guilty to eight counts of high treason. This was, in effect, committing suicide as the judge had no option other than sentencing Amery to death.

It is reckoned he pleaded guilty to spare his family prolonged distress during what would have been a long trial. Despite a plea from South African Field Marshall Smuts to Prime Minister Attlee and one from Amery's mother to the king, there was to be no reprieve.

There is a bizarre footnote to this good-looking, dissolute and misguided young man's story. While in his broadcasts he was forever warning of world domination by Jews, there was a secret tucked away in the Amery family background. Was it possible that he actually knew that his father's mother was a Hungarian Jewess? Leo Amery, aware of the rampant anti-Semitism within the establishment, had managed to successfully bury this fact, which would have scuppered his rise through the political jungle.

John Amery was transferred to Wandsworth prison. On meeting the executioner, he was reported to have said, 'Mr Pierrepoint, I have always wanted to meet you, but of course not under these circumstances.' Pierrepoint was later to claim that Amery was the bravest man he had ever met. John Amery was hanged at 9.00 a.m. on 19 December. He was thirty-three. In death he had, at least, sought some late redemption for his flawed and tragic life.

William Joyce was another influential figure whose backing of Germany was to lead to his execution. Born in New York to naturalised US parents, who had emigrated from Ireland, the family arrived to live in England in 1922. Joyce was then sixteen and the following year he joined the British fascists. He was slashed on his face with a razor at a public meeting the year after. He insisted this was inflicted by a communist Jew. An intelligent man, he had graduated from London University with a first-class honours degree. Later he was to join Oswald Mosley as a leading spokesman for the British Union of Fascists as its director of propaganda. He was narrowly defeated in London county council elections for Shoreditch in 1937, by which time his extreme racist views led to a split from Mosley's party. Worried that the government was contemplating the internment of known fascists, Joyce left for Germany. He was gratefully recruited by the German Radio Corporation. On 14 September 1939 Joyce started his *Germany Calling* programme. He continued with these broadcasts throughout the war where he was sometimes joined by John Amery. Joyce acquired the name of Lord Haw-Haw, after the *Daily Express* said he spoke with the ultra-refined accent of the 'haw-haw, damn-it-get-out-of-my-way variety'. By 1940 almost a third of the population of Britain was reckoned to tune in regularly to his broadcasts. At first the authorities were worried at the torrent of propaganda aimed to raise doubts about Britain's ability to fight and survive. They even arranged for popular radio programmes to be broadcast at the same time as Joyce to act as a spoiler. Before long it became obvious that Lord Haw-Haw's claims were vastly inflated. His appeals for Britain to surrender were counterproductive. Soon apathy about his claims changed to ridicule, helped by spoof send-ups by the popular comedians of the day.

Although he lived in Britain for most of his life, Joyce had never taken out British nationality. He fraudulently acquired a British passport in 1933, which enabled him to travel to Germany. In 1940 he took out German nationality. None of this was to help him at his trial. The attorney general, Sir Hartley Shawcross, maintained that his British passport had entitled him to diplomatic immunity in Germany and therefore he continued to owe allegiance to Britain at the time he started to work for the Germans. It was, therefore, claimed that he had committed treason by broadcasting for Germany between September 1939 and July 1940, when he officially became a German citizen. The evidence for this was purely anecdotal, but the government, rather than the public, needed a conviction. There was a degree of sympathy for Joyce who was not seen as a threat, rather as a butt for jokes. A comical and pathetic figure, but one who remained defiant, he said, 'In death, as in life, I defy the Jews who caused this last war, and I defy the colour of darkness they represent.'

At the age of thirty-nine, Joyce was led to the gallows on 3 January 1946, just a couple of weeks after John Amery. In a war that killed millions, sympathy was short lived for Britain's traitors, however ineffectual they had been.

The Treachery Act of 1940 was introduced to deal with the expected surge in the number of spies operating in Britain. A total of sixteen were executed for their actions (nine at Wandsworth and seven at Pentonville). While Albert Pierrepoint praised John Amery for his bravery, earlier it was a German spy who had offered the most resistance as he was taken to the gallows. Karl Richter hailed from the Sudetenland. He was convicted at the Central Criminal Court after a four-day trial in October 1941. His appeal was dismissed a month later. Despite this he appeared surprised by the arrival in his cell of Pierrepoint and his assistant Harry Allen. Throwing himself violently across the cell, he smashed his head against the wall. A strong and powerful man, he fought ferociously as the executioner attempted to strap his arms behind his back. Warders had to be called in an attempt to restrain him. Still he fought and with a supreme effort brought on by desperation, managed to snap the stout leather strap. He was half carried, still struggling, to the gallows and even then he was not done. As the lever was pulled he leapt forward. This had the effect of loosening the noose, which caught his top lip rather than under his jaw. Although distressing for all those present, the force of the drop broke his neck and he was declared dead.

Josef Jakobs was the last man to be executed at the Tower of London. In February 1941 he was parachuted into a field just outside Ramsey in Huntingdonshire. Unfortunately for Jakobs, he did not have a happy landing. Two farm workers heard what they thought were gunshots. They found poor Josef nursing a broken leg covered by a camouflaged parachute. On being discovered he threw his pistol away and surrendered. He was lying on top of an attaché case that contained a wireless transmitter, a torch with a flashing device and a map with local airfields highlighted. He had already torn up a code that would have enabled him to contact his controllers in Germany.

He was taken to the Duke of York's HQ, Chelsea, where he was charged with 'committing treachery in that [he] ... descended by parachute with intent to help the enemy'. Jakobs admitted that he was an officer in the intelligence section of the German General Staff. The court martial found him guilty and, as such, he was sentenced to be shot. At 7.15 a.m. on 15 August 1941 Jakobs was taken to the Miniature Rifle Range at the Tower. This was where spies from the First World War had been executed. Due to his broken leg Jakobs was shot while seated. A white target was pinned to his chest. He was executed by an eight-man firing squad drawn from the Scots Guards. So it was that Josef Jakobs joined a long and illustrious line of people executed at the Tower over the centuries. He will surely be the last.

6

Wartime Entertainment

Wearing his white Stetson and mounted on Trigger, his Palomino horse, Roy Rogers is again being chased by an ugly gang of bandits. Across London thousands of children shout out in alarm. Of course they have no need to worry, 'the good guy' always wins and soon they will be laughing at the antics of Laurel and Hardy or Charlie Chaplin. Welcome to Saturday morning 'pictures', where for a couple of hours children can forget the hardships of a war-torn London and give vent to their feelings without any form of parental control.

For adults too, a visit to the cinema was not a passive activity. It was often raucous and emotional. Newsreels showing British success in battle were greeted with thunderous applause and stamping of feet. The sight of Hitler or of German troops led to whistles, boos and, frequently, verbal abuse. The unruly tradition of the music-hall audience had transferred to the silver screen. Today's sophisticated audience, which appears not to outwardly react to even the most extreme scenes, would have been shocked at what almost amounted to audience participation.

Attendances at cinemas during the war soared to record levels. The blockbuster *Gone With The Wind,* starring Clark Gable and Vivien Leigh, was released in April 1940. It proved a massive success, running uninterrupted in the West End for four years. It was difficult for the British film industry to compete with its powerful Hollywood cousin. There was a shortage, not only of actors, but technicians too, and yet the period of the war saw a revival in the industry. According to critic Dilys Powell, 'It took a war to convince the British to look at themselves and find themselves interesting.' It needed time to evolve, with the quality of British films tending to improve as the war progressed. This was not apparent in the 1940 offering *Bulldog Sees It Through*, starring Jack Buchanan and based on a story by Sapper. Bulldog Drummond was a character locked in the past. An ex-officer with time on his hands setting out to defeat an assortment of crooks, most of whom were, of course, foreign. It was a genre wittily described as 'snobbery with violence'. Comedy was popular, however puerile, and a film of *Just William* featuring Richard Lupino and Fred Emney also attracted mixed reviews. Things had to improve.

After the horrific impact of the Blitz on London, audiences increasingly sought escapist fare. *The Wizard Of Oz*, although a children's film, attracted huge adult audiences too. Everyone was desperately seeking their own somewhere over the rainbow, longing for better times. On a more mundane level, well-known entertainers Flanagan and Allen appeared in *Gas Bags*, while American couple Bebe Daniels and Ben Lyon starred in *Hi Gang*, a spin-off from their popular radio programme. Improvements in Allied fortunes from 1942 were reflected in the type of film being made. Comedy and escapism still featured strongly, but now films shot to stir the patriotic spirit were starting to appear. *The First Of The Few* (released as *Spitfire* in America) showed how the legendary fighter plane was developed, against the odds, by R. J. Mitchell. It was tragic that he died of cancer (officially of tuberculosis – the 'c' word was unacceptable to a wartime audience) just as the first prototype was produced. Maybe it was because he didn't live to see the huge impact of his legendary fighter plane that the film was made, featuring Leslie Howard and a young David Niven, with music by William Walton. *In Which We Serve* could have been renamed 'The Noel Coward Show', written, directed and starring 'the dear boy'. He was also responsible for the music. Based on the exploits of Louis Mountbatten, it received rave reviews on both sides of the Atlantic. Starring John Mills and Celia Johnson, the film gave Britain a much-needed propaganda boost in the States.

The film was also notable for the first appearance of Richard Attenborough.

Propaganda was on the mind of the Ministry of Information and the Crown Film Unit that came under its jurisdiction. During the war the MOI made close on 2,000 films and were also responsible for the vetting of newsreels. In 1942 the Crown Film Unit made *Coastal Command,* which featured regular RAF and Royal Navy staff. It brought a sense of realism and was well received. The film was enhanced by the score composed by Ralph Vaughan Williams who, like his contemporary William Walton, produced memorable music for the cinema.

The war was to see the production of several films that are now regarded as classics, together with actors, directors and producers who have subsequently become household names. Michael Powell and Emeric Pressburger always pushed boundaries with their productions, including *49th Parallel* and *Canterbury Tales. The Life of Colonel Blimp* was based on the frighteningly reactionary character created by the cartoonist David Low. Perhaps it was too well targeted because some establishment figures reacted furiously, damning the film as subversive. The outstanding talent of English director Carol Reid was reflected in 1940 by *Night Train to Munich,* followed later by *The Young Mr. Pitt* and the classic *The Way Ahead.* Anthony Asquith was the son of former Prime Minister Herbert Asquith, who had been at the helm during the First World War. In 1940 Anthony Asquith was responsible for *French Without Tears,* based on a play by Terence Rattigan, as was his classic *The Way To The Stars,* starring Michael Redgrave and John Mills. The fact that Rattigan became such an influence on wartime films was due in no small part to the intervention of Winston Churchill. In August 1942 the Prime Minister went to see *Flare Path,* which had opened at the Apollo Theatre. He declared the play to be a masterpiece and, with his ringing endorsement, Rattigan was released from his duties as a rear gunner in the RAF to write more patriotic offerings.

Noel Coward continued to be another huge influence in British film-making. *Blithe Spirit,* which had received a mixed reception as a stage production, was made into a 1945 film by David Lean, who also wrote the script. It was a rather zany comedy, featuring psychics and clairvoyancy. It starred Rex Harrison and the wonderful Margaret Rutherford. Unusually for a British production at that time, it was filmed in Technicolor. *Brief Encounter* was an altogether more serious and impressive film. It involved the intense and emotional relationship between a couple already married but not to each other. It was all repressed passion and yearning. Being British, of course, Trevor Howard and Celia Johnson never made it to the bedroom. The film struck a nerve with the public, many of whom were doubtless encountering similar problems, although not necessarily with the same outcome. British film-makers did not want, or more likely were not allowed, to condone adultery. Helped by David Lean's wonderful direction and the music of Rachmaninoff's searing Second Piano Concerto, there was scarcely a dry eye in the house.

It was left to good old William Shakespeare to prove that a work written centuries before could re-emerge as a modern-day hit. *Henry V* was released in 1944. Surely it was its patriotic theme that appealed to the public. Never mind the fact that half the audience only had the very vaguest idea of what the dialogue was going on about. It was a Technicolor spectacle and the English were victorious. It raised the spirits. For the French at Agincourt, one could substitute the much-loathed Germans. It was a triumph for Laurence Oliver, who was the director and who also took the star role. Swept along by William Walton's Academy Award-winning score, the film was indeed a morale booster 'for England, Harry and St George'.

While a visit to the cinema was the most popular form of entertainment, the West End theatres also enjoyed good times, except during the Blitz and later with the arrival of 'flying bombs'. Then, for a time, central London remained eerily empty.

With all places of entertainment closed down at the outbreak of war, it took only a few weeks for the ban to be lifted. The British public sought any escape from the impact of war – the constant worry, the drabness, and the endless queues. Yet queues outside one theatre became a trademark feature. For the thousands of servicemen flocking to the West End, their first port of call was often the Windmill. A small theatre with seating for under 400, each day queues snaked their way down Great Windmill Street. This was one of the few places that a young man could legally see nude girls on stage. True, they were static and about as sexy as the marble statues in the British Museum, but it was a start. A start for many young men who were being introduced to the excitement and perils of a big city for the first time. Despite the lure of bare flesh the Windmill actually offered bright, professional and wholesome fare. The girls had to exude personality as well as good looks. There were up to six shows a day and two separate companies. So the girls were either performing or constantly rehearsing. It was a tough schedule and with the onset of the Blitz a decision was made for most of the company to live in the theatre. They showed great courage and spirit each night as they went on stage against a backdrop of ack-ack fire and falling bombs. On 19 October 1940 a bomb demolished a café directly opposite the theatre, also killing a seventeen-year-old electrician working at the Windmill.

Margaret McGrath was generally acknowledged to be the Windmill's number-one pin-up in 1940. On that awful October night, she volunteered to look for the missing electrician. It was a gruesome business. There were over a dozen mutilated bodies covered by blankets lying in the street, and none of the Windmill men could face the task. So it was left to the glamorous Margaret to identify the poor boy.

Within days, Margaret was back in action. She was in one of the remaining cafés in Great Windmill Street with her friend Annie Singer. Hundreds of firebombs were being released by the Nazi planes above. As the girls ran towards the theatre they heard the whinnying of horses. The stables at the back of Ham Yard were ablaze. The horses were frantic but the girls, undaunted, plunged in and released them. Eventually, holding onto their halters, they led three horses each out onto the street. Trying to calm them down was not easy with the sound of gunfire and fire alarms going off. In due course, with the help of passers-by, they managed to pacify the poor horses. What do you do with six horses in the middle of an air raid in the heart of the West End? First they tried a garage but were turned away by the fire brigade. So they set off down Shaftesbury Avenue. When they encountered a perplexed policeman, he suggested taking the animals to the nearest police station. So they set off around a still-crowded Piccadilly Circus. Trying to lead three horses each isn't easy at the best of times. They received many offers of help, not all of them related to equine safety. What a sight, two very pretty girls leading six bucking horses. For a moment, it was possible to forget the falling bombs. But not for long. They drew even more attention to themselves by singing 'I've got Sixpence' as they went along. They felt a strange sense of exhilaration until another bomb fell nearby and the horses broke loose. It was half an hour before they managed to catch them all, firstly from Regent Street and later from Burlington Street. Eventually, the horses were passed for safekeeping to an astonished duty sergeant at Vine Street police station.

Under the protective eye of the managing director, Vivian van Damm, working at the Windmill during this time was likened to a boarding school. Sleeping quarters were set up in rehearsal and dressing rooms, with the sexes duly segregated. A curfew was strictly enforced for those not appearing in the evening's show. Even so, the doorman became a key figure in dealing with stage-door Johnnies. Generally speaking, it was air crew who were the favourites with the girls. They tended to have a taxi waiting and a table booked. There were breathless romances and a few broken hearts. There were deaths and news of hideous injuries to young men who only a few weeks earlier had kissed the girls a tender goodnight. Life for the Windmill girls was a whirl. An exhausting schedule of singing, dancing and snatched kisses, all conducted against a background of searchlights, bombs and real danger. High-octane stuff. This was a time still remembered with affection by the few remaining girls surviving. 'We never closed' was their proud claim or, as the alternative version had it, 'We never clothed.' Whichever it was, the old showbiz saying, 'the show must go on', has seldom been upheld with such courage.

A dapper little man who rarely sought publicity came to dominate West End theatre for forty years. Still only in his early thirties at the outbreak of war, Binkie Beaumont, joint founder and managing director of A. M. Tennant Ltd, was a figure admired and feared in equal measure. From a tiny office above the Globe theatre in Shaftesbury Avenue, he spun his web of lavish praise, veiled threats and intrigue. To upset him was likely to consign you to the sidelines, so they came, the actors and playwrights, to pay homage. Authors, including Noel Coward, Terence Rattigan and Emlyn Williams, sent their plays to him first. Designers Cecil Beaton and Oliver Messel were in his thrall, while he kept star actors of the day, including John Gielgud, Peggy Ashcroft and a host of others in permanent work. At the height of his power he had fourteen productions running in the West End simultaneously. Vivien Leigh, who had returned to Britain after her triumph in *Gone With The Wind*, decided she wanted to drive an ambulance as her contribution to the war effort. Binkie was horrified. He lectured her 'on her duty to her public rather than putting herself in danger'. She concurred, as did most people.

His early wartime offerings included *Cousin Muriel* at the Globe theatre, starring Peggy Ashcroft and a young Alec Guinness. One of his few setbacks during the war came when the Luftwaffe very inconveniently dropped a bomb on the Queen's theatre in Shaftesbury Avenue in September 1940. The front façade was destroyed and the auditorium wrecked. Thus ended a successful run of Daphne du Maurier's *Rebecca* in which Margaret Rutherford had enjoyed rave reviews as the frightening Mrs Danvers. Beaumont, the 'master fixer', continued to spread his influence during the war years, feeding the public with a diet of classics and light comedy. It was later that he woke up to the potential of musicals with his staging of *My Fair Lady*. Before then he had viewed musicals with some distaste, despite the fact that *Me And My Girl* ran to over 1,600 performances. Could anyone really imagine him having anything to do with a show so vulgar that it featured the 'Lambeth Walk'?

Vulgarity appalled Binkie, but not the British public. Max Miller, 'the cheeky chappie', told very risqué jokes at breakneck speed. Wearing loud suits and his hat at a rakish angle, he belonged to a generation who learnt their trade on the music hall circuit. He appeared at the Holborn Empire in the review *Haw-Haw* and then at the same theatre with Vera Lynn before bomb damage forced the show to transfer to the Palladium. Flanagan and Allen also pulled in the crowds when in 1941 they appeared in *Hi-De-Hi* at the Victoria Palace, which was later to become their base in successive productions featuring the 'Crazy Gang'.

Bomb damage to costumes and scenery was one of the problems that even Binkie sometimes found difficult to overcome. Once destroyed, with wartime restrictions in place, replacements proved impossible. Bare stages, destined to become popular by choice after the war, were perhaps unplanned trendsetters. A season of Gilbert and Sullivan was ruined for devotees when *H.M.S. Pinafore*, *Ruddigore* and *Cox and Box* all had to be omitted from the repertoire.

Binkie had similar problems with a season of Shakespeare's plays in 1943. He modestly claimed in 1945 that 'it may sound cynical but the war has been the making of me. And to think I owe it all to Hitler.' Beaumont had indeed enjoyed a good war. He had presented fifty-nine plays in the West End, of which only seven had failed. Many had run for over a year and gone to over 1,000 performances. He reflected on his luck, in that so many of his rivals were in the forces and conveniently out of the way. It was Binkie's connections who had smoothed his path with the Minister of Labour, Ernest Bevin, able to grant him exception from military service. In the world of theatre, as in life, it's not so much what you know, as who you know.

The summer exhibition at the Royal Academy was among one of London's leading social events before the war. It was good to be seen staring intently at some modern daub to prove you were not a total philistine. Better still to purchase a painting or two to grace your Kensington flat. The great and the good were pretty thin on the ground for the 1941 exhibition, but by the following year it was again the place to be seen. Augustus John managed to extricate himself from his complex love interests for long enough to offer a portrait of the Viscount Caldecote, but by 1944 he was much more in his element showing chalk studies of Poppet, Lauretta and Mary. In the same year Britain's favourite equine artist, Alfred Munnings, was knighted. He celebrated by exhibiting nine works, including the much-admired *Start at Newmarket*. 1944 proved to be the most generally successful year for sales at the Royal Academy. Evidently, buyers were out in strength, sensing that art as an investment was about to take off after the war.

Music is central to all our lives and even more so during times of stress. It affects our mood and heightens our emotions. Uniquely, popular music comes to represent past eras as we look back. London was awash with music during the war, fuelled in part by a love of dancing. There were hundreds of dance halls scattered all over the capital, from Hammersmith Palais to the Astoria in Charing Cross Road and the giant Locarno in Streatham. London was rocking – well, not actually rocking (that was still to come) – but jitterbugging and boogieing. The major dance halls, like the huge West End cinemas, offered a glimpse of glitz and glamour. Those wearing uniforms were often allowed in for half price (that is if they agreed to remove their boots to help protect the highly sprung floors). Waltzes and foxtrots were still popular with the more buttoned-up clientele, but the days of when the hokey-cokey and hands, knees and boomps-a-daisy cleared the floor were numbered. With the arrival of the Americans it was time for change. A wide-eyed British public looked on as their girls were thrown about like rag dolls. Victor Sylvester fought manfully to retain strict tempo dancing, but the free expression of the jitterbug gradually emerged as jive. It was no longer necessary to learn all those tedious steps. This was dancing to mirror the age, fast, breathless, exciting. Driven on by the sounds of Glenn Miller, Artie Shaw and Benny Goodman, British bands from Lew Stone to Joe Loss and Harry Roy quickly mugged up on the latest American hits and belted out reasonable cover versions. Ladies who are now very old speak nostalgically of those exciting times. Whisked into the arms of someone they might never meet again, emotions were raised, and often dashed, to a background of unforgettable dance music.

New British singing stars now emerged as solo artists. Previously, their role had largely been consigned to provide what was known as a vocal refrain. Employed by the band leader, it was he who was lauded as the star. Vera Lynn, a young London singer in her early twenties, had previously worked for Charlie Kunz and Joe Loss, but her recording of 'We'll Meet Again' changed her life. With music and lyrics by Mancunian Ross Parker, the lilting song exactly caught the mood of hope and anxiety that war creates. It catapulted her to stardom. Her voice was strong and emotive, even today pulling at the heartstrings. Good-looking in a homely way, she became known as the 'Forces' Sweetheart'. The girl next door, a sister, welcoming yet unthreatening. She was to be the perfect link between men away at the front and their wives or girlfriends. She fulfilled this role in her radio programme *Sincerely Yours*, where she passed messages between separated loved ones. In 1940 she married Harry Lewis, a player in Lew Stone's band. Harry went on to be her manager. By 1943 she recorded another song which was to become a classic, despite the stupid lyrics that suggested there would be 'bluebirds over the white cliffs of Dover'. Well, Walter Kent and Nat Burton were Americans so we can forgive them their ignorance of British bird life. The song, like her later recording of 'A Nightingale Sang in Berkeley Square' (more bird-sighting problems here), were massive hits.

There are similarities between Vera Lynn and another London singer, Anne Shelton. She too was attractive, but no glamour-puss. She spent six years with Bert Ambrose and his orchestra. She was still a teenager when she recorded 'I Don't Know Why I Love You, But I Do' in 1941, and three years later her voice had matured and lowered when she recorded 'Lili Marlene' with Stanley Black and his orchestra, which became her signature tune. Here was a song written by a German in 1916, which had a global, emotional appeal. Anne Shelton's wonderful, deep voice attracted the attention of Bing Crosby and Glenn Miller. Anne did record six shows with his band but, at her mother's prompting, decided not to join him on a trip to France. Miller's concerts recorded in Versailles were to be his last. On his next trip to the Continent he took off from an airfield near Bedford on 15 December 1944 but his plane disappeared over the English Channel. No trace of the aircraft was ever found and the legendary band leader was declared missing in action.

Strangely, British male singers failed to make a huge impact during the war. Perhaps the only one to achieve status only managed it after his death. Born in Mozambique, Al Bowlly came to Britain in the 1920s and by 1941 had made over 1,000 records. He had great success with Ray Noble, including the haunting

'The Very Thought of You'. He also enjoyed considerable success in the States, but he returned to London just before the start of the war. His absence had dented his popularity with British audiences. An operation to remove a vocal wart weakened his voice and he was forced to take bookings in second-rate venues. In 1940 he started a double act with Jimmy Mesene, whose own career was also in decline, due in part to his heavy drinking. On 17 April 1941 the pair appeared in Oxford Street – not the West End version, but the Rex cinema, Oxford Street, High Wycombe. They were offered digs for the night but Bowlly chose to return to his flat in Duke Street. As he slept a parachute bomb landed in the street outside. He was discovered totally unmarked, killed by his bedroom door, which had been blown off its hinges and had landed on him.

The imposition of the blackout led to a boom in reading. My mother would make weekly trips to our local library or to the Boots lending library, and return with an armful of books. Reading for her was pure escapism, not so much from the war but the drudgery of housework. With few modern appliances, most women were consigned to a life of washing, ironing, cleaning and endless queuing. So her escape was to get stuck into a book. She cooked while reading (sometimes with pretty dire results) and even sat on the loo reading. It was her passion. Having never travelled abroad, books about faraway places fascinated her, particularly India. Some of my earliest memories are of a hissing gas fire, the smell of hide leather armchairs and everyone in our family with their noses stuck in a book.

A mass observation report suggested that as well as fiction, gardening, cooking and do-it-yourself craft books were the most popular. Paperbacks, introduced by Penguin in 1935, also helped popularise reading. Although published on poor-quality paper, their green-covered detective and crime series were snapped up as soon as they appeared on the shelves. In 1941 the company started publishing Puffin story books aimed at children in the nine- to thirteen-year-old group. Previously Puffin had only offered picture books for children.

The bestsellers during the early 1940s revealed a desire for turning away from the impact of the war and the intrigue of world politics. In 1940, a story about life in a Welsh mining town topped the list. *How Green Was My Valley* was written by Richard Llewellyn (who, despite his denials, was born in London). The book was also a massive hit in America and in 1941 a film based on the story was made starring Walter Pidgeon and Maureen O'Hara. It was nominated for ten Academy Awards, including the producer Darryl Zanuck for Best Picture and John Ford for Best Director, both of which they won. In 1941, it was the turn of Scottish writer A. J. Cronin to take the honour of bestselling book with his *The Key to the Kingdom*. Set in China, it follows the fortunes of Father Francis Chisholm and his attempts to set up a mission in unfriendly territory. It too was made into a Hollywood film in 1944 starring Gregory Peck and Vincent Price. *For Whom the Bell Tolls* by Ernest Hemmingway was in the bestseller list for over a year, but it was to be other American authors who became wartime publishing sensations.

The Robe, written by an ex-cleric Lloyd Douglas, was published in the States in 1942 and it appeared in Britain the following year. A book based on events after the crucifixion of Christ hardly suggested massive sales but within weeks the book headed the bestseller list. It was seen through the eyes of Roman tribune Marcellus Gallio, who witnesses the crucifixion and subsequently takes possession of the robe worn by Jesus. Not convinced of the prophet's guilt, he begins to believe that the robe has some supernatural powers. It is a story that crosses continents and sees Marcellus convert to Christianity, before he is eventually executed on the orders of the insane Emperor Caligula. It took until 1953 for the blockbuster film to be made starring Richard Burton.

Forever Amber, published in 1944, was the all-time bestseller for the entire 1940s. Set in Restoration England, it too was written by an American, who was as outrageous as her heroine, Amber St Clare. The book, by Kathleen Winsor, sold over 100,000 copies in the first week of publication in the States. Ridicule and slating by many reviewers did nothing to stem the sales. It was banned in fourteen states for being pornographic. In truth, the sex scenes are fairly tame, appearing only on a few occasions in a monstrous text that ran to almost 1,000 pages. A pretty girl and a cast of dastardly men, all set against a background of major historical events, including the great fire of London, proved irresistible to a public hungry for glamour, scandal and romance. The film, directed by Otto Preminger and starring Linda Darnell as Amber, was made in 1947.

The success of her book had the author behaving very much like her heroine. In 1946 she ditched her husband who had been away fighting in the Pacific. She was a celebrity now and within weeks she had married the serial bridegroom, bandleader Artie Shaw, to become his sixth wife. They were divorced two years later. Undeterred, they both had a few more marriages to go through yet. Kathleen Winsor died in 2003 at the age of eighty-four.

Radio was as important to wartime Britain as television or the internet is to us today. It was a constant companion, feeding its listeners a diet of news, drama, music and comedy programmes. It provided another escape from the grinding effects of the war and served as a much-needed morale booster. With the outbreak of war, the BBC abandoned its existing schedules and for a short period the listeners were subjected to a meagre offering of news bulletins, propaganda and endless organ recitals played by Sandy MacPherson. Within weeks the Home Service was formed following the merger of the national and regional programmes. By 1940 the *Forces Programme* was created. An entertainment network for forces personnel, it proved to be the forerunner of the *Light Programme* and, subsequently, Radio 2.

Although John Reith had resigned as the first director-general of the BBC in 1938, his mantra of 'inform, educate and entertain' was the core mission of the corporation. Programmes continued to be largely sanitised. Scandals, particularly involving sex, were ignored. Swearing was unheard of and the cut-glass accents of announcers were the norm. A BBC pronunciation unit was deferred to by staff, including announcers Alvar Lidell and Stuart Hibbert (reputedly the last man in London to wear spats). Decency, high standards and fair play all reflected the Reithian concept. Despite the disruption of having four separate director-generals during the war, the organisation grew in output and confidence. Its rather coy, protective attitude towards its listeners led to the BBC being affectionately known as 'Auntie'. The appointment of the economist Frederick Ogilvie in succession to Reith was not considered a success. In 1942 joint director-generals were introduced. A decision that was bound to cause problems. It was solved with the resignation of Cecil Groves due to ill health the following year. Robert Foot carried on to March 1944, when at last some continuity was offered by William Haley who continued in the post until 1952.

The war years output at the BBC are remembered mostly for entertainment and comedy shows. Some programmes featuring the spoken word also had massive followings. Perhaps the least likely of these was a programme of real intellectual quality. *The Brains Trust* started life as *Any Questions* in 1941, but changed its name the following year. Who could imagine that today an audience of 12 million would listen to three old buffers discussing why it is that flies land upside down on ceilings, or if they considered that the world is worthless. A panel of Julian Huxley, Commander A. B. Campbell and Professor C. E. M. Joad grappled with the most opaque questions. Transmitted each Tuesday evening, *The Brains Trust* became something of a national institution. It was regarded as being entertaining as well as educational. Far more down to earth was the radio doctor Charles Hill. His talks were broadcast each Friday morning after the eight o'clock news. They started in May 1942 and attracted an audience of 14 million. In his bluff, down-to-earth manner, the doctor gave advice on any number of everyday medical problems. He was particularly concerned with the population's bowel movements and encouraged listeners to use 'those little black-coated workers'. The sales of prunes soared following each of his frequent promptings.

Music While You Work was a live programme that went out twice a day. Aimed at factory workers, it featured a different band for each programme and was relayed through tannoys at work in an attempt to boost morale. A regular favourite was Geraldo and his orchestra whose record sales were increased as a result. His wartime recordings included 'Over the Rainbow', 'Pennies from Heaven' and 'I've got a Gal in Kalamazoo'. Music also featured in Henry Hall's *Guest Night,* which was in effect the BBC's first chat show. The unscripted programme had the greatest stars like Gracie Fields and Noel Coward lining up to appear. The informal format was one that was increasingly copied and popularised. Each show was signed off with Henry Hall's nostalgic signature tune 'Here's to the Next Time'.

Perhaps the most iconic of all radio programmes is *Desert Island Discs*. Created by Roy Plomley, it started life in 1942. Like many great ideas, the basis for the programme was simple and remains unchanged. Each castaway is allowed to take eight records and one luxury item with them to the mythical island. To be asked to appear on the show has been regarded as a huge accolade. The list of castaways has included royalty, prime ministers, stars of film, radio and sport, and an army of the great and good. The original theme music, 'A Sleepy Lagoon', by Eric Coates, has also remained and is now always associated with the programme even if played elsewhere. The first castaway was Vic Oliver von Samek, an Austrian comedian. It was in many ways a strange choice. Despite opposition, Oliver had married Winston Churchill's daughter Sarah in 1935. Strange because by 1941 the couple had separated and it was known how much the Prime Minister loathed the comedian, who had become engaged to Sarah while still married to his Austrian wife. The couple were finally divorced in 1945. The first female castaway was the actress Pat Kirkwood. By the end of the war the impressive list of those marooned included Ivor Novello, C. B. Cochran, Stewart Granger and the Dambuster pilot Wing Commander Guy Gibson.

Another programme that became an institution and was fondly remembered by all those growing up during the 1940s was *Children's Hour*. It was a unique mix of serials, plays and features on history and wildlife. It was introduced by Derek McCulloch who was known to all as 'Uncle Mac'. He really was a kindly uncle to a whole generation of children who still remember him with affection. The programme was particularly important for children who had been evacuated and felt isolated. It was also a comfort for those caught in the trauma and horror of inner-city bomb devastation. *Children's Hour* projected what was essentially a middle-class, middle-brow view of how children should develop. It was an attempt by 'Auntie' BBC to help guide their listeners to be polite, caring and yet inquisitive. Despite this, millions of children tuned in each afternoon at five o'clock with a sense of anticipation. Uncle Mac finished each programme with the words 'goodnight children' and, after a pause and with great emphasis, 'everywhere'.

Some of the most popular programmes attracting huge audiences were those devoted to comedy. Tastes obviously change over the years, but listening to most of them now they seem fairly puerile. Despite this it must be remembered that these shows were breaking fresh ground by creating a totally new genre. The stand-out show was *ITMA* (It's That Man Again), starring the Liverpudlian comedian Tommy Handley. It had a regular audience of 20 million, making it the most popular British radio programme of all time. *ITMA* was launched in 1939 but was taken off air to return much stronger in June 1941. The original plan was to base the programme on an American show starring George Burns and Gracie Allen, but this was quickly abandoned. Instead, the fast-talking, wise-cracking Handley was surrounded by a bizarre group of characters who relied on constantly repeated catchphrases for many of their laughs. The drunken old soak Colonel Chinstrap and the hopeless German spy Funf became stars whose escapades were endlessly discussed in offices and factory canteens. For Chinstrap (played by Jack Train) to turn any conversation round to be construed as an invitation to have a drink with the phrase 'I don't mind if I do' was enough to have the entire country laughing helplessly. The same reaction came when Mrs Mopp enquired of Handley, 'Can I do you now sir?', or by the character Mona Lott saying mournfully, 'It's being so cheerful that keeps me going.'

ITMA was breaking new ground with the speed of its delivery. The script writer Ted Kavanagh attempted to get a laugh every ten seconds. He failed, but his ambition is to be admired. In any event the show ran to 300 performances and was only brought to an end by Tommy Handley's death in 1949.

A low-key event in October 1940 illustrated the pent-up anxiety felt by many Londoners as they sought to escape for a few minutes from the grinding presence of war. The concert pianist Myra Hess approached Sir Kenneth Clark, the director of the National Gallery, about the possibility of giving a lunchtime recital. With many of the paintings having been sent off to North Wales for safety, much of the huge building was empty. Clark suggested a series of concerts, but could hardly have expected the massive public response, which resulted in performances being given every weekday for the duration of the war.

Crowds poured in for the first recital, having paid their one shilling admittance, with many having to sit on the floor. Hess played Beethoven's 'Appassionata', followed by her own arrangement of 'Jesu, Joy of Man's Desiring'. This sensitive performance released an extraordinary tide of emotion with many, including Clark, in tears. He said, 'This is what we have been waiting for – an assertion of eternal values.' Similarly, British reserve was uncorked at the Last Night of the Promenade Concerts, which had transferred to the Royal Albert Hall in 1941 following the destruction of its previous home, the Queen's Hall in Langham Place. The encores were so prolonged that finally the conductor, Henry Wood, brought the evening to a close by appearing on the rostrum in his hat and coat. It was escapism that Londoners craved. Jitterbugging worked for some, Beethoven for others. A visit to the silver screen or reading poetry, it didn't matter which. There was one other important escape valve – anyone for tennis?

7

Sporting London

London has had a long sporting tradition. Happily, it has moved on from bear-baiting and cock-fighting pits. During the 1930s the hordes came each Saturday in their thousands, heading towards London's numerous football stadiums. They were tribal, proudly sporting scarves and rattles bearing their team's colours. In summer, many of these fans would head for Lords or The Oval to watch Wally Hammond or the new record-breaking batsman, Len Hutton. In every park across the capital, coats or jumpers marked out imaginary goalposts for youngsters kicking a ball, or a noisy, improvised cricket match was taking place. Sport had become central to Londoners' lives, particularly as more leisure time had generally become available. With the outbreak of war everything changed. The demand was as great as ever, but the supply, at least for spectator sport, was abruptly curtailed.

As ever, sport tended to be segregated by social class. As spectators, only an ability to pay separated the wealthy from the working man, while shared participation was rare. In the gentlemen's clubs of St James, dinner-jacketed toffs enjoyed a game of billiards, while in the pubs and snooker halls not far away there was a similar sense of enjoyment, albeit in far scruffier surroundings. While snooker had rather aristocratic origins, having been developed in India during the Raj, it now found a mass audience, while billiards tended to remain the preserve of the well-to-do. Both games were played professionally and were dominated by the Davis brothers, Fred and Joe. Joe Davis was world champion from 1927 to 1940, and again after the war.

It was, perhaps, that most English of games, cricket, where people from different social groups actually first played alongside each other. Initially, at the game's inception, the toffs found bowling rather too arduous and it was a key factor in allowing working men to play alongside their 'betters'. Much had changed in the intervening years, but the Gentlemen *versus* Players fixtures dragged on until 1962. Cricket established a significant role in English society. It was played at every school and it was considered essential in teaching the young about teamwork and fair play.

None of this seemed to matter too much as the bombs rained down on London, but sport was not going to be totally sidelined by the Luftwaffe. True, many of London's major sporting venues were requisitioned by the government. The Oval was turned into a prisoner of war camp, while rugby's headquarters at Twickenham suffered the indignity of having its turf dug up and the whole area made into allotments. The hallowed lawns of Wimbledon were converted into a decontamination unit, while Highbury, home of the mighty Arsenal, was taken over by the civil defence authorities. Another barrier to top-class sport was the number of stars who had been called up to serve in the armed forces, and yet, with ingenuity and goodwill, sport continued to flourish. The annual boat race was rowed at Henley and the Varsity rugby match alternated between Oxford and Cambridge.

Football was already established as the national game. It bore little relation to today's 'beautiful game' with its minimal physical contact and multi-millionaire players. Football in the 1940s was tough and abrasive. Shoulder charges, crunching tackles and elbows working overtime. It was played with a heavy, leather ball and boots with reinforced toecaps. It was not for the faint-hearted.

The outbreak of war led to a complete re-jigging of the professional leagues into regional competitions. London had sufficient clubs for them to be split into two divisions. With the authorities worried about the potential danger to large gatherings, crowds were initially restricted to 8,000, later increased to 15,000. By June 1940 initial concerns about danger to crowds had been further relaxed as 40,000 attended an unofficial cup final at Wembley, in which West Ham won 1–0 against Blackburn Rovers. The 1941 game featured two brothers who had made their name in both cricket and football. Centre-half Leslie Compton had the misfortune to miss a penalty but his brother Denis compensated by scoring the equalising goal against Preston North End. Denis Compton was part of a rare breed who played for England both at cricket and football. He was to go on to be one of the first sports stars to make money out of advertising when he became the face of Brylcreem. These unofficial matches continued throughout the war, with Chelsea recording a rare triumph with a 2–0 win over Millwall in 1945. The previous year the old rivalry between England and Scotland was revived with an unofficial international at Wembley. This attracted a crowd of 80,000 and £18,000 was raised for charity. The armed forces also organised an inter-Allied service cup with Dutch and Belgian sides competing against London teams.

With The Oval out of commission, the emphasis for cricket focused on Lords. The ground was requisitioned in 1941 to act as an RAF induction centre. The Long Room was stripped of all its historic memorabilia, which was stowed safely away in the basement. Although a visitor described a visit to the ground as 'a sobering experience with sandbags everywhere', it didn't take long for matches to be arranged. Again, these tended to be inter-services events, with school and invitation matches also popular. The ground sustained minor damage during the early years of the war. Two bombs landed at the nursery end and incendiaries caused a blaze on the pavilion, but the fire was quickly doused. More damage was done when a barrage balloon broke free, ripping the famous Father Time weathervane from its moorings. It was left to the V1 'Buzz Bombs' to cause the most consternation. Flats and the synagogue opposite the Grace Gates were hit early in 1944. Later in July a game between the RAF and the Army was underway when a 'doodlebug' cut out above the famous ground. Players and spectators threw themselves on the grass. The bomb landed just north of Regent's Park, just a few hundred yards away. Showing no concern at the near miss, the game continued.

By way of celebration Jack Robertson, the Middlesex opening batsman, despatched the next ball for a resounding six.

An astonishing 242 MCC members were killed on active service during the war. It's instructive to learn that among this number were a vice-admiral, a major-general and an air vice-marshal, while the total number of NCOs amounted to just a sergeant and three private soldiers who perished. This, again, underlines the social and class divide that continued to dominate society. Five 'victory' test matches were staged between England and an Australian service side in 1945. Honours during this series ended all square.

Horse racing was also severely curtailed during the war. Londoners were denied their annual trip to Epson Downs to watch the Derby, with the Classic being transferred to Newmarket until 1945. The other suburban racecourses popular with Londoners were all requisitioned. Sandown Park became a training ground for the Welsh Guards, while Kempton Park was used as a prisoner of war camp for captured Germans and Italians. Hurst Park served as a motor transport depot and school of instruction. It was left to the quirky Alexandra Palace course in North London to keep the capital's racing alive. Known as 'Ally Pally', it was 'the most peculiarly shaped course in Britain' according to *Copes Racing Encyclopedia*. Nicknamed the 'frying pan', its shape restricted races to being run only over three distances and was considered to be dangerous by many jockeys. Certainly, horses frequently fell, which was unusual in flat racing. Race horse ownership had slumped from the 1930s, when almost 5,000 thoroughbreds were in training, to less than 1,500 in 1940. National Hunt horses were down to just 700. Surprisingly, the prices at the Newmarket sales held up quite well with an average figure of 787 guineas (over £30,000 at today's values). While Lord Derby and the Aga Khan continued to lead a blue-blooded elite of owners, 'Ally Pally' was the preserve of the cockney. Race days were noisy, chaotic and occasionally violent. The first meeting of the war was held in April 1940, when the favourite Ipswich won a selling handicap. Reckoned to be the worst viewing course in the country for spectators, it struggled on until it finally closed in 1970.

'The sport of kings', even at unfashionable Alexandra Palace, saw spectators drawn from all sections of society. It was part of racing's unique attraction, yet its poorer cousin, greyhound racing, acquired a dubious reputation after its arrival in Britain from America in 1926. It unleashed a tidal wave of interest for the working man. By the outbreak of war a staggering 25 million spectators a year were attending British tracks. Gambling among the well-to-do was, on the whole, accepted by society, but a perception grew that 'going to the dogs' attracted the feckless and criminally minded. Its astounding success did little to alter this prejudice in the mind of Middle England. With the introduction of the blackout, meetings had to be organised in the afternoons when honest folk should have been at work. London was still peppered with nineteen dog tracks holding regular meetings, although the war saw a decline in its popularity that continued into the 1950s. The White City at Shepherds Bush was one of greyhound racing's most popular venues, pulling in crowds of up to 90,000 during the 1930s. With the arrival of GIs in London, a bemused local crowd watched the introduction of American football to the stadium.

The need for the greater utilisation of dog tracks led to a very happy coincidence with the arrival of speedway racing. Popularised in the States and Australia, it involved four to six motorcycles competing against each other over four laps. The bikes had only one gear and no brakes. The rasping noise of the engines and the smell of scorched cinders also attracted large crowds but, again, traditionally races had been run under floodlights and only a few meetings were held at West Ham and Haringey, terminating in 1942. Speedway went onto enjoy huge success in the years immediately after the war.

Despite most professional fighters serving in the armed forces, boxing continued during the war, attracting sell-out crowds. The Royal Albert Hall, Haringey Arena and Earls Court were regular venues for leading bouts. A forty-year-old showman emerged in 1940 to become Britain's leading promoter. Jack Solomons was an extrovert, larger-than-life character. He had learnt his trade running the Devonshire Sporting Club in Hackney. His first major success came in a sensational fight staged at White Hart

Lane between the champion Len Harvey and his challenger, the charismatic Freddie Mills. The bout attracted a crowd of 30,000 to the home of Tottenham Hotspur football club. Harvey, at thirty-five, was a veteran of over 100 fights. Mills, an all-action boxer of amazing courage, had come up through the tough ranks of fairground boxing booths and was still only twenty-two. Within two rounds Harvey found himself on the seat of his pants, having been knocked clean through the ropes by a savage left hook. It was only the second time in his career that Harvey had ever been stopped. Devastated, he retired, leaving his heavyweight title vacant.

Giving away over 3 stones in weight, Mills was out-pointed in a final eliminator for the heavyweight crown by Jack London in 1944. The following July, Jack Solomons again chose White Hart Lane to stage the championship bout between Jack London and another emerging heavyweight star, Bruce Woodcock. This ended with Woodcock knocking London out in the sixth round, setting the scene for a boom in British post-war boxing, featuring both Woodcock and Freddie Mills.

Cycling, as a leisure pursuit, became a craze in the 1920s. With petrol rationing, bikes again became a prized possession. It didn't take long on largely deserted roads to reach the leafy suburbs and the open country beyond. Wicker panniers were attached for housewives to do their shopping, while legions of office and factory employees pedalled to work. Cycling had also flourished as a competitive sport with Britain excelling in both track and velodrome racing. Herne Hill in South London became the focus for British cycling, with crowds of 10,000 regularly attending the Good Friday meeting. During the war the velodrome briefly became the home of Crystal Palace football club. The track itself was damaged, having been used by an artillery anti-aircraft battery. By 1942 it was covered in weeds with small trees growing through the cracks in the racing surface. A young Reg Harris, due to become Britain's first cycling superstar, was waiting in the wings. Discharged as being medically unfit from the Army in 1943, he was soon to prove the medics wrong.

Back in the 1880s, there were still only twenty golf courses in England. The early part of the twentieth century saw a massive expansion. London was not about to miss out on the chance to indulge in a little light exercise. The expansion of suburban railways led to a rapid proliferation of courses surrounding the capital. Hampstead Golf Club, which had opened in 1894, was the most centrally located. Golf had many social advantages, not least because, as A. A. Milne said, 'It is the best game in the world at which to be bad.' During the 1930s the golf club became an important centre for the well-to-do middle class. You didn't have to be young. You didn't have to be fit. For married couples it was a game that could be enjoyed together. You were made to feel important. You referred to staff, including the club professional, by their surname and they deferred back to you. The club secretary tended to be an ex-military type who saw to the upholding of standards. You were cocooned in a safe, familiar world. No foreigners. No Jews even, after all they did have their own clubs. Then, dammit, all blown off course by this infernal war. Ingenuity was required. Richmond Golf Club issued temporary rules in 1940 to help cope with the possible unwelcome conditions. Players were requested to collect bomb or shrapnel splinters to save damage to the mowers. There were to be no penalties incurred for members taking cover during a bomb attack. Known 'delayed action' bombs would be marked by red flags. Generously, members were allowed to replace a ball moved by enemy action. More harshly, a player whose stroke was affected by a simultaneous explosion of a bomb could play another ball but incur a one-shot penalty.

Several of London's golf courses were returned to agriculture for the duration of the war, while others were requisitioned, like Shooters Hill Golf Club, where the back nine was given over to an anti-aircraft battery. Later, the club, in common with others, including Trent Park Golf Club, became a POW camp. Coombe Hill Golf Club was not alone in sustaining numerous bombings of their fairways, including a V1 bomb which caused a massive crater in front of the tenth tee. Coombe Hill was also the secret hideaway of the golf-mad General Dwight Eisenhower. He stayed in Telegraph Cottage, just behind the fourteenth tee. They were an intrepid lot, these golfers, as were most Londoners who scorned the daily dangers to enjoy their particular sporting love, even if it was only a game of darts down at the local.

8

British Restaurants and Swanky Hotels

Every Monday morning the pupils of Barking Abbey School would sing 'Eternal Father, Strong to Save', the hymn of the British Armed Forces. Then in total silence, the headmaster, Colonel Ernest Loftus, would read out a list of former pupils who had either been killed or were missing. It was a stark reminder that although children are astonishingly adaptable, it was impossible for them to ignore the consequences of a war that left no-one untouched.

Jean Clarke was thirteen in 1943 and had done well to gain a scholarship to attend Abbey School. That same day a five-year-old boy attended his first-ever day at Edgware Elementary School. My mother led this very reluctant student by the hand, occasionally having to drag him. Although it was a walk of over a mile, it must have seemed much longer to her. I joined a gaggle of children, who were to be my classmates, and our intimidating teacher, Miss Arnold. By the arrival of the first break-time my mind was set. School was not for me. While the others gathered in the playground I slipped away. Down the high street and then off into the tree-lined streets where I knew I would find him. For weeks during the long summer I had helped Jack the milkman. It may seem strange to us today but my mother had been happy for me to walk the mile or so to the United Dairies depot early each morning. At the back behind the stacked milk crates were the stables. I loved the smell of the hay and of the gleaming horses as they munched on their breakfast. I never tired of seeing them being tacked up. More smells, leather this time. Head collar and reins, all shining. Then I watched as the horse was manoeuvred between the wooden shafts. While the milk crates were loaded it was my job to fill the horse's nose-bag. Holding the reins as we clip-clopped along the suburban streets was a particular treat. Jack was probably in his thirties and had suffered from TB and, therefore, had been excused military service. Sometimes we would stop for elevenses at a wooden-shedded workmen's café. It was warm, welcoming and smoky. Not just from the men with their Weights and Woodbines hanging from their mouths, but also from giant kettles bubbling away on a hissing gas cooker. Of course, the school rang my mother who didn't take long to find me. With blood-curdling threats still ringing in my ears, I did manage to complete a full day's schooling. But by the next day I decided my initial assessment of school had been correct. Again I slipped away and went in search of the milkman. This time he took me straight home and the reluctant student was forced to accept the inevitable.

In the East End, having survived the Blitz, the arrival of flying bombs raised fears to new levels and it was impossible not to pass this concern onto children. School for most was frequently interrupted by air-raid sirens. At Barking Abbey School the young pupils were given time off to allow fifth- and sixth-formers to take their exams in the relative safety of the shelters. While most parents tried to shield their children from the most distressing aspects of the war, this was not always possible. Jean Hewitt can remember her mother clutching her with frightening strength and crying uncontrollably on learning her brother had been killed at Arnhem. Later the reaction to her mother's younger brother's death from Beri-Beri while working on the Burma railway was even more upsetting. Like many of her generation, to be caught up so young with raw grief was not just distressing, but also gave these youngsters reason to doubt the sanity of a flawed adult world. Luckily, some had happier tales to tell. Brenda Burns was born in Willesden in 1939, already sporting two baby teeth. When they fell out her father kept them on him all the time as good luck charms. It was while he was serving in Burma that he developed a nagging toothache. As was quite common at the time he decided to have all his teeth extracted (supposedly to avoid any further dental problems). He was excused duties for forty-eight hours and while he was recuperating the whole of the patrol of which he should have been a part was wiped out. Good luck or coincidence, who knows.

Although most of us who grew up during the war appeared to cope well with its consequences, strange, unexplained, irrational fears sometimes built up. Bizarrely, I remember being scared by the image of the 'Squander Bug', a cartoon character created by the British National Savings Committee in an effort to discourage wasteful spending. In my childish mind, the bug-like creature came to represent the Germans who, due to constant background propaganda, I really imagined were not human at all. It came as a great shock to me when I actually got to see some Germans at close quarters. A team of prisoners of war were set to work repairing a wall at our school. Although we were told not to go near them, our curiosity was too great. When the teacher overseeing playtime disappeared for a few minutes, we sidled self-consciously towards the work gang, which was being supervised by a couple of armed 'Tommies'. They didn't look sub-human, these Germans, in fact several were blond and very good-looking. They were friendly too, talking to us in broken English and smiling. The boys in our group were shy and held back, unsure if it was wrong to be seen talking to the enemy. The few girls with us had no such doubts. Although at that age none of us understood flirting, its ability is obviously an integral part of some young girls' make-up. They were all fluttering eyelashes, coquettish smiles and giggles. They were hooked. That was it. No more kiss-chase in the playground for me while this lot were around. Were these young men really our enemy? Had they really been some of those responsible for dropping bombs on us? It was all so confusing.

School dinners bring back painful memories for those growing up during the war. The smell of strained cabbage permeated every corner of the building. Indescribable slithers of meat and lumpy mashed potato served by ladies with the scowls of prison camp warders. Food for our generation at that time was just about filling your stomach. For adults it was a preoccupation, a constant topic for conversation. Glassy-eyed, they would remember delicacies that we kids had never experienced. Small treats like a jar of chocolate spread were drooled over. For us it was eat whatever was put in front of you or go hungry. Yet we all managed to grow up – skinny, but healthy. It was unusual to see overweight people and obesity was virtually unheard of. Some of us had a glimpse of what we had been missing when food parcels started arriving. We had one sent from Australia with a range of basic foodstuffs, but also I remember a bag of delicious sugar-coated almonds.

The introduction of food rationing meant that, theoretically, every household would have to compromise their diets, and yet obviously the wealthy were less affected by shortages. While coupons regulated fair distribution of essential items, other foods were not rationed and buying these relied only on the ability to pay. So the price of fish, poultry and game soared as did rare supplies of exotic fruit that had made it to London. Previously in 1940, the likes of 'Chips' Channon and Harold Nicolson had been able to gorge themselves at the Dorchester. With friends they quaffed four magnums of champagne and reported, 'London lives well – I've never seen more lavishness, more money spent or more food consumed tonight.' Most were less fortunate, having to rely on 14 ounces of meat, 4 ounces of bacon and a cheese ration that by 1944 had fallen to a miserly 2 ounces. Each person was also allocated twenty coupon points to splash out on say, a tin of tomatoes, which took six points, or perhaps to really go mad and buy a tin of peaches (if you could find one), for the loss of eight points.

A burning resentment that the rich were able to sidestep austerity finally began to concern the government. In the summer of 1942 a fixed maximum price of 5s for all restaurant meals was introduced. This was largely to counteract criticism that those who could afford to eat in restaurants were able to consume more than the rationing scheme would allow, without having to forfeit any coupons. While on the surface, this appeared a fairer system, it didn't take long for creative managements to render the new limits meaningless. Huge cover charges were introduced by most leading hotels and restaurants, while for the more modest establishments the menu ranged from 2s 6d to 3s 6d. Special dispensation was granted to the six swankiest London hotels. The Ritz, Savoy, Dorchester, Claridge's, Grosvenor House and Mayfair were authorised to charge an additional 6s for the privilege of eating in the most refined settings that London had to offer. For the hungry gourmet the charges didn't stop there. With wine in short supply, prices soared. Smoked salmon was likely to set you back an extra 5s 6d, while coffee was 1s. Worse, customers complained that for their shilling they were restricted to just one lump of sugar. The cover charges kept coming, with an extra 2s 6d being added for those dancing. Another source of resentment related to the fact that there was nothing to stop the wealthy diner from gorging himself on two or even three five-bob meals. Most establishments did try to limit the outward signs of ostentatious consumption. Inspectors from the Ministry of Food were making regular undercover visits, and prosecution was not just embarrassing but ultimately bad for business. Food was generally in short supply even for the elite hotels, and dining rooms filled up early at lunchtime to avoid the disappointment of a severely restricted menu. The establishment clubs of St James prided themselves on their austerity. Wine stocks were severely depleted and the food on offer was often restricted to the type of fish which previously would only have been served to one's cat.

A very popular innovation was the introduction of the 'British Restaurant', scheduled initially to be called Communal Feeding Centres. It was Churchill who realised that 'British Restaurant' created a much more welcoming and patriotic image. Run by local authorities, initially it was designed to provide hot food for those whose houses had been bombed. The scheme was rapidly expanded. The fairly basic restaurants were open to all with the aim of serving a three-course meal for under 1s. The London County Council provided around 250 outlets in halls, municipal and temporary buildings. Each offered a self-service cafeteria, which was new at the time and was soon copied by commercial enterprises. Soup was priced at 2d, while the main course consisting of meat and two veg was 8d, and a filling pudding was on offer for 3d. I can remember eating at our local branch. It was popular. There were constant queues at the servery with people looming over you as you ate, waiting for a space to sit down and eat their own meal. The food served was marginally more appetising than the foul school dinners we endured, but not much. It was as far away from what today is referred to as 'fine dining' as it was possible to be. However, British Restaurants did help fill stomachs in a generally warm and friendly atmosphere. For many it was their first experience of eating outside their own kitchen or dining room.

It is doubtful that many of the patrons staying at London's most prestigious hotels ever set foot in a British Restaurant. Neither did they seek shelter in underground stations during the Blitz. They slummed it, using the basements and corridors of the hotels for their protection. These guests had one thing in common – money. They were a weird collection who could have been drawn from Central Casting. There was royalty from across Europe, aristocrats, film stars and captains of industry. There was new money, con-men, high-class tarts, senior military men, suspected spies, deserters and queers, many uncomfortable in each other's company but drawn together as if by a magnet in their search for a little luxury and a need to be acknowledged as someone of substance. London's prestige hotels found wartime conditions particularly difficult to adapt to. Surrounded by walls of sandbags, with increasing shortages of supplies and staff either whisked off to serve in the armed forces or interned. Previously held high standards had to be compromised. The dress code for male guests was relaxed as uniforms came to dominate. With the advent of the Blitz the upper floors at the Savoy and Dorchester were closed off, being thought too dangerous for their illustrious guests. Above, on the rooftops, ARP wardens kept an eye open for enemy aircraft. Although there was no official pecking order, among London's four most prestigious hotels they each tended to attract their own brand of clientele. Claridge's was much favoured by royalty and senior politicians from across Europe, as was the Ritz. The Savoy attracted film stars, including Bob Hope, Edward G. Robinson, Danny Kaye and the acting fraternity, while the Dorchester welcomed not only the establishment but also the generally reviled nouveau riche. If you could pay, you could stay. They did attempt to improve the calibre of their guest list by offering concessionary rates to those they thought brought increased social standing. Of course they could boast that General Eisenhower was a permanent fixture, but Emerald Cunard, who decamped from the Ritz, fitted their desired image rather better. She was allocated a three-roomed suite, which she stuffed with priceless artefacts and furniture removed from her Grosvenor Square mansion. To Cecil Beaton, the Dorchester was 'reminiscent of a transatlantic crossing in a luxury liner, with all the horrors and enforced jocularity and expensive squalor.' Some of the jocularity was supplied by Lew Stone and his band as they performed in the huge mirrored ballroom to a background of ack-ack fire coming from across the road in Hyde Park.

Some of the most expensive suites at the Savoy overlooked the broad sweep of the Thames. While of great advantage in peacetime, it made the hotel particularly vulnerable with the outbreak of war. Within days of the start of the Blitz the glass-domed restaurant was closed. Each night witnessed the bizarre sight of guests, some in pyjamas and dressing gowns, mingling on the stairs with others in evening finery. A receptionist called out, 'Diners to the left, sleepers to the right.' Clutching their hot water bottles, those seeking rest nodded off to the background noise of Carol Gibbons and his band, while their fellow guests danced into the early hours. Booking a table for dinner normally ensured a bed for the night in the comparative safety of the hotel's shelter.

One night at the height of the Blitz, a bomb falling nearby threw Carol Gibbons and his band off their rostrum. Amid the ensuing mayhem Noel Coward took to the piano and in his stilted voice calmly sang 'A Nightingale Sang in Berkeley Square'. A surreal scene set to a background of ack-ack fire and the dull thud of falling bombs.

In November 1941 the hotel received a direct hit in which two people were killed, including the Belgian minister of finance. The following April, extensive damage was inflicted on the hotel when a land mine exploded outside the Embankment entrance. Despite these setbacks, by 1943 the hotel was fully booked and recording record profits.

At Grosvenor House, the safety of their guests was a top priority. A loudspeaker system was installed throughout the building and

100 trained staff were assigned specific safety responsibilities, ranging from rooftop aircraft spotters to a small team of qualified nurses. The hotel invested in 5 miles of blackout material to line their windows. Outside, the building was protected by 10,000 sandbags which were increased to 30,000 with the advent of the Blitz. The Silver Restaurant was closed because of its vast expanse of plate glass windows and the main restaurant became the Tudor Grill located safely below ground. Here each night guests could dance to the music of Sydney Lipton and his band. At midnight the guests would stand for a rousing chorus of the National Anthem. The restaurant then became a giant dormitory, with an undignified rush for the restaurant banquettes that were reckoned to offer the most protection from a possible bomb blast; the less nimble were forced to bed down on the dance floor. There were two other large air-raid shelters for guests, where playing cards, crossword puzzles and even a darts board were supplied for insomniacs. A bomb falling nearby in April 1941 broke 2,000 window panes, and a delayed action bomb caused the north block of the hotel to be evacuated for a few days. The singer and songwriter Douglas Byng owed his life to Grosvenor House. Repeated encores for his rather risqué act ensured his late arrival for an appearance at the Café de Paris on the night it was destroyed.

Grosvenor House was also the venue for many grand social gatherings, including the annual Queen Charlotte's Birthday Ball. There were not so many aristocrats present for a huge party held at the hotel in June 1943. Some 2,000 gathered to celebrate the downing of 1,000 Luftwaffe aircraft in the sector covered by RAF Biggin Hill. It was organised by South African air-ace Wing Commander 'Sailor' Malan. The cabaret that night was organised by Vivian van Damm and featured the girls from the Windmill Theatre. The debt owed to the young airmen was generously illustrated by London cabbies who laid on a fleet of taxis to take the air crew back to their base free of charge, when the party eventually broke up at three o'clock in the morning.

As in all the leading hotels, the luxury ceased abruptly below stairs in the vast network of kitchens. Working conditions were dreadful for the poorly paid staff, which led to numerous industrial disputes. Clement Freud worked as a trainee chef at

the Dorchester in 1941. He described the kitchen as 'a hell-hole
of a huge, dark, dank building, built regardless of inconvenience
to the staff'. He summed up the resentment felt by most catering
staff when he wrote of the hotel's clients in his book, *Freud Ego*,
'When your weekly salary was what they spent on a portion of
grilled lamb cutlet with broad beans a la crème and allumette
potatoes, the feeling that we were part of the same human race
flew out of the window.' He continued, with feeling, 'We hoped
the bombs would kill our customers.'

Staff conditions and labour relations were no better at the
other leading hotels. Staff tended to receive only a nominal
wage and most relied on the tronc system. This involved a
pooled distribution of tips for their livelihood. The stark
differences between the served and those supplying this service
caused a number of bitter disputes, particularly at the Savoy. In
September 1940 about seventy Stepney Communists led by Phil
Piratin invaded the Savoy, demanding to be allowed access to
the hotel's shelter. It was an effective way of pointing out the
lack of adequate public shelters for ordinary Londoners, while
the privileged living in hotels hunkered down each night in
considerable comfort. The widely reported invasion was a major
factor in the government agreeing to open up the tube stations
for night-time shelters.

Sir Michael Duff had an altogether rosier recollection of the
Ritz in its halcyon days just prior to the war. 'The Palm Court was
always filled before luncheon with society beauties, debutantes
and their boyfriends.' The Ritz, he reckoned, was more like a club
than a hotel. It had a combination of elegance and cosiness. He
maintained the Ritz had an essentially happy atmosphere, which
radiated from its staff. How little, it appeared, the privileged few
understood the resentment felt by most of those staff he assumed
to be happy with their lot.

At the outbreak of war, 'Chips' Channon recorded in his
diary, 'Ritzes always prosper in wartime as we are all cook-less.'
He noted the hotel 'had become fantastically fashionable, all
the great, gay, the government; we knew ninety-five percent of
everyone there'. This was a small 'club' of just a few thousand; the
dukes, duchesses, cabinet ministers and those who had inherited

vast estates and huge wealth. To some, they were the idle and undeserving rich, to others, the upholders of all we British cherish and the cream of society. The Ritz, like the Dorchester, claimed to be one of London's safest buildings. Despite this, the sixth and seventh floors were covered in dust sheets and closed down. During the worst of the bombing, the hotel's corridors were lined with chaise-longues for guests to sleep on, and in the basement camp-beds were provided.

On 21 January 1940 the first recorded birth took place in the hotel. Not some poor chamber maid who had succumbed to the persistent charms of a famous guest, but to Lady Howland. Two suites were set aside for the birth of a future Duke of Bedford. Later that year saw the arrival of King Zog, the distinctly dodgy King of Albania. He also brought his wife, the infant crown prince, his six sisters, a few nephews and nieces, his American mother-in-law and a few very heavy suitcases. These contained gold bars which he had filched, and represented a sizeable percentage of his impoverished country's wealth. The loot was transferred to the Bank of England vaults and each week the king's secretary would draw out £1,000 as loose change to pay a few bills. Soon a procession of European royalty was seeking out the Ritz to act as a temporary bolt-hole. This included the formidable Queen Wilhelmina of the Netherlands, the kings of Greece, Yugoslavia, Norway and Denmark, not forgetting the Grand Duchess of Luxembourg. King Zog was always among the first to reach the underground shelter during an air raid, but he and his retinue decamped to the safety of the Buckinghamshire countryside following a bomb landing in Piccadilly.

Considering that the Ritz was a bastion of the establishment, the 'goings-on' in their bars must have caused a number of well-plucked eyebrows to be raised. How was it that an openly homosexual bar was allowed to flourish? It was a time when 'queers' were routinely harassed by the Met. Even allowing for the fact that the police were probably paid off, what of the hotel's management? Why did they risk the reputation of the hotel? Above ground was the 'hetro' bar and even here convention appeared to have been cast aside. A very good friend of mine (now sadly dead) worked at the secret Bletchley Park establishment.

Most of the girls working there appear to have been recruited purely because they were drawn from solid, upper-middle-class families and on this basis alone could be trusted. The plummy-voiced girls would travel up to the Ritz on their night off and, although only afforded the rank of private, would hob-nob at the bar with senior officers. On a visit to her London flat after Bletchley had been declassified, she described the excitement of those times. The romances, the flings, punctuated by the sorrow on the death of a young lover. 'They think today is a permissive society, but, believe me,' she said, 'whatever they do today my generation tried it first.' As I gazed at her society portrait, painted when she was nineteen, all blonde and demure, it was only the fact that the artist had captured the twinkle in her eye that made me believe her. Meanwhile, in the downstairs bar...

Laura, Duchess of Marlborough, was recorded as saying, 'A lot old queers remember the wartime Ritz with nostalgia, because the Ritz bar had a cachet for pick-ups.' Felix Hope-Nicholson agreed it was 'notoriously queer'. A few women appeared to enjoy the outrageously camp atmosphere, including Pauline Tennant, whose father ran the Gargoyle Club in Soho. The woman most adored by 'the boys' was Edomie Johnson, known affectionately as 'Sod'. She was a plump, not very attractive, middle-aged woman who would rise late and go shoplifting before devoting the rest of her day to some serious drinking. She held court in the downstairs bar and could always be relied upon to arrive with an attractive young serviceman on her arm, who would be disgorged into an admiring crowd wanting to make his closer acquaintance. She was happy to be known as 'the buggers' Vera Lynn'.

Today, Old Compton Street is the centre of London's gay scene. Away from the relative safety of the Ritz basement bar, homosexuals lived in constant fear. Homosexuality was illegal and generally condemned, except in theatrical circles. Even within Soho, generally so accepting of minorities, gay men had to be relatively discreet. Many resorted to speaking Polari, a street slang formerly popular with dockers and sailors. This allowed like-minded men to make contact. Attitude to 'queers' was generally savage and the homosexual act continued to be known as the 'abominable crime'. Generations of British men were either forced to deny their natural instincts or to live a lie, constantly worried about blackmail or arrest. Quentin Crisp, who was in his thirties during the war, went on to become Britain's best-known gay man. He explained he always felt safer in Soho where, caked in make-up, he minced through the blacked-out streets in search of accommodating GIs. Crisp was rejected by the British Army who declared he was suffering from 'sexual perversion'. Over at the Ritz, many of a similar persuasion seemed to have passed muster.

So it was that Soho offered places where gays were tolerated, if not exactly welcomed. The Swiss Tavern in Old Compton Street was described as being 'not entirely straight'. Today, the pub trades as Compton's, one of Soho's best-known gay watering holes. Round the corner in Dean Street there were two other pubs, the Golden Lion and the Crown and Two Chairmen, who also offered a fairly safe retreat for homosexuals. As always, all strands of humanity could thrive or destroy themselves in Soho.

Back in London's grandest hotels, it was business as usual. It is difficult to find much to like or admire in their rich and pampered guests. The triple sins of snobbery, xenophobia and anti-Semitism bubbled away just under the surface. It was the writer Sydney Horler who declared that fellow novelist Michael Arlen (born Dikran Kouyoumdjian) 'was the only Armenian who never tried to sell me a carpet'. Worse was the loud remark made in the Ritz by Alice Keppel, the former mistress of King Edward VII. A bomb fell nearby in Green Park, causing a Jewish guest to call out in alarm. Stiff backed, the old Keppel strutted across the room and boomed, 'Madam, this is not the wailing wall.' Hopefully, today's guests are more enlightened. It is left to the Canadian diplomat and diarist Charles Ritchie to give his verdict on the types of clientele drawn to London's finest hotels. 'In the Dorchester, the sweepings of the Riviera have been washed up – pot-bellied, sallow, sleek-haired, nervous gentlemen with loose mouths and wobbly chins, wearing suede shoes and checked suits, and thin, painted women with fox capes and long silk legs and artificial curls clustering round their bony sheep-like heads!'

Full house! Sydney Horler the xenophobe, Alice Keppel the anti-Semite and Charles Ritchie the snob, and he was not even British.

9

Buzz-Bomb Terror

Our family only visited a public shelter once. It was a squat, brick-built building situated at the bottom of our suburban road. The only safety advantage it offered was that it had no windows. Flying glass was one of the major factors in injuries sustained by bomb damage. I can still remember the dank smell as we entered the darkened space, complemented by the vague whiff of stale urine. While this alone would probably have been enough to have my mother making for the entrance again, it was the vigorous activity coming from one of the bunks that settled matters. An Army corporal was getting to know one of the local girls. There was so much groaning and panting that, in my innocence, I imagined the soldier was trying to kill the poor girl. Ignoring the wail of the air-raid siren and the vague rumble of approaching aircraft, my sister and I were marched home again; our mother's concern for our moral well-being outweighing that surrounding our immediate safety.

By the beginning of 1941, it was reckoned that over 90 per cent of Londoners could be accommodated in public or private shelters. For those who didn't have a garden, or preferred to have a shelter inside their house, the Morrison shelter was an important alternative to the Anderson version, which was built below ground. The Morrison was constructed of sturdy steel in the form of a large, ugly table with room beneath for mattresses to be laid for sleeping. A metal grill could be fitted to reduce the effect of flying glass. The metal monstrosity half-filled our dining room and I can remember lying alongside my sister and listening to the drone of German bombers as they made their way northwards.

Jean Sporle's parents, who lived in Hammersmith, also opted for a Morrison shelter, but after a couple of days it was abandoned, only in future to serve as a table. Jean's mother became convinced that they would be buried alive if they continued to climb into this claustrophobic cage. The family arranged to use their neighbour's Anderson shelter, constructed safely underground. When the siren sounded, Jean was instructed to run as fast as she could next door. A problem soon emerged. The old couple were both deaf and the door had to be almost battered down for them to stir. Sheltering at home had its compensations. Sweets were dispensed and games were played. The radio was kept on, anything to distract the children from the boom and thud of falling bombs. Iris Chapple, living in Brixton, sheltered in the coal hole under the stairs. She can remember her mum making toast in front of an open fire when the all-clear sounded. As Ivy Robinson's parents waited for their Anderson shelter to be completed, her father turned to his carpentry skills to give the family extra protection. He constructed what appeared to be a massive wooden wardrobe which was laid side on between the sleeping family and the window. Rather than give protection, Ivy was convinced that if a bomb had fallen nearby they were more likely to have been killed by her father's handiwork than the Luftwaffe.

At the same time, across London almost 200,000 people slept on the platforms of London's tube stations. Rocky Knight can remember being taken each night from The Angel to the Bank underground, which was reckoned to be one of the deepest and safest shelters in town. They slept on the hard concrete platforms, covered with warm blankets. Endless lines of people, crushed close together like sardines in a tin. Rocky and his friends loved what to them was a great adventure. They played hide and seek and joined in raucous sing-songs, while those trying to sleep cursed and moaned.

Children are incredibly adaptable and most took what positives there were from the war situation, but it was impossible to shelter them from the mayhem going on all around. Many were killed or seriously injured and those who survived were often exposed to horrendous events. Jean Sporle can remember visiting her grandmother, who lived just off Fulham Palace Road, and seeing bodies mutilated by a recent bomb. Dead cats and dogs were left in the road while the bodies were covered with sheets and blankets. People were sobbing. It was a scene from hell. Brenda Burns witnessed similar scenes following a raid on Kilburn. Brian Abbott remembers, as a five-year-old, sheltering in a church during a raid and an old lady being brought in badly hurt from shrapnel wounds. She looked ghastly and this image from the relative safety of suburban Penge remains with him today.

Fire watching was an essential part of trying to keep London safe. Volunteers worked in shifts and it was often extremely dangerous. Jean Sporle's father and his mate Joe were on 'fire watch' on the roof of British Home Stores in Hammersmith. The job alternated from long periods of boredom to sheer terror. They used to take it in turns to make tea in an old shed, whose shelves were lined with tins of paint and an array of workmen's tools. Although it was her dad's turn to make the tea, Joe was thirsty, so he went instead. It was as he entered the shed that the bomb fell. The whole area was devastated. The police arrived to tell Jean's mum that her 'old man had bought it'. Joe, it appeared, had survived and his wife went to the hospital to see him. When the survivor was cleaned up (he was covered in paint) it turned out to be Jean's dad. It was poor old Joe who had 'copped it'.

Although the underground stations accommodated by far the most people sheltering in London, underground car parks were also put into service. In Brewer Street, Soho, the Lex Garage became a focal point for locals. The building was converted at night to one of the best shelters in London. It had a canteen and even its own surgery. There were comfortable bunks for many while others brought their own chairs or laid mattresses on the floor. The building developed its own sense of community, with card schools and sing-songs. It was a colourful cast of people who gathered there each night. Waiters from local restaurants, barrow boys, the odd down-and-out and a few street girls after they had concluded their business for the night. Strangely, as the Blitz intensified, fewer people took to the shelters. Maybe it was a feeling of claustrophobia, being cooped up with so many strangers, but a feeling of invincibility developed in some. It became commonplace for many not to even take cover during intensive raids. Another factor was the feeling that underground shelters were not that safe after all.

The first deaths recorded at a tube station actually occurred above ground at Colindale on the Northern Line. The bombs were probably intended for nearby RAF Hendon, but much damage was done and eight people left dead. Two weeks later, a bomb crashed through the roof of Charing Cross station and, although only one person was killed, it was perhaps a warning of worse to come as the Blitz intensified. On 12 October 1940, Trafalgar Square station took a direct hit. The bomb punctured the road surface and exploded close to the top of the escalator. It created a collapse of the steel-and-concrete casing, causing a deluge of sodden earth to engulf waiting passengers, killing seven and injuring many more. The following day, Bounds Green was hit. Here the damage was so severe that the station had to be closed for a full two months. There was carnage, with a death toll of nineteen, including fifteen Belgian refugees who, having successfully escaped the clutches of the Nazis, were finally tragically caught hundreds of miles from their home.

On 14 October, the claim that sheltering in underground stations was completely safe was finally and frighteningly undermined at Balham. A bomb landed close to the station, causing a section of the road to collapse. The explosion severed the water mains and water gushed through the station, carrying with it ballast, sand and rubble. This formed a foul smelling, moving blanket of sludge and slime, which quickly submerged people sheltering from the raid. A record sixty-four people lost their lives in what was at the time the worst accident to affect an underground station. Sadly, this was not a record that lasted long. At the beginning of 1941 one person was killed at Turnpike Lane, but the relative calm of the past few weeks since the firestorm of 29 December was about to be shattered. It was a catastrophe that was to strike at the very heart of the financial centre of the City of London. It was preceded by a bomb falling on 11 January outside Liverpool Street mainline station. This caused widespread damage, both inside and outside the station and also a massive crater in the road. Forty-four people were killed, including many on board a double-decker bus that was passing the station.

Just before eight o'clock that same night, a massive bomb landed in the booking hall of Bank station, where it killed thirty-five people outright. The blast continued on down the escalators, killing most in its path, and onwards to the platforms where there were horrific stories of passengers being blown onto the line and electrocuted. Including fatalities in the road outside, the death toll rose to 111. The road, already weakened by the firestorm in the city on 29 December, now had a massive crater that was so wide the Army had to construct a temporary bridge to enable City workers to get to their offices. Later in the month, further deaths were recorded at the stations, including Green Park, Lambeth North, Kings Cross and Chalk Farm. So, while bombing continued, albeit at a lesser rate, it was to be a new devastating type of device that would bring another wave of terror to London, but not just yet.

While news on the war front began to slowly improve, disaster was always waiting in the wings. Disaster that again centred on a London transport tube station. On the night of 3 March 1943, fate conspired to claim the largest number of lives in a single non-military incident. Although air-raid warnings had declined since the Blitz, they were still part of London's everyday life, so, at the sounding of sirens, most people made their way calmly to the nearest public shelter. What was it that caused the panic that led to such devastation? As the siren went off there was an explosion that sounded very close to Bethnal Green station. It had been a refuge for East Enders at the height of the Blitz, so it was natural that soon a crowd was making its way down the steep, narrow steps leading to the booking hall. It is thought a mother carrying her child stumbled as she reached the bottom of the staircase. Above, at street level, there was another loud explosion. Those outside pushed forward to what they imagined was safety. The pressure from behind caused a number of people further down the steps to fall over the prostrate figures of the young mother and child. In vain, those struggling to stay on their feet pleaded for those behind to stop pushing. They couldn't. There were no hand rails to hang onto and the lighting was dim to conform with blackout regulations. Hundreds of people were still joining the queue at the top of the stairs. Below there was panic as crowds of people toppled over like a pack of cards. It was to resemble a scene from your worst nightmare. There were screams of agony and the sobbing of terrified children. The force of a crowd now out of control careered down the stairs. Those at the bottom of the stairwell were being crushed further by each new arrival as they toppled over, crushing those beneath. Before the swell of humanity could be stemmed, it was reckoned that 300 people were locked in a twitching, gasping heap. About half were eventually extricated, leaving a horrific death toll of 172, of which sixty-two were children. The dreadful irony only surfaced much later. The explosions that started the panic were not caused by enemy fire or bombs. Rather, nearby in Victoria Park, new anti-aircraft weapons were being tested by the Army. Our own troops had inadvertently inflicted on Londoners one of the most tragic incidents of the entire war.

The authorities were so alarmed at the effect the disaster would have on morale that although the incident was reported, the location was not. The East End had endured much over the preceding years and this tragic accident was one of the hardest for them to bear.

Churchill was always sensitive to the suffering of East Enders and frequently turned up after particularly heavy raids, where he generally received a warm enough reception. His morale-raising visits also widened out on occasions to the suburbs. Brian Abbott can recall him visiting Penge. Driven in an open car and dressed in RAF uniform, a large cigar clamped firmly in his mouth, he waved, smiling broadly to the wildly cheering children gathered in the school playground.

With news of the successful D-Day landings by the Allies, Britons were entitled to think the worst was over. Certainly, Londoners felt they could relax somewhat and dream of peace returning. Few now believed German propaganda that they were harbouring some secret weapon that would bring total destruction to Britain. John Betjeman was, however, as gloomy as the wet, cold summer of 1944. Writing to Geoffrey Taylor, he predicted, 'I don't see any end to the war – not for two years at least in Europe and another three for Japan on top of that!' He was right to be gloomy, even if his predicted time frame was somewhat out.

Just a week after Allied troops stormed the beaches of Normandy, the Germans flexed their muscles once more and so started another period of terror and destruction to be unleashed on poor old war-weary London. Perhaps the number thirteen was to blame, for on 13 June a strange black object crossed the Kent coast heading towards London. It was surrounded by a red glare and an engine that sounded like a car in low gear. While not quite the last throw of the dice, the V1 bomb was known in Germany as 'the revenge' or 'retaliation weapon number one'! It was designed to bring terror to London and break civilian morale. The ten rockets launched that day met with very mixed success. Half failed to make it across the Channel, but the one that did reach its target gave an indication of what was to follow. While only six people were killed in Bow, there were many injured and hundreds made homeless. There were no reports in the papers about the new threat. Within days the number of rockets launched at London made denial counterproductive, but still no locations were given. The first major assault occurred on 15 and 16 June. Almost 250 missiles were launched and over seventy reached London. On Sunday 18 June, 121 worshippers at the Guards Chapel in Birdcage Walk were killed as they rose to sing the *Te Deum*. Just three days of 'Buzz Bomb' or 'Doodlebug' activity had seen 500 people die, thousands injured and huge destruction of homes and factories. The terror of the Blitz had returned, almost more frightening because of the haphazard nature of these unmanned rockets. People now stared skywards as the missiles became an everyday sight above London. When the engine cut out it was time to dive for cover.

Young Iris Chapple, living in Brixton, had already been re-housed twice with her mother during the Blitz. Now the young girl had the added responsibility of having to listen out for the doodlebugs, as her mother was deaf. It was just as well, for their whole house was demolished by a V1. Bizarrely, Iris can remember that among all the carnage, her clothes hanging on the washing line in the kitchen were still clean and totally unmarked.

Although inflicting massive destruction to hundreds of thousands of properties, the V1 produced virtually no craters where they landed. Despite this, their blast power was greater than conventional bombs. This strange effect was illustrated when a rocket hit the bottom of the road where I lived. The explosion blew our windows out. Luckily, I had been sleeping close up to the window and the glass showered over me and I survived without a single cut. The bomb had landed hundreds of yards away and people living in the house next to my best friend had been killed, and yet his house remained untouched. This quirk of fate was endlessly repeated across London during the V1 bombings.

It was reckoned that the accuracy of the rockets was variable but that the overall target set by the Germans was Tower Bridge. It is probable that double agents working in London gave false reports as to where the rockets were exploding. Most were landing short, ensuring that South London was taking the brunt of the attacks. Herbert Morrison was particularly concerned that in, effect, the government was orchestrating which part of London should take the heaviest punishment. Why should predominately working-class South London protect fashionable Mayfair and Westminster? He warned, 'We must not play God.' Did anyone listen? In any event, it was areas like Croydon which suffered repeatedly.

The V1s being launched from France had their range pre-set at 140 miles. They flew at over 300 miles an hour at a height of 2,500 feet. Their speed increased as their fuel lightened. On average, just under 200 rockets were being launched every day. Each site was firing off every half hour. With the government only giving scant news about the V1s, public morale plummeted. The wet, gloomy summer and cold autumn didn't help, it just reflected the depressed mood. Just when victory seemed a real possibility, a new form of terror was unleashed on poor, punch-drunk London. Maybe it was as well that the public did not know what a sizeable percentage of the authorities were thinking. It was being predicted that if the attacks continued with the same ferocity, within weeks London would suffer the same death and destruction endured during the whole of the Blitz. For a further three months the flying bombs continued to arrive day and night. No air-raid warnings were given, as shooting down missiles over heavily populated areas was just as dangerous as letting fate take its course. People were nervous, twitchy. Many were unable to sleep, listening and at the ready to dive under the bed at a moment's notice. Walking through London didn't help, with smouldering piles of fresh ruins and the screaming alarms of ambulances in the background. When would it all end? Not yet, but Allied troops were beginning to knock out the launch sites, leaving Churchill in a bullish mood. He knew this was a last-ditch attempt by the Germans, some of whom had thought the bombing campaign would be a persuasive bargaining counter in pursuing a truce.

At last the sun appeared on 30 June, a cause in itself for celebration. Shirtsleeve order and summer frocks were paraded along Aldwych. Then came the familiar sound of a V1 cutting out and diving towards the packed street. The summer sun was clouded by dust and debris. Lines of burnt-out buses emerged like ghosts, and on the pavements the sprawled bodies of forty-two dead and hundreds of injured. Surely the people of Croydon might have been forgiven for thinking that it was time for central London to take some of the punishment. They had seen thousands of their homes totally destroyed and close on 60,000 severely damaged. The West End was hit again a month after the Aldwych disaster, when forty-five people were killed in Kensington, but earlier on that morning of 28 July South London again convulsed under a horrendous attack. Lewisham street market was in full flow when a bomb dived down on the helpless shoppers. Lewisham hospital was overwhelmed with the dead, dying and injured. Marks & Spencer was on fire and the street was littered with burnt out vehicles. Some of those only slightly injured were screaming hysterically. A nurse commented that 'no battlefield could be worse or more bloody'. Earlier, American soldiers, billeted in fashionable Lower Sloane Street, had been killed. The V1s were indiscriminate in seeking out their victims.

The colossal damage to housing was now creating additional problems. For the second time since the outbreak of war, there was an exodus from London to the country. Some 20,000 houses a day were being damaged. It was impossible for teams of builders brought in from the provinces to keep up. Over 5,000 bombs had fallen on Kent, Sussex, Essex and Surrey. Places that previously had been considered safe were themselves now in the firing line. It was in this 'alleyway' to London where efforts to intercept the flying bombs were made, leaving even those living in rural areas wondering if they were safe.

By the end of August it appeared the V1 attacks were tailing off. Virtually all the launching sites in France were now in Allied hands. With the false confidence that seems to be the preserve of prominent politicians, Duncan Sandys, the minister of supply and also Churchill's son-in-law, pronounced that the threat from flying bombs was, to all intents and purposes, over. His announcement to the press on 7 September was followed within twenty-four hours by the arrival of the V2. This was a monster missile. It was almost 50 feet long, carried a ton of explosives and travelled faster than the speed of sound. War for Londoners was just about to get even nastier. The rockets were launched from Holland, some 200 miles distant from London. Their launching platforms were easily transportable, making it very difficult for Allied planes to target them. Now it tended to be Northern London and the East End that experienced the most attacks. Once more, the government went into its shell. A total news blackout was implemented. The first V2 landed in Chiswick and for a time it was supposed that the explosion was the result of a gasometer blowing up. It was another month before Churchill finally 'came clean' with the public. The speed of the rockets meant there was almost no warning of the calamity just about to engulf you. The loud, double bang that announced a V2's arrival could be heard many miles away. Although there were less V2s launched, if anything they were feared more than their predecessor. Swathes of buildings were swept away in seconds and those hundreds of yards away were stripped of roof tiles, with crockery and household utensils smashing to the floor. A most distressing attack on the Woolworth store in New Cross occurred on 25 November. People reported a blinding flash and a demonic boom of an explosion. The store was packed with early Christmas shoppers. There was total chaos. Dazed survivors, half-blinded, groping through the dust and rubble. Screams from the injured, cries for help and a sense of disbelief at the damage done. Reserve workers, numbering in their hundreds, frantically searched for survivors for two whole days. The death toll was 168, with many seriously injured. Robin Burns's father, working for the heavy rescue unit, was directed to another horrific scene with the bombing of Smithfield Market on 8 March 1945. The bomb landed right in the centre of the market, causing its total collapse. Robin's father didn't spare the young boy his graphic description, insisting it was difficult to distinguish the difference between the sheep and cattle carcases and the human dead. A death toll of 110 was recorded.

Only weeks before, the Allies had carpet-bombed the beautiful old city of Dresden. The ensuing firestorm had killed thousands. Was it 20,000 or perhaps 50,000? No-one seemed to know. Opinion was divided. The bloody Krauts started it and deserved whatever was coming to them. London's pain was dreadful but not on the scale of Dresden. Life was becoming de-humanised. Weapons were being used, decisions made that cheapened life. War had always been brutal, but modern war was now cold and calculating. Our baser instincts held sway, above honour, if that had really ever existed. In the last gasps of the European war, these questions and doubts were beginning to take root. But there would be time for those discussions later. All through March the rockets kept on coming, fulfilling their death mission. The East End was ending its war as it had begun, with Stepney and Petticoat Lane being hit. A second, more devastating V2 hit Stepney on 27 March 1945. Here was the final insult for the East End to endure. A black tragedy. A final gift from Hitler that smashed its way through two blocks of flats. It was like an earthquake scene. Huge piles of rubble, desperate rescuers digging, digging. Sniffer dogs and small groups waiting for news of their loved ones. Today it is just another statistic, but 134 died and many more were injured. Crushed, in body certainly, but possibly in mind too. Nothing goes on forever, surely that was the last punch, albeit a body blow that old London would have to take. Well, almost.

Most who lived through the Blitz and the doodlebugs have their own stories to recall. Jean Sporle tells of her mum, having just made lunch, throwing herself to the floor as a bomb landed nearby. It brought the ceiling down, covering the food in a thick mixture of dust and plaster. 'Waste not – want not' was a favourite saying. So, undeterred, they sat amid the chaos of their ruined kitchen and steadfastly ate their crunchy roast.

I remember my father arriving home one night with his suit torn. I think it was the day of the Aldwych bomb. Hearing the engine cut out, he threw himself under a stationary taxi, hurriedly joining a rather startled cabbie. They both survived with minor cuts and bruises.

It's rotten luck to be the last civilian to be killed in the war. Poor Ivy Millichamp had lived in relative suburban peace until a bomb landed near her bungalow in Orpington. The date was 1 April 1945 but it was no April Fools' joke for poor Ivy, who joined the many thousands of Londoners who had been killed since 1939. The war in Europe still had some way to run, but the assault on London was over. It had taken a terrible pounding, by far the worst in its long history. Vast chunks of it had been destroyed. Historic buildings, churches and thousands of ordinary homes had been turned to rubble and dust, but the City was still standing. Sometimes stately, often brash, London was ready to rediscover, reinvent itself again, but for the moment it must wait. Symbolically, the harsh, cold winter of 1945 was gone and London embraced the coming of spring and a brief summer of victory and hope.

10

Time to Celebrate

London is like some huge prehistoric animal, capable of enduring terrible injuries, mangled and bleeding from many wounds, and yet preserving its life and movement.

Winston Churchill

Sipping at her gin and orange, my grandmother declared that after five years of war, 1944 was the most miserable Christmas ever. The half-bottle of Booths had been acquired by her rather dodgy lodger. Gin, like almost every prized commodity, was in short supply. Turkeys were just a distant dream. A scrawny chicken, or more likely a rabbit, was possibly to be the best available treat for most Christmas lunch tables. Even the huge retail palaces of the West End had little to offer. Bare shelves ensured that central London was strangely quiet. Children eagerly searching through their Christmas stockings often had to make do with second-hand toys.

For most living in London, life was grim. John Betjeman went further; writing to Geoffrey Taylor, he declared, 'I will never live in London again, it's death.' Certainly London looked tired and down at heel, as did most Londoners. Threadbare overcoats and shiny suits were now standard wear for many men, while even the prettiest young woman struggled to look glamorous in an age of 'make do and mend'. The weather didn't help. A damp, foggy autumn had developed into a bitterly cold winter. Waking up each morning it was impossible to see outside for the frost that lined the inside of the windows.

There was constant talk of victory, but little sign of it. During 1944 there had been continual industrial disputes. That year witnessed more days lost to strikes than in 1939. The continual devastation caused by flying bombs was also affecting public morale. The break out of the Allied troops from Normandy was initially slower than had been anticipated. Each reported military success appeared to attract an immediate setback. The most depressing was the disaster at Arnhem. The airborne and glider operation planned by Montgomery involved some 10,000 troops, of whom only 2,400 managed to escape. The raid left 1,200 servicemen dead, with thousands being captured. The Allies now reverted to Eisenhower's broad-front strategy, while to the east the Russians were surging across Central Europe.

In Islington, having survived a family Christmas Day, many sought refuge in a couple of pints at their local on Boxing Day. The Prince of Wales was packed with customers anxious to get a drink before the beer ran out. Suddenly, without warning, the earth shook and there was a deafening blast. The V2 landed nearby, causing the demolition of the pub and an area of devastation covering hundreds of yards. Many were trapped in the rubble and debris, leaving sixty-eight dead and hundreds injured. Bomb sites, ugly and overgrown with weeds, were now commonplace across London, a constant reminder of the remaining danger posed by the V2s. Although the bomb was silent until impact, many still lay awake at night listening, hoping it was not about to be their turn. What they did often hear was the rumble of Allied bombers as they made their way south to inflict terrible damage on the major cities of Germany.

In March 1945 the Luftwaffe staged what was to be their last airborne attack on Britain. Some seventy fighters and bombers managed to drop a few token bombs over London. Six enemy aircraft were shot down before the rest headed back to war-devastated Germany. A month later, there was more bad news with the announcement of the unexpected death of President Roosevelt from a cerebral haemorrhage. There was genuine grieving for a man who had proved to be a great friend and, to some, the saviour of Great Britain. C. P. Snow wrote, 'I don't think I have ever seen London quite so devastated.' Again, it was as if every piece of good news had to be paid for. A memorial service was held at St Paul's Cathedral, attended by King George, his queen and an emotional Winston Churchill. He sent a telegraph to his wife Clemmie, who was on a goodwill tour of Russia: 'Sarah and I attended the service at St Paul's for Roosevelt, which was very impressive.' He doesn't dwell on his sadness, adding, 'The weather here is bright and delightful. Everyone is as much astonished by the rapidity with which Germany has been over-run.' So although the general public didn't know it, the end was at last in sight.

For years there had been rumours of barbaric behaviour by German troops. This had largely been attributed to action in the heat of battle and even Allied propaganda, but news of horrendous concentration camps changed those perceptions. In the same month of Roosevelt's death the British public was confronted by more excruciating news. Throughout London news cinemas started showing films in graphic detail of Belsen and Buchanwald. Queues stretched into the distance as if the public was waiting to see a Hollywood blockbuster. It was curiosity and a sense of disbelief rather than voyeurism. Audiences watched in total silence. Nor was there any conversation between them as they left the cinema. It was almost as if they too shared some of the guilt that had led to such depravity. Public reaction was one of horror and a further nagging sense of unease at the casual anti-Semitism that existed throughout British society. For many this hardened into a desire to wreak revenge on Germany and to show them no mercy as the Third Reich tottered towards defeat.

There had been, and continued to be, a steady return to pre-war conditions. In October 1944 the home guard had been stood down with a final parade, held at Horse Guards Parade. Firefighters were also dismissed, but told they would be able to keep their uniforms. Public shelters were closed and the bunks used for sleeping removed from underground stations, much to the annoyance of an army of down-and-outs who had come to regard tube stations as their home. By April 1945 blackout curtains were allowed to be taken down. Typically, some had become so used to the privacy the curtains gave them that they continued to hide away from the prying eyes of their neighbours.

Many of the artistic masterpieces were returned to the National Gallery from North Wales, and the royal horses were welcomed back to their stables in Windsor. Gradually, London was losing its cosmopolitan atmosphere as thousands of foreign refugees returned to their liberated homelands. There only remained a relatively few American servicemen to spice up the atmosphere of central London. There were no more air-raid sirens to be heard, and again in April lighting returned to some London streets. This and the lack of GIs was a lethal combination for the prostitutes of the West End. Together with small-time crooks, they had enjoyed the cover of darkness and with the lights back on the police suddenly became more active. It was still to be a few months before full lighting would be restored, but a symbolic event took place on 30 April. The shrapnel-pocked faces of Big Ben had been restored and after a gap of over five years the world's most famous clock chimed out a message of hope.

Britain was limping, rather than marching, towards peace. The sales of flags and bunting soared. All that was needed now was the official announcement. It was as if the authorities were taking a perverse pleasure in dampening down expectations and keeping the public in the dark. The ministry of food decreed that no extra food was to be distributed to hotels and restaurants. The five-shilling limit on restaurant meals was to remain. Stocks of beer were low, while wines and spirits were unobtainable for most. It appeared that killjoys were in control with the news that pub hours were not going to be extended. 'Chips' Channon noted that even the guests at the Ritz were on edge and in a restless mood as they awaited the formal announcement. Channon picked up a communiqué issued by SHAEF on tape that the Germans had capitulated in Holland, western Germany and Denmark and a ceasefire would come into effect the following day at 6 p.m. He celebrated with a few glasses of Kummel with some of his aristocratic chums.

As a seven-year-old, I was still sent off to bed early. I was awoken by a frightening scream. I dashed downstairs, thinking something terrible had happened, to find my parents and older sister celebrating with some of our neighbours. My father had produced a bottle of Haig whisky that he had been saving for this day. I was kissed and hugged, and realised that life from now on was going to change. At the same time, over at her boarding school in Potters Bar, the seventeen-year-old Pat Desbruslais was showing real initiative. Having heard the unemotional voice of BBC announcer Stuart Hibbert state that tomorrow would be VE Day and Churchill would address the nation at three o'clock, she rushed to the school chapel. There, alone, she rang the bell. It was the first time it had been heard since the outbreak of war.

There was a strange meteorological coincidence that linked the duration of the war in London – a form of weather-related bookends. In the early morning of VE Day 8 May, there was a massive thunderstorm of Wagnerian proportions over London, just as there had been on the morning of the outbreak of war. Just as 3 September developed into a glorious late summer's day, so did VE Day offer a cloudless spring sky with temperatures soaring into the mid-twenties. Although there was a flu bug sweeping the capital, it didn't take long for huge crowds to gather in the West End. To start with, they wandered aimlessly or sat on the steps of public buildings waiting for a focal point of interest to develop. Not everyone was up for a party, with Kensington reported to have been as quiet as a tomb. At least the East End was decked out in flags and bunting, and here and across most of London parties were being organised. By midday huge crowds swirled around the West End. Many carried Union Jacks or were decked out in red, white and blue. By afternoon loudspeakers relayed speeches by the king and Prime Minister Churchill in which he said, 'We may allow ourselves a brief period of rejoicing, but let us not forget for a moment the toil and effort that lie ahead.' With his voice cracking with emotion, he concluded, 'Advance Britannia, long live the cause of freedom! God save the King.' Across London crowds cheered while many wept as they gave way to the outpouring of emotion. Clementine, Churchill's wife, was still away in Russia. She sent a telegram from Moscow, 'All my thoughts are with you on this supreme day, my darling. It could not have happened without you. All my love, Clemmie.'

Crowds spilled down Shaftesbury Avenue towards Piccadilly Circus. There were young girls in cotton dresses, children carried aloft on their parents' shoulders, old couples arm in arm. There

Unity Mitford in Munich, in Mosley's fascist uniform, talking to an SS colonel in front of Brown House, Munich.

October, 1939

See inside cover
for descriptive details.

PETER JONES
SLOANE SQUARE, LONDON, S.W.1.   SLOANE 3434

Left: Peter Jones' *Fashion Gazette* 1939.

Below and opposite page: London fashions in 1940 before rationing was imposed.

Chic without measure

John Lewis, Oxford Street, in 1939. The building was destroyed by an enemy bomb in 1940.

Above left: January 1940. Evacuees departing for the countryside.

Above right: It's off to war, but it's all smiles for the time being.

Above left: A night on the tiles looking out for enemy planes.

Above right: Preparing a warm welcome for the Luftwaffe.

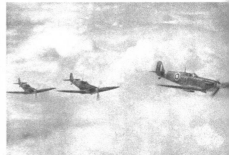

Above left: Nazi bombers in the sky above London.

Above right: Spitfires and Hurricanes won air supremacy in the Battle of Britain in 1940. Here, a Spitfire patrol is seen on duty, ready to attack.

Left: The king and queen see bomb damage. Bombed areas in London's East End were visited by the king and queen on 11 September 1940, where they talked sympathetically with people whose homes had been destroyed.

Below: When a bomb fell near a parked London taxi cab, the force of the explosion lifted the vehicle into the air and hurled it into a crater. Not a single window was broken in this freak journey.

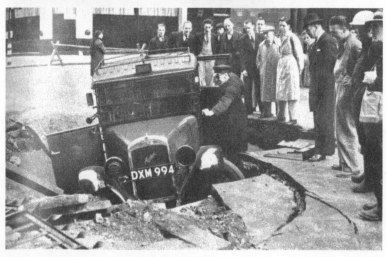

Nazi raiders penetrated the London defences during the rush hour on the morning of 8 October 1940. In a low-diving attack, bombs were dropped on crowded streets and two buses were wrecked.

Freak effect of a bursting bomb. Blast of a bursting bomb in the night attack of 8 September 1940 flung a stationary bus against a building, pinning the radiator to the windowsills of an upper floor. Passengers, driver and conductor had taken shelter.

Children playing in a bombed-out street in 1940.

Mannequins, not corpses, lying outside the ruins of John Lewis in Oxford Street.

Life in Oxford Street goes on despite the damage. 'Never knowingly undersold' was taken to new limits after the John Lewis store was bombed out.

Shopping in Oxford Street is temporarily suspended.

In September 1940 Buckingham Palace was hit and a policeman on duty was killed.

Above: At the Windmill Theatre, the artistes slept on site as the bombs fell all around.

Right: Margaret McGrath, the Windmill glamour girl who bravely led trapped horses through the streets of the West End to safety.

Scene in the Aldwych shelter, the stretch of underground railway between Aldwych and Holborn which was taken out of service to accommodate Londoners in night raids. Railway lines and platforms provided relatively safe sleeping accommodation.

Musical entertainment being provided for the sheltering crowds.

Above left: St Bride's church, Wren's beautiful church known as the 'Cathedral of Fleet Street' was gutted by Luftwaffe incendiary bombs.

Above right: Guildhall was one of many historic London buildings destroyed by Nazi fire raiders on 29 December 1940, in what was the Second Great Fire of London.

A good read amid the carnage of Holland House library in Kensington.

St Paul's stands defiant while all around the City burns.

Fires rage in Chancery Lane.

Above left: Firefighters tackling a blaze caused by incendiaries.

Above right: Paternoster Row, the centre of London's book trade, was decimated, with the loss of millions of books.

Above left: The empty windows of a blazing building frame a view of St Paul's.

Above right: The raid of 29 December also targeted Guy's Hospital.

Death on the dance floor at the Café de Paris. The fashionable venue is left in ruins after a freak attack on 8 March 1941.

Ludgate Hill takes its punishment.

Some of Goering's captured blond bombers.

Above left: Even Westminster Abbey is not spared by the Luftwaffe in May 1941.

Above right: The City of London became a special target for night bombers. Here, Cannon Street lies in ruins.

The Houses of Parliament still stand as an important symbol amongst the mayhem.

Left: A present from the Luftwaffe in 1941. This used to be home.

Below: The delights of utility furniture were unleashed in 1942.

Furniture for the
BEDROOM

Furniture for the
DINING ROOM

Right: Rainbow Corner. This was the Red Cross club for GIs and a magnet for armies of girls, also spivs and small-time crooks on the lookout for fun or the chance to sell goods purchased on the black market.

Below: A little Allied co-operation.

The Messina brothers, London's kings of vice.

Above left: The Savoy offered a comfortable billet for the lucky few.

Above right: At the Savoy the manager presented firewatcher William Lewes with a 200-guinea raccoon fur coat to ward off the cold. It had been left at the hotel by a guest who did a bunk without paying her bill.

As well as providing shelter, the Savoy hotel also offered board games and newspapers to pass the time.

Left: The basement bar at the Ritz attracted and welcomed the wartime gay community.

Below: Whilst some slept, others danced the night away. The floor at the Savoy was raised for cabaret performances.

Above left: Not exactly the Ritz, but safe.

Above right: A government poster forms the backdrop for those seeking shelter for the night.

Buzz Bombs brought a new form of terror for Londoners to endure.

Promise not to snore! A family of nine prepares for a good night's sleep in South London.

Some injured people being taken to hospital.

Above left: Old-timers, who had served in the Great War, joined the Home Guard.

Above right: A rather stylish 'postie' making a delivery.

Time for a cuppa served by ARP women workers.

Above and next page: Women were essential in Britain's armaments industry.

Left: A view of St Paul's.

Above left: Charlie Weber before being severely wounded.

Above right: Rose Sheran captured two men's hearts.

Left: Phil di Meglio having a good time.

Phil di Meglio, charming and fun to be with.

Rose Sheran with baby Tony, who lived to trace his true father.

Above left: The Women's Land Army and Timber Corps were a vital part of the war effort.

Above right: The 'New Look' brought glamour and curves back to austerity Britain.

Fanny Blankers-Koen, Sportswoman of the Century, competing in the 1948 Olympic Games.

Above left: Not all was glamour and luxury in London's swankiest hotels.

Above right: Nubar Gulbenkian, regular Ritz hotel guest.

Oswald Mosley addressing a meeting of the Union Movement in 1948.

A department store in 1948.

West Indian passengers aboard the *Windrush*.

were soldiers, sailors and airmen from around the world. An officer from the tank corps was the first to clamber up to the top of the boarded up Eros. He was joined by a paratrooper who hauled up an attractive young blonde. The crowd cheered as two GIs joined them and soon the wooden pyramid was invaded by a rush of young people. In the background the bells of St James in Piccadilly rang out. Police, who had been advised to take a low profile, looked on as bonfires were lit in the street and an effigy of Hitler was burnt to loud applause. US sailors formed a conga down Piccadilly, while Londoners responded by linking arms to do the Lambeth Walk. It was a heady day. A mass expression of thanks and relief. This was their magic moment. This is what victory felt like and it was exhilarating. In Trafalgar Square the fountains proved irresistible for many, whose drenching did nothing to temper their determination to enjoy this special day. Huge crowds cheered as the royal family appeared on the balcony of Buckingham Palace. The image of Humphrey Lyttleton swaying on a handcart playing 'Roll Out The Barrel' remains as a reminder of a day that nobody who was present would ever forget.

That night Vivian van Damm allowed members of the armed forces into the Windmill Theatre free of charge. As was to be expected, the atmosphere was even more uninhibited than usual. To help restrain the audience, wire netting was erected to protect the performers whose songs were drowned out by shouting and wolf whistles. Champagne and prized vintage wines which had been saved for this day were uncorked at the swanky hotels and restaurants.

The Savoy offered a special VE Day menu for 5s but with a 3s 6d surcharge. It sounded exotic, yet patriotic also. The offering was: La Tasse de Consommé; Niçoise de la Victoire; La volaille des îles Britanniques; La citronneuse joyeux délivrancé; La Coupe Glacée des Allies and La Médaille du Soldat. There are no records of what the food tasted like, but hopefully it was a meal to remember. Meanwhile, at a be-flagged Ritz, 'Chips' Channon was celebrating with old Mrs Keppel and the Duchess of Rutland. He reported everyone was kissing him, but outside 'the streets were almost empty, as there is a bus strike and taxis refused to go out – there were a few singing people, that's all'. So a momentous day fizzled out. Tomorrow was also to be a public holiday, but that would be dedicated to a mass hangover. It would also be one of reflection on a conflict that left very few families untouched.

Within two weeks of the VE celebrations, party politics were back on the agenda. The Labour Party formally left the coalition and the date for a general election was fixed for 5 July. The overall consensus was that Churchill would be swept back into power on a tide of emotion and thanks for his enormous wartime contribution. The experts chose to ignore the warning signals of a by-election held at Chelmsford in April. Perhaps it was because a Commonwealth candidate and not Labour had overturned a Conservative majority of 16,000. On 26 May Churchill resigned but stayed on as caretaker Prime Minister. Although looking tired and every bit his age, he set out on a triumphal tour of the country. Posters of Churchill were plastered over London urging voters to 'help him finish the job'. Tory candidates continued the theme with their election leaflets imploring 'don't let him down'. Even in Labour strongholds he usually received an affectionate welcome. A visit to Walthamstow perhaps pointed the way to the future. Here, his reception was particularly hostile. He made the mistake of saying that Labour 'would have to rely on some sort of Gestapo' to implement its policies. He suddenly appeared out of touch in a peacetime environment. Lack of decent housing was top of most Londoners' agenda, but what would a Tory toff know about that? Despite the warning signs his advisers seemed unaware of the changing tide. They even managed to dismiss a Gallup Poll taken two weeks before the election that showed 45 per cent intending to vote Labour, while the Tories languished on 32 per cent, with the Liberals weighing in at 15 per cent. Even Labour politicians couldn't quite believe that the electorate would turn their backs on Churchill. The press were hopeless tipsters, maintaining that a Conservative majority of up to 100 was to be expected. It was not until actual polling day that the Labour Party finally realised that there was a seismic switch underway. There was a three-week wait after the election for the votes of the servicemen stationed abroad to be counted. Still, Conservative central office and the press continued to predict a Tory win. The bookies were more savvy and by 26 July, the day the results started to filter through, they were offering 100–1 on a Conservative victory. The swing to Labour in London was 18 per cent. It was a landslide for the socialists and the establishment was horrified and angry that an unthankful Britain had rejected the architect of victory. At Claridge's, Lord Beaverbrook had arranged a party to celebrate Churchill's victory. As the result became clear the old press baron barked out to his guests, 'This occasion was intended to be a victory feast,' he paused, 'in the circumstances it now becomes the last supper.' When the pain of his defeat really sunk in, Churchill was quoted as saying, 'I won the race and now they have warned me off the turf.' At 7.30 p.m. on the evening of 26 July 1945 Clement Attlee, together with his wife, drove their own family car to Buckingham Palace. There he shook hands with the king and was confirmed as the new Prime Minister. The British electorate had demanded change and they were about to get it. It was perhaps symptomatic of that change that as Attlee drove cautiously into the palace forecourt in his modest Standard saloon, a chauffeur-driven Rolls-Royce swooped by in the opposite direction. In the back sat a thoughtful Winston Churchill. Lighting up a Havana, no doubt his mood improved somewhat. Out of office and with Chartwell, his country house, uninhabitable, the Churchills decamped to a flat lent to them by Duncan Sandys. While Clemmie attended to the restoration of Chartwell, Winston went for a well-earned holiday on Lake Como with his daughter Sarah.

With the battle for Europe won, now attention was switched to the war in the Far East. Although Allied advances had been made, there appeared to be no immediate prospect of victory and the fear was that the conflict would drag on for years. The mood was reflected in the first weather forecast to be broadcast since 1939. The day after VE Day the BBC warned of a deepening depression approaching. Many imagined that the end of the war would lead to a radical improvement in their lives. This was not to be. Rather than a relaxation of rationing, the allowance for bacon and lard was cut. There were even long queues for potatoes and other basic vegetables. Lack of available accommodation was chronic and there was huge resentment at the number of large, neglected houses in central London that lay empty.

On 6 August an atom bomb was dropped on the Japanese city of Hiroshima. Most Londoners had only a vague idea of the frightening power and destruction of the bomb. Even when it became clear that a huge area had been incinerated, there was little sympathy expressed. Few had any knowledge of the sinister effects of radiation, nor did they care. As with the Germans, news of Japanese atrocities encouraged the view that the Japs had it coming to them. The newspapers did their best to convey the previously unimaginable area of destruction caused by an 'A' bomb. It was pointed out that a bomb falling on Tower Bridge would see total devastation spreading out in all directions for 4 square miles, taking in St Paul's, Shadwell and the Old Kent Road. The effects of radiation would silently cover a greater area still. It certainly prompted Londoners to pause for a moment, but generally they were convinced that as the bombs shortened the war the consequences were worth it. On 14 August the Japanese duly surrendered. The news was given in a midnight bulletin, so it was the following morning before most people learnt that at last the world war was over and victory achieved. Once again a two-day public holiday was declared for 15 and 16 August. The crowds were back, 100,000 filling the streets and squares of the West End. Many of the rituals from VE Day were re-run. They danced and swayed to the music of barrel organs, while searchlights swept the sky. The royal family appeared on the balcony of Buckingham Palace, with crowds stretching up the Mall. Church bells pealed and bonfires were lit across the country. Young stomachs groaned under the weight of jam sandwiches, home-made cakes and lemonade as street parties took over the capital. London was full to bursting. It was impossible to find a vacant hotel room. Pubs were granted an extension, but most had run out of beer before closing time. The lack of available booze ensured there was little drunkenness reported, but the crowds were in good humour. There were fireworks and singing in the streets. It was as if for one evening a collective weight had been lifted from the population. London and its citizens deserved some joy. Soon it would be time for reflection. London had taken dreadful punishment, enduring the most damage it had experienced since the Great Fire almost 300 years before.

There had been over 100,000 deaths or serious injuries. The City of London had witnessed the destruction of some 30 per cent of its buildings and Stepney and the rest of the East End didn't fare much better. Throughout London 80,000 houses had been totally destroyed. As Bertrand Russell said, 'War doesn't determine who is right – only who is left.' While few Londoners would have supported Russell's pacifist views, London was left – left with much of its fabric in need of repair. Not just bricks and mortar, but its social fabric too. Did London have the ability to recover and meet the new challenges, or had the struggle weakened it so badly that a slow decline was inevitable? Only time would tell, but generally London could look back on the war years with its head held high.

PART 2

Peace

11

Austerity London

London in the years immediately after the war was like a famous old film star who has fallen on hard times. There was still a hint of glamour, a whiff of seedy opulence, but the confidence had gone. London was sad, drab and down at heel. It was almost as if Londoners couldn't quite believe that the country had been victorious. They scurried across the streets of the capital like figures from a Lowry painting, heads down and slightly stooped. In the backstreets, women in snoods, headscarves and wrap-around aprons stood chatting. They stood in queues. Endless queues for food, for buses, for cinemas. Trains arriving at London's mainline stations were dirty, overcrowded and often hours late. There were no dining cars and there were long queues for tea on the platforms, which was often served in chipped cups. Queuing had become a way of life, second nature. Many men were still in uniform, while others wore ill-fitting brown de-mob suits. As winter drew in, more layers were added. An army of bulky Michelin men and women trying to combat the cold. Children wearing woollen balaclavas to protect their chapped ears. In the gutters of the major thoroughfares, shabby ex-servicemen stood, rather shame-faced. A few joined some mates in a makeshift band, while others with medals pinned to their lapels were reduced to selling matches. So this is victory.

Britain was broke. The cost of the war ran into billions of pounds. The country's gold reserves had been savaged and massive outstanding debts run up. Within a week of the Japanese surrender the American president, Harry S. Truman, axed the existing Lend-Lease agreement. Economist John Maynard Keynes, acting as a treasury adviser, was packed off to Washington to negotiate a loan of almost $4 billion on none-too-generous terms. The British were now in hock to our American cousins. Our position in the world had changed – at home too.

Chubby-faced Welsh firebrand Aneurin Bevan suggested to a leading Tory, 'My class is on the up and yours the down.' Few could disagree. Change (that word so coveted by contemporary politicians) was in the air. Fundamental, far-reaching change. Despite the acknowledgement that the country was all but bankrupt, the Labour government embarked on a massively ambitious and expensive welfare system. There was a pledge to significantly expand state ownership. By the beginning of 1946 the Bank of England was nationalised, to be followed by the railways, road transport and civil aviation. A peaceful revolution was underway. The dramatic shift was to affect everyone and yet everyday living for most remained a constant struggle.

During winter, just trying to keep warm became a major preoccupation. Outside the main living room, most houses were freezing with only a tiny proportion enjoying the benefits of central heating. For many, they had to rely on an inefficient two-bar electric fire which hardly took the chill off the room. An alternative was a dangerous, hissing gas fire that had to be lit with a match. I remember an evil-smelling paraffin stove being brought into my bedroom as I lay languishing with mumps. Many in London were living cheek-by-jowl with their neighbours and sharing a toilet on a draughty landing. Hot water was often only obtained from noisy, unreliable gas geysers. Baths, if you were lucky enough to have one, were normally restricted to one a week; alternatively a trip to public baths was an option. In crowded spaces BO, rather than aftershave, was the over-riding perfume of London. There were still tenements that had no electricity. For the majority that did, it was a ritual feeding of the meter with a shilling coin, and dim, naked light bulbs. Telephones had become an important part of life. No mobiles, of course, but heavy, black Bakelite versions with dials so stiff that you needed a strong index finger to dial a number. Long-distance calls were made via the operator. This was usually a swift and efficient service where, unlike today, you actually spoke to a human being. For many, making a phone call required a visit to the nearest street corner. Here, inevitably, stood a red public phone box that required a penny or two in the slot for local calls.

The streets of London in the 1940s were already clogged and choked with traffic. This is one of the few direct comparisons that can be made with our contemporary capital. True, many streets and famous buildings survive today, but the whole atmosphere would seem alien to the twenty-first-century onlooker. While red double-decker buses and taxis fought an ongoing battle for space, there were also trams and trolley buses. The one clanking, the other silent, but both constrained by either rails or overhead cables. There was still a sprinkling of horse-drawn waggons clip-clopping their way through the traffic as well as sweating traders pulling handcarts. Beer deliveries were made with gleaming shire horses, their huge, dinner-plate feet a reminder of London's real horse-power heritage. Steam rollers, the smell of tar and traction engines were common sights as repairs of bomb-damaged roads were undertaken. Bombsites already overgrown with weeds denied the sadness that their destruction must have brought, as children were drawn to them as dangerous adventure playgrounds, childish cries of excitement replacing those previous cries of despair.

There were rag-and-bone men calling out for 'any old iron' or anything else you wanted rid of. There were rat catchers with their metal cages and street cutlery grinders. This London was noisy and ribald, little changed from previous centuries. There were also spivs with suitcases of 'knocked off' goods. Sell quickly was their motto, and move on in an attempt to avoid 'the rozzers'. Away from central London's massive stores, there was a sea of independent retailers and corner shops. Some multiples did fan out from the centre, with Boots, Timothy White and Taylors tending to dominate the chemist trade. Supermarkets had yet to become a way of life and leading grocers included Cullens and the Home and Colonial stores. However, Sainsbury's were already the major player in London. A visit to one of their shops was a totally different experience to that of today. To a young boy they resembled a tiled cathedral, grand and imposing. Two long granite counters ran down either side of the shop. Behind each section, assistants were immaculate in white uniforms, the women's hair covered in a fetching mob cap, while butchers' aprons were worn in the bacon department. Shopping then had an air of tranquility about it as each item was individually wrapped. It was all butter pats, greaseproof paper and tea weighed from a row of tea chests. Here came the death throes of civilised shopping. High bent-wood chairs were even available for customers waiting to be served. Despite the incessant queues, shopping had the rhythm of an age where life was not so frantic and time seemingly less precious.

London was a city of smells which varied with the seasons. In a heat wave, the stench from the abattoirs or the gasworks floated on a breeze for miles. Fish arriving by train from Grimsby hung in the air long after it was trucked off to Billingsgate. As autumn arrived smells were often cloaked in a cloying fog. Most households continued to use coal for their heating. From every street, belching chimneys conspired to produce air so foul that it attacked the throat and lined the lungs. Clothes worn for just a day were covered in specks of soot, particularly if you lived near to one of London's mainline stations. Buildings and monuments were dark and begrimed. For youngsters, travel by train was a journey of excitement. Walking down the platform past the snorting, belching monster of the engine created a sense of anticipation amid the hustle and bustle, with porters wheeling heavy luggage on barrows before hoisting it onto the luggage rack in the small compartments that normally only seated eight people, then waiting, hand outstretched, for the expected tip. Outside in corridors crowds stood, many of them still in uniform. It was a London set in monochrome. Drab, dirty but nostalgic and etched in the memory.

On 8 June 1946 London hosted a vast victory parade. Not everyone wanted to celebrate – victory, if anything, had brought even worse conditions. The weather didn't help, dawning damp with rain in the air. The killjoys were proved wrong, with crowds lining the route, twenty to thirty people deep in places. Leaving early by tube, my mother, sister and myself secured a good viewing point on The Mall. Despite the drizzle, I was absolutely captivated by the magnitude of the event, the crowds and the uniformed servicemen lining the route. The procession started with the top Allied brass saluting languidly as they were driven by in their chauffeur-driven staff cars. They were followed by a 500-strong mechanised column representing all sections of the war effort. There were tanks, mounted ack-ack guns, massive missile-like bombs carried on groaning trailers and amphibious landing gear. Civilian organisations included a vehicle from the ARP heavy-lifting unit, ambulances and gleaming red fire engines. Then in the distance the sound of approaching military bands. First though, servicemen from each Allied nation bearing their flags. Then a swell of cheering as, in waves, troops from the armies, navies and air forces from across every continent and of every colour. They marched with a precision that must have taken weeks of practice to perfect, each intent on outdoing the rest. There was the skirl of bagpipes and the sway of kilts as a Scottish contingent passed, to huge applause. This was matched by the Aussies, a particular favourite with the crowds, but so too for the Canadians, Kiwis and South Africans. The Yanks attracted wolf whistles, while the Indian troops were perhaps the most spectacular, resplendent in their turbans and with the fierce looks of a group of men not to be taken lightly. Politics ensured that there were no Poles or troops from the USSR making an appearance. The Cold War was setting in and sadly the fantastic heroics of the Polish airmen were unable to be publicly acknowledged on that rainy day in London. Eventually, the royal family appeared in the State Landau, and then it was all over. We spilled down The Mall, swept along in a human tide as we waited outside Buckingham Palace for the royal family to appear on the balcony. Nobody wanted the day to end. That evening, crowds swirled round the West End and lined the Embankment. Although public buildings and monuments were floodlit, the future for most attending that day didn't seem so bright.

The young tend not to worry about the future. They have an in-built optimism which, unfortunately, tends to drain away in adulthood. In Islington, twelve-year-old Rocky Knight was nervous but excited about starting at a new school The Dame Alice

Owen School had been founded in 1613 for twelve poor students and 300 years later had built up a fine reputation. Rocky spent the next six years there, tramping the 2 miles back and forth through all weathers. A year later he joined the Crown and Manor Boys Club. These institutions were a feature of London inner-city life and for many they were almost more important than their formal schooling. Sport was obviously the main attraction, with top-class professionals available to offer coaching. As well as soccer and cricket, athletics featured, together with rifle shooting. Tuition was given in art and essay writing, with the debating society also very popular. For those interested in improving themselves rather than hanging around street corners looking for trouble, these clubs were invaluable. Added to the school curriculum, it offered kids from less privileged backgrounds a combined syllabus that was not so different from the leading public schools. These clubs were the springboard for many young Londoners to achieve success far beyond their expectations. It certainly worked for Rocky as six years later he went up to Cambridge to study history and then on to McGill University in Montreal, where he took his masters degree.

Sylvia Cooney, as a fifteen-year-old, had her sights set on the bright lights rather than academia. She had taken tap dancing lessons at a studio in Great Portland Street since she was eleven. A born entertainer, accompanied by an accordionist she had entertained crowds using the underground shelters during the war. On leaving school, she went touring with her sister and a friend appearing as the Alpine Trio, but soon became disenchanted with rotten digs and horrible landladies. In 1945, without her father's knowledge, she auditioned at the Windmill Theatre. Anne Mitelle, Vivian van Damm's assistant, was difficult to please but the lovely-looking Sylvia was quickly accepted. Her father was horrified and was only placated by being offered four free tickets a month to see the show. Much to Sylvia's shame, he insisted on collecting her from the stage door each night. She stayed at the Windmill for two years and was unusual in that she refused to appear at the theatre in the nude. As pressure for her to do so increased, she resigned. Following appearances at Café Anglaise in Leicester Square and a succession of West End clubs, she married her long-time dance instructor. Still quite stunningly attractive at eighty-three, we were perhaps denied a star of the future.

The desire for normality and a return to pre-war conditions was answered in part for sports lovers, with the resumption of the first class county cricket in May 1945. Tellingly, in a game still influenced by social class, only one county had a professional player as their captain. Les Berry captained Leicestershire, but other counties often opted for establishment figures, some of whom would not normally have had the ability to play in the first-class game. In June, the first of three test matches against India was staged at Lords. Getting an early morning bus, I arrived with my father before eight o'clock to find queues already snaking round the ground. I was really concerned that we wouldn't get in but after a couple of hours we struggled through the turnstiles at the Nursery End. Then, armed with cushions and a scorecard we entered the mound stand and claimed our seats. My two heroes, Len Hutton and the charismatic Denis Compton, managed just seven runs between them against what was judged to be a poor Indian attack. The Nottinghamshire batsman Joe Hardstaff eventually ground his way to a double century but by today's standards the run rate was pedestrian. I didn't mind, I was captivated as, seemingly, were the rest of the full-house crowd. How wonderful it must have been to be worrying about dropped catches rather than falling bombs. That year Yorkshire retained the championship they had won in 1939 and Wally Hammond headed the batting averages, while leg spinner Eric Hollies was the leading bowler.

At the end of August the first full season of professional football kicked off, with over 60,000 cramming into Stamford Bridge to see Chelsea beat Bolton Wanderers 4–3. Earlier in April the first post-war Cup final was held at Wembley. With ten minutes to go there was no score, but by the final whistle both Derby County and Charlton Athletic had netted chances and the match went to extra time. Derby eventually ran out 4–1 winners and their veteran half-back, Bert Turner, earned the distinction of scoring for both teams (with an own goal and one for his own side).

A symbolic sporting event surely underlined the slow return to normality. The sixtieth All England Tennis Championships started on 24 July 1946. Maybe the strawberries were less in evidence than before the war and champagne a distant memory, but tennis, even more than cricket, represented a peacefully tranquil English summer. The fact that our players were fairly hopeless hardly seemed to matter. We knew how to stage these grand sporting events better than anyone and surely that was just as important. The men's singles was won by the Frenchman Yvon Petra. In a five-set match he eventually beat the Australian Geoff Brown 6–4 in the final set. The ladies' final was an all-American affair in which Pauline Betz Addie beat a young Louise Brough 6–2, 6–4.

Back in July 1945, the launching of the BBC *Light Programme* had been an early pointer towards a more relaxed and enjoyable life. It replaced the popular *General Forces Programme*. While retaining many favourites like *ITMA* and *Variety Bandbox* made popular during the war, the service was expanded in scope. The connection with many troops still serving abroad was maintained with the introduction of *Two-Way Family Favourites*. It was an immensely popular record request programme which linked up families with British forces posted abroad. Music programmes were now as popular as comedy and another institution, *Housewife's Choice*, was introduced in 1946. For over twenty years it retained its regular 9.00 a.m. weekday slot and mirrored the shifting tastes in music. The generally more informal approach of the station proved really popular with the public and pointed the way towards the style of radio we listen to today.

Cinema attendance in 1946 reached an all-time record of 1.6 million visits in the year. The biggest British success was a film version of Charles Dickens's *Great Expectations*. Directed by David Lean and starring John Mills, Alec Guinness and Valerie Hobson, it won two Academy Awards. One of the year's most popular Hollywood offerings was *Blue Skies*. Starring Bing Crosby and Fred Astaire, it was the ultimate escapist film, featuring the music of Irving Berlin. The highlight was the routine 'Putting on the Ritz', performed by Astaire, backed by nine images of himself as the chorus, which was filmed separately and superimposed.

For those seeking more serious music, Benjamin Britten's *Peter Grimes* was first performed at Sadlers Wells in July 1945.

The following year the Proms kicked off with Basil Cameron conducting the London Symphony Orchestra performing Beethoven's 'Egmont No. 1 Overture'. That year the last night was largely given over to Sir Adrian Boult conducting performances of works by Berlioz and Elgar. He left the traditionally rowdy finale of Henry Wood's 'Fantasia on British Sea Songs' to be handled by Basil Cameron.

Although it was natural for Londoners to indulge in a little escapism, the hard reality of the country's plight continued to gnaw away. Not only had the government committed itself to an astonishingly expensive welfare system at home, it was still trying to fulfil what it saw as its international obligations. In 1946, troubles in Palestine culminated in the bombing of the King David Hotel in Jerusalem, with many British deaths. Throughout the Empire, massive problems were evident and Britain also shared in the expense of governing Germany, Austria and Italy. Sir Henry Tizzard warned, 'If we continue to behave like a great power we shall soon cease to be a great nation.' Money had to be raised to help meet our commitments and the rich were targeted with punitive tax and death duties. Although Ernest Bevin, Nye Bevan and Herbert Morrison represented the working class within the cabinet, they were in a minority. Even here the old school tie still held sway. Most of these politicians were intelligent and well meaning but with very little experience of the world of business and finance. The industrial supremo was the austere Sir Stafford Cripps, who had at least married into a business fortune. Ursula Davy was the heiress to the Eno Salts company. The couple married in 1936 but the business was sold to the Beecham organisation two years later. Ironically, Stafford Cripps suffered from constant colitis, which only a vegetarian diet helped alleviate, rather than the famous effervescent fruit salts. As president of the Board of Trade, he truly represented the austere face of Britain. Prim and puritanical, he appeared to embrace sacrifice and hardship. His father had been a Tory MP and Cripps, like many of his colleagues, enjoyed a privileged upbringing, having been educated at Winchester and University College London.

Another well-connected socialist emerged in 1945 as the new Chancellor of the Exchequer. High Dalton was the son of the chaplain to Queen Victoria. Educated at Eton and Kings College, Cambridge, like so many he discovered socialism while at university. He built up a reputation as an economist, having obtained a doctorate at LSE. Unfortunately, the step from theorising to becoming the chancellor is huge, and despite his outward bravado he was quoted by a City friend as 'seemingly utterly ignorant of the workings of the monetary system'. Not a ringing endorsement for the man running the nation's finances. Despite this, he oversaw the nationalisation of the Bank of England in February 1946. Reforms to change the face of Britain were being applied, with free school dinners and free milk which was supplied in dinky little third-of-a-pint bottles. Further nationalisation and other more sweeping reforms were soon to be introduced. A country run by technocrats rather than entrepreneurs was being envisaged. Middle England was beginning to get nervous. Many who had voted Labour were having second thoughts. If this lot were so clever, how come that at the end of June bread rationing had to be introduced? Bread coupons were to cover seven categories for consumers and included bread, flour and cakes. The idea was to eke out supplies until the next year's harvest. The rationing eventually ran on for two years. As ever in Britain, we seemed to take two steps forward and one back. It didn't stop the Ministry of Food issuing a stream of advice, with tips for healthy living. They ran advertisements extolling 'Nature's Beauty Foods' and 'Green For Go', but lettuce was a poor substitute for a population starved of fondly remembered treats. Empty slot machines stared out balefully on crowded platforms. Even fags were in short supply. Notices in tobacconists' windows proclaimed the bad news. Furtive requests of 'have they come in yet?' were met with a terse 'no', except for the few favoured customers.

The acute lack of housing in 1946 led to the largest mass squat in British history. It was reckoned that about 45,000 people without homes took part. Large empty houses in London were taken over, but it was mainly disused military camps that gave these desperate people temporary accommodation. Bomb damage, returning troops and building material shortages conspired to highlight the very pressing human problem. Squats were set up at the Ivanhoe Hotel in central London and a block of flats in Kensington. There were also camps dotted around London in Watford and Bushey Park. A military camp that was taken over in Gladstone Park upset their more fortunate neighbours, while others ranging from Victoria in central London to the outer reaches of Eastcote and Richmond underlined the severity of the problem. The long-suffering mentality of the Blitz had evaporated. People were angry and disillusioned. In 1945 George Orwell had his *Animal Farm* published to great acclaim. Now it did seem that everyone was equal but some more equal than others.

By the end of 1946 almost 4 million service personnel had been demobbed. There had been huge criticism about the time it had taken, but for many their return was either an anticlimax or, indeed, traumatic. This was not the glorious return of conquering heroes to a new land of promise and hope. To many returning to London, nothing much seemed to have changed. London was just dirtier and more run down than many remembered. They were shocked by the extent of the bomb damage. True, there were a few prefabs appearing and repairs being made to houses, but for most, London had lost its verve and vibrancy. While in 1946 'Chips' Channon was able to say to Emerald Cunard 'how quickly London had recovered from the war and how quickly normal life had resumed', few would have been able to agree with him, except in areas where they would have liked to have seen change. Britain remained a Conservative country despite the new socialist government. It was Conservative in its social outlook, where class barriers remained seemingly unaltered. It was still a place of deference. A hat-doffing society that looked up to class and position rather than money. Doctors, school teachers, even politicians were normally admired as figures of authority. Swearing in public and unruly behaviour were roundly condemned, even at football matches. It was a prudish place, a land where censorship held sway across the arts. London remained a city where foreigners were the butt of most jokes and there was a general, thinly veiled anti-Semitism. It was a sanctimonious place of double standards, where a blind eye was turned to adultery and yet for most divorce was unthinkable. It was a place where many husbands physically abused their wives and yet were rarely condemned. It was a place where man as head of the household held sway, and yet it was here that the returning troops did experience change at first hand. Many women had gone to work during their husbands' absence. They had become self-sufficient and independent. This put massive strain on many marriages and, although most survived, life with a virtual stranger was going to prove extremely difficult.

12

A London Love Story

Bomb sites were not the only scars of war that continued to haunt London. They could be repaired or rebuilt, but emotional scars are more difficult to cure. Between June 1945 and January 1947 some 4 million service personnel were demobbed and returned to civilian life. As is so often the case, expectation and anticipation led to disappointment, resentment and sometimes anger. There was to be no heroes' welcome home, just a sense of anti-climax.

On arriving back in Britain, the troops were herded off to a dispersal centre. There they were issued with a large cardboard suitcase. This contained a 'demob' suit, a shirt with two detached collars, a tie, two pairs of socks, a pair of cufflinks and a hat. Now dressed to conquer the world, they were despatched to the nearest resettlement office where they were given some basic advice on their return to civvy street. Having been issued with travel documents to take them home, they queued to get their last military pay packet. This amounted to eight weeks' wages, plus an extra day's pay for every month they had served overseas. They were then cast off, after years of obeying or issuing orders, to face the world. Away from their mates, with whom they had experienced so much. A fair proportion were now institutionalised by the cloak provided by military life. Many were concerned, rather than excited, by the thought of being reunited with their wives, family and loved ones.

Some reunions were joyful. An explosion of love, the more intense for the time spent apart. These were the lucky ones. For most the re-establishing of relationships was often awkward and for some extremely difficult, or sadly traumatic. Many children resented this strange man who came between them and their mum. A mother who had previously devoted her sole love and attention to the child. Wives found their husbands had become strangers. Changed, certainly, sometimes haunted by their war time experiences. Nightmares and mood swings were common, but they were difficult to understand or to respond to appropriately. Many women had gained a sense of independence by working in an office or factory. They saw no reason to revert to the old ways of waiting on their menfolk like servants. All of these tensions led to arguments and a feeling on both sides of being trapped. The house or flat seemed too small to accommodate this irritable newcomer. Resentment replaced love, for a time anyway, until gradually they learnt to live together again. Not many men had to confess to having a fling or a visit to a brothel in some far-off land. After all, it had only been a bit of harmless fun, but few took such a tolerant line concerning their wives' or girlfriends' romances. Some women openly confessed, while some returning servicemen were told by well-meaning or nosy neighbours. Tongues wagged and hearts were broken. Some suspected, but never dared ask. Although the divorce rate soared to ten times its pre-war level, for most it was never on the agenda. In a judgemental world, scandal tended to be avoided even if it meant living the rest of your life in a marriage of constant recrimination.

Like so many youngsters at that time, Tony Weber couldn't really remember his father returning home after the war. He was little more than a baby, but his parents were central to his formative years. Like many boys he was particularly close to his mother. He was proud of her. She was pretty, affectionate and outgoing. His father, by contrast, was quieter and rather thoughtful. Although he never spoke of his war experiences, the result was evident and painful to see. Charlie Weber had served with the Desert Rats and survived. It was later in Italy, still serving with the Eighth Army, that he was injured. In a bizarre series of events a mate on sentry duty panicked and attempted to run away, and was shot in the process. Charlie volunteered to stay for the second watch and was shot several times in the back by enemy snipers. He was left bleeding and paralysed before being transferred to a hospital ship where emergency surgery was performed. Months later Charlie was shipped home and sent to Stoke Mandeville Hospital. After intensive treatment he gradually regained movement in his right side that enabled him to walk. Until the day he died he had open wounds that had to be dressed daily and he was often in agonising pain.

It was only after his death that the family learnt that, as well as the Africa and Italy stars, he had also received the King's Commendation for bravery. So no wonder this brave man, whose own family had come to Britain after the Great War from Alsace, seemed somewhat preoccupied to his young son, haunted, no doubt, by his wartime experiences. As the years progressed, there were additions to the Weber family, with Tony being joined by three sisters and a brother. Gradually, seemingly irrational doubts began forming in the young boy's mind. Despite his father being invariably kind and supportive, he tended to show more outward affection to his other children. By the time he entered his teens another worry niggled away. Tony was short and stocky with a swarthy complexion, while the other children were tall, slim and fair.

Unable to sleep on a hot, sultry evening when Tony was about fourteen, he decided to go downstairs to get a drink. Stopping for a moment on the landing he could make out his mother chatting to her sister. They were talking about him. No youngster can resist eavesdropping. The conversation was confusing. There was constant reference to someone called Phil. Tony crept down a few more stairs so that he could hear better. There was talk of Glastonbury. Tony knew his mother had served near there during the war in the Timber Corp. Then the bombshell. It appeared that his mum had fallen for a GI and the man he loved as his dad was not really his father at all. It explained Charlie's rather measured attitude and only increased Tony's admiration for him. Realising the sensitivity of the situation, Tony didn't confront his parents, but it created a deep-rooted desire to eventually trace his biological father.

It was a couple of years later that Tony interrupted a huge row between his parents. Alarmed, he pleaded with his dad to calm down. 'Dad! Dad! Who are you calling Dad?', Charlie responded. Obviously it wasn't only his war wounds that remained raw and painful. As in all family rows, there were tears and banging of doors. In typical British fashion nothing was said the next day. Instead, rather awkwardly, Charlie offered his stepson his first cigarette. This was a peace offering. A Woodbine and a squeeze of the arm. Mutual love and respect restored. For them, the subject was closed. It was never discussed again. Tony obviously quizzed his mum, but for the moment she refused any discussion. Gradually, over the years, she weakened slightly and with the help of other family members Tony was able to slowly reconstruct his parents' story.

For some, love triumphs despite massive setbacks and heartbreak. First love has an intensity that is seldom forgotten, even in old age. Charlie Weber was eighteen at the outbreak of war. Born in Lambeth, his family, along with many from the East End and others from deprived areas of London, were housed by the London County Council on the Watling estate in Burnt Oak. A few years earlier, Burnt Oak had been a small, rural hamlet just off the Edgware Road (the ancient Watling Street). Thousands of homes were built and a tube station enabled residents to commute to work in central London. There was also plenty of employment to be had locally with factories, including Rawplug, Duples and the de Havilland aircraft factory nearby. The estate attracted many left-wing activists and for a time the area was known as 'Little Moscow'.

Charlie had already been called up for military service by the time he met Rose Sheran. Her family had moved to Burnt Oak from St Pancras. She was a petite, lively brunette two years his junior. He tried to pick her up in their local pub, but she wasn't playing, not yet anyway. He insisted on walking her home and by dropping his service cap under a bush in her parents' front garden, gave himself the excuse to return. She relented and they started going out together. They were a good-looking couple. He was a tall, slim young man who was rather shy and reserved, but a perfect foil for the chatty bundle of energy that was Rose. For the weeks before Charlie was posted they were inseparable. They went dancing and like most youngsters loved going to the pictures at the Gaumont in Burnt Oak and the Essoldo in Colindale. They became engaged just before Charlie was posted to join the Eighth Army, serving first in Egypt and Libya. For a couple of years they kept in touch by letter. Eventually he stopped writing and Rose assumed he had tired of her or had fallen for some exotic girl in a far-off land.

As the war progressed, Rose decided that she really didn't fancy working in a factory. She managed to join the Women's Land Army, being assigned to the Timber Corps. She was surrounded mostly by girls who had grown up in the country, so she was something of a curiosity, this little London sparrow. Her unit was billeted just outside Glastonbury in Somerset. During their six-week training they were given lectures on tree recognition and the uses for different types of timber in the war effort. They were sent out with experienced staff and were taught how to fell trees and to plant saplings, as well as undertaking nursery work. The workload was physically tiring and the days long. They started early in the morning and, with only a short lunch break, they carried on to 5.30 p.m. in the summer or until dusk during winter months. At night there was little to do except listen to the wireless or play cards. All this changed with the arrival of the Americans in 1943, who were stationed in nearby Street. British and New Zealand troops had been stationed nearby previously and there had been a few romances, but the GIs were in a different league. To start with, they had money and were happy to spend it. Dances were organised at US camps. There was live music and gifts of stockings and food that the girls had not tasted for years. They were different, these Yanks. Outgoing, generous and so self-confident. The girls (at least some of them) were caught up in the excitement of it all. It was at one of the dances that Rose met chubby-faced Private First Class Phil di Meglio. Was it unconsciously an attraction of opposites? Not of Rose and Phil, but the difference between Charlie, her first love, and Phil was extreme. Phil was a fast-talking wise guy, always the centre of attention, the exact opposite of the gentle, thoughtful Charlie. Phil was ten years older than Rose and perhaps it was a confidence that maturity brings that swept her off her feet. She was bowled over by his sense of fun and zest for life. They met as often as they could and once again Rose fell in love. Not for her was the idea that there is only one person in life you can fall in love with, but she knew there were thousands of potential suitors with whom no romantic feelings would ever surface. Wartime, with all its dangers and the prospect of parting, heightened the emotions. British reserve was cast aside and instincts rather than convention held sway.

The tide of war in Europe was changing. The D-Day Landings in Normandy took place on 6 June 1944. For weeks the roads in the south of England had been clogged with military hardware. There was little chance of a lingering farewell as Phil's unit joined the exodus of Allied troops across the Channel. The couple never met again. On 25 October 1944 Rose gave birth to a little boy christened Anthony Charles. It was to be almost half a century before Philip di Meglio was to learn that he had fathered a son. He maintained that he had tried to contact Rose, but she had moved away from Glastonbury and her home in Burnt Oak had been destroyed by a V rocket. So life moved on, but he didn't forget her.

When Charlie Weber finally arrived home after the war, thinner than ever and full of shrapnel, he immediately set about finding Rose. It must have been a terrible shock to learn she had given birth to a baby boy. Male pride can be destructive. At first he felt hurt and let down. Circumstances had changed, but Rose remained as attractive and challenging to him as ever. It was time for him to swallow his pride and follow his instinct. He hated the fact that Rose had snide remarks made about her behind her back. He decided he would bring the child up as if it were his own. In the summer of 1946 Charlie and Rose were married in Hendon. For the next forty-seven years the couple enjoyed a good and companionable marriage, successfully bringing up their large family. Tony looked back on his childhood with affection, but the need to trace his natural father seldom left him.

Philip di Meglio was discharged from the US Army on 1 November 1945 in Belgium. Later he sailed from Le Havre to New York, eventually arriving on the Wheaton Victory on 15 May 1946. He then rejoined the di Meglio clan who lived in Chester, Pennsylvania. The family were involved in a variety of businesses, based mainly around the catering industry. The fast-talking Phil branched out on his own, opening Phil's Autos, tapping into the Americans' love of their cars and the open road. He married Helen, a girl of Polish descent, and they had a son, Philip di Meglio junior.

By contacting US Army Veterans Associations, Tony was able to compile a list of di Meglios who had served in the war. He had no idea how extensive it would be. There were over two dozen Philip di Meglios listed. He wrote the following to each of them:

Dear Messrs. di Meglio,

I am writing to you in the belief that you may know the Philip di Meglio who served in the U.S.A. Army in Wiltshire, England during 1944.

The substance of this enquiry stems from a reunion commemorating the war years here in England recently. Philip's name cropped up and there are people here who would like to know if he is alive and well and how he has fared over the years.

I realise, of course, that this is an exercise in nostalgia stretching over nearly fifty years, but I would appreciate any light that you may be able to shed on this matter.

Looking forward to hearing from you.

Yours sincerely,

Tony Weber.

P.S. He was originally known to come from Pennsylvania.

Within weeks he received a reply from a Philip di Meglio living in Chester, Pennslylvania. A photograph taken in service uniform was also enclosed together with a telephone number. With his heart thumping, Tony dialled the number. A rather frail voice answered the phone. Having established it was Philip di Meglio speaking, Tony came straight to the point. He asked, 'Did you know a Rose Sheran back in England during the war?' There was a long pause. After what seemed an age the voice, quieter still, now said 'Rose Sheran'. He sounded wistful, obviously casting his mind back. 'Rose Sheran.' There was another long pause. 'Rose Sheran, I sure did.' There was a woman's voice in the background demanding to know what was going on. Tony took a deep breath. 'Phil, my name is Tony, I'm your son.' There was a sharp intake of breath, a strangled cry, 'Oh my God, my God.' Now the phone was grabbed from the old man and an angry voice demanded to know who the hell was upsetting her husband. Then his father was back on the line. He was crying. It was impossible to tell if they were tears of joy or anger.

Tony could only imagine the impact on the di Meglios of this unexpected bombshell. More composed now, the old man kept repeating, 'My God, it's my son.' It can't be easy for a wife of almost fifty years to learn her husband had fathered a long-lost love child. Diplomatically, Tony told them he would ring back the next day.

That afternoon an excited Phil di Meglio took on a new lease of life as he danced round his small garden. Even Helen, his wife, calmed down. After all, it had happened a long time ago and if the news made Phil so happy, who was she to spoil everything.

There were several more phone calls and plans were made for the two families to meet in Chester. The bookings were confirmed, although Rose decided to stay at home with her husband. She did, however, get to speak to Phil on the phone. No-one listened in on the call, but it must have been overwhelmingly heartrending.

Some months later, ringing to finalise the arrangements for their planned visit, Tony didn't get the response he expected. Phil di Meglio whispered, 'You are too late, I'm dying, I've only been given a week to live.' It was obvious the old man was extremely distressed, each breath was rattling across the airwaves.

Although their flight was re-scheduled, it was two weeks before the Webers arrived in Chester. There was a strained silence in the hire car as they made their way down the main street and past the eighteenth-century courthouse. They were shocked by the run-down nature of the neighbourhood as they approached Phil's small house. Now the moment had come to meet his father, Tony held back. The knowledge and planning of this meeting had taken years and now he felt an irrational fear that it would all turn sour. They were met at the door by Helen and at once Tony was struck by the obvious physical likeness to his own mother. With a dry mouth and a thumping heart he was shown into a small bedroom. The meeting of father and son combined pain and joy. They fell into a fumbled embrace. Nothing was said, but tears flowed. The old man grasped his son with a strength that belied his appearance. No longer portly, Philip di Meglio had been reduced to skin and bone by the cancer that was killing him. His own son, Philip junior, looked on and the following day Tony was introduced to other members of the di Meglio family who had gathered in curiosity to see this man claiming to be their relative. He certainly had the di Meglio looks. He had a sturdy physique, darkish complexion and was starting to lose his hair. They liked his easy going, informal manner, which was not how they imagined Englishmen to be. OK, he talked funny but they would forgive him that. They formed a huddle in the corner of the crowded bedroom, while the English guy held Phil's hand. Eventually, they declared with a theatrical flourish, 'OK, this boy is a di Meglio, welcome to the family, Tony.' Then, formally, each in turn embraced him.

Tony spent several days at his father's bedside. Phil was becoming progressively weaker and not much was said. His father moved in and out of consciousness, but always holding onto his son's hand with a firm grip as if this alone was his passport to life. With the timing that only a film director could get away with, Philip's body was being carried out to a funeral car as Tony arrived on the last day of his visit to say his final farewell. It was as if the desperately ill man had hung onto life just long enough to meet his son and now he was going home it was time to take his leave. He died aged seventy-eight and the date was June 1992.

Here was just one of thousands of love stories thrown up by the war gently moving to its conclusion. Three people, two of whom had never met each other, yet remained linked together. It was as if their lives had been choreographed so that they all left the stage in quick succession. Rose died in February 1993, to be followed by Charlie shortly afterwards. Ordinary people have extraordinary lives, which are magnified in times of war. True love never dies but it can be impossibly complicated.

13

The Great Social Divide

In November 1945 some 3,000 guests crammed into the Great Room at the Grosvenor House Hotel. The food was pretty grim, but the music was great. This was the largest American dance ever held in London, with music played by the United States Navy Band. Soon, most of those attending would be returning home with their memories of London and still confused by their British allies. They were frankly bewildered by the unbreakable thread that ran through British society – class. It dominated, it divided. Here was a country that placed more importance on where you came from rather than what you had achieved in life. In truth, it was far more complicated and nuanced than that. Even after the war, class continued to intrude on everyday life and many feel it helped fuel Britain's decline in the world.

At the top of the social pyramid was the old order, the aristocracy, high society. Since the turn of the century it had been infiltrated by a number of leading financiers who had themselves become establishment figures. Edward VII had always been attracted to money and a slightly more raffish set, but on his death much of the old order was restored and it again became difficult to penetrate a way into this elite group. Many of the Bright Young Things who had driven their parents mad with their infantile behaviour were now despairing of their own offspring, some of whom were even claiming to be socialists!

A cut-glass accent was one of the most obvious ways of defining your background. The foppish drawl of the Regency playboy had developed into a clipped, staccato way of speaking that sounds so dated and affected to us today. Although two world wars had gone some way to loosening the traditional social ties, they were still central to British life. The ruling class remained on top and in control. Society continued to be run by influential cliques based on shared experience at public school or Oxbridge. Time spent serving in the forces was also an important pointer. In the Army the regiment you served with spoke volumes. You may have been an officer in the infantry but not necessarily a gentleman. If, however, you served in the cavalry or guards, you most certainly were. Being commissioned in the Royal Navy also cut the mustard, while those minor public school types in the RAF were not quite the thing. Very brave and all that, but still suspect socially.

Unlike in the Great War, the aristocracy had made substantial sacrifices during the latest hostilities. There had been a cull of dukes and sons from leading families. The 6th Duke of Wellington had been killed in 1943 at Salerno, leading a group of commandos. He was joined by the Dukes of Connaught, Westmorland and Kent. Anthony Eden (later Lord Halifax) lost his son. No-one could accuse the aristocracy of not doing their bit. It was reckoned that in the First World War strings were pulled. Of the 1,500 members of the elite enlisted, more than a third managed to avoid the trenches altogether, where the life expectancy of a junior officer was just a few weeks.

After the Great War the social life of the old order was still defined by the London season. Since 1780, traditionally this had followed the movements of the royal family while they were in residence in London. It covered a period from April to July and then again from October to Christmas. While in town it was the done thing to be seen at the Chelsea Flower Show, Royal Ascot and possibly the Summer Exhibition at the Royal Academy. Showing up at the Trooping of the Colour was also a plus. Then, of course, at the beginning of August there was Cowes Week on the Isle of Wight, which came after a few days spent losing money at glorious Goodwood. Next, the social elite trekked north to Scotland to shoot grouse and stalk deer. Whoever suggested the rich are idle – they work very hard at their pleasures. The season culminated with the year's debutantes being presented to the king. Before this they had to endure four months of endless balls and parties. A sort of seemly meat market intended to introduce well-connected daughters to suitable suitors. It was a wickedly expensive round of entertaining. It often resulted in the joining of two influential families which consolidated their shared strength. Marriages were also still arranged by parents, often to create an escape route from debt. Here, penniless title holders married their daughters willingly to 'new money'. So, loveless marriages continued to be launched. With divorce out of the question, a blind eye was frequently turned to infidelity. The knowing glance over a dinner table continued to lead to steamy love affairs. The upper classes were certainly not squeamish about lust, providing discretion was exercised. Many a pretty housemaid was compromised. She was normally sent home to her parents, hopefully with some financial support. Some whose female ancestors were in service may well have blue blood coursing through their veins. It was not unknown for the lady or the daughter of the house to have a fling with a groom or footman. Most were resolved when the initial passion cooled and ranks closed. It was the occasional 'bolter' that brought disgrace and scandal, giving the lower orders the opportunity to laugh and sneer.

By the end of the war attitudes were already beginning to change. For the past five years people of all social classes had been thrown together as never before. Although many longed for a return to the old order, the few hundred families who had held sway over London's social scene were now increasingly being infiltrated by those with money. Talent also provided an entrance for people like Cecil Beaton and Noel Coward to hob-nob with the grandest. But 'new money' (however despised) was staking its claim in the social hierarchy. Like adultery, money should be handled with discretion and certainly never discussed in public. The old order thought a flaunting of wealth vulgar, but this never bothered the likes of Nubar Gulbenkian. He was holed up at the Ritz after the war, maintaining a permanent suite. His father, Calouste (known as Mr Five Percent), was a virtual recluse, but Nubar by contrast was an extravagant extrovert.

Born in Armenia, he was educated at Harrow and saw himself as typically British despite retaining both Iranian and Turkish citizenship. His miserly father only left poor Nubar 2.5 million dollars from a fortune valued at over 400 million dollars. No matter, Nubar added to his inheritance by successful oil dealings and was soon setting new standards of extravagance in post-war London. He demanded that all his food should be in season, no matter where it came from. Delicacies were flown in from around the world just to please him. Grouse had to be served at his table on 12 August whatever the cost. At first he was seen in London being driven around in a Rolls-Royce, but the capital's clogged traffic irritated him so he invested in a London black cab, but one with a basket work body and powered by a Rolls-Royce engine. He reckoned it could turn on a sixpence, not that anyone had ever seen him handle small change. He was a legendary tipper, even palming money to the liftman at the Ritz for every short ascent to his suite and back down to ground level. When asked to state his position on a form he was asked to fill in, he wrote 'enviable'. Gulbenkian was perhaps the most noticeable proponent of lavish wealth in London, helped no doubt by his bearded, rather satanic appearance, but there were others not far behind. London's plushest hotels were welcoming a mixture of people who had made their fortunes during the war, together with free-spending American film stars. It was impossible to get a room at the Savoy and profits at the Grosvenor House and the Ritz were soaring. In June 1946 Heathrow airport opened for civilian flights and soon a regular stream of wealthy Americans were making their way to London.

With price controls still in effect, Grosvenor House sought extra revenue by staging the Antique Dealers Fair in the Great Room. Later, 30,000 people visited the International Stamp Fair at the same venue, including the king. His father, George V, was reckoned to have built up one of the world's greatest stamp collections.

Money and influence are of little help when personal tragedy seeks you out. Peter Beatty was the good-looking son of Admiral Lord Beatty and the grandson of the fabulously wealthy Chicago store owner, Marshall Field. He was a leading racehorse owner and a prominent figure among that set which included the Aga Khan and Lord Roseberry. Unfortunately, Beatty had been born with a degenerative eye condition which worsened to the point where he was having difficulty seeing. Now, if you want to commit suicide there can surely be few better places than the Ritz. Taking no risks, he went to the sixth floor and jumped.

It was not just the super rich who monopolised London's grandest hotels. Pat Desbruslais remembers having her joint twenty-first birthday and engagement party at the Savoy in 1948. The menu was still very restricted, but the evening was made memorable by dancing to Carol Gibbons and his orchestra. The Savoy was also the setting for the first public dinner party attended by Princess Margaret. Shortly after midnight her elder sister gave a signal that it was time to leave. In a sign of things to come, Margaret sought out the tallest member of the party and, so hidden from sight on the dance floor, she was able to eke out a few more minutes before finally having to depart.

It was the death of royal courtesan Alice Keppel in 1947 that was somehow symbolic of changing attitudes. It was she who had perfected the prized art of discretion. Within weeks of meeting Edward VII she had become his mistress, despite the twenty-seven year age gap. Not only did she manage to maintain her own reputation, she also schemed to keep both the king and her husband happy (on the surface at least). Her husband, George Keppel, was made a member of the Royal Victorian Order by Edward (assumingly for services rendered). How long would this unquestioning sycophancy last? Not just for cuckolded husbands deferring to royalty, but for society in general. Looking up to social position and authority was in the early stages of being diluted.

Until the outbreak of war, class division was almost as divisive as a caste system. Patriotic pride was one area where generally the classes were united; there was an inbuilt feeling that one Briton was worth several Johnny Foreigners. Despite evidence to the contrary, it was felt that British goods were superior to those manufactured abroad, that British sportsmen were the best and only normally beaten by rotten luck or cheating foreigners. Even British food was reckoned to be better than all that foreign muck. We were deluded but unshakeable in our beliefs. It was a dangerous mindset, but one that was commonly held. There was a link too, between the old order and the working man in their distaste for the thrusting, bourgeois middle class, with their neat semis and pompous affectations.

It was reckoned that over 60 per cent of London's population was working class. This was roughly defined by those who were paid for their labours in cash or were wage earners, rather than being salaried. It was a complex mix with many subsections. London remained a series of interlinked villages, each with its own distinct character. In the 1940s this was underlined by many areas being given over to special traditional trades. It was a time of limited social mobility, where families lived in the same district for generations. Sons followed their fathers' trade or line of employment. Skilled cabinet makers were found in Bethnal Green, while boot and leather handbag manufacturers were grouped around Hackney. Hatton Garden flourished as the centre for diamond dealing, while down in Clerkenwell watches and clocks were the speciality. Across the East End tailoring was undertaken in overcrowded sweatshops, where families worked in one room and slept two or three to a bed. The West and East End were two totally different worlds joined by commerce. The society ladies of Mayfair and Knightsbridge linked in part with the girls of the sweatshops; the one was living in airy comfort waited on by servants, the other in appalling squalor, but each in part was reliant on the other. Both were tough, both survivors. These groups are still with us today, or their children and grandchildren are. The one, having sold their grand town houses to Russians or Arabs, but still doing well, living in Hampstead or Islington; the other, having left the East End to a new wave of immigrants, now generally liberated from their former poverty. Life moves on. Away from a time where infant mortality claimed hundreds of babies each week in London alone. A time where, until the National Health Service was introduced, many literally could not afford to be ill. A time of hand-me-down clothes and ill-fitting shoes. A time when Iris Chapple, living with her mum in Brixton, was sent out as a seven-year-old to collect a hundredweight of coal and lug it home on a pram. A different age so alien to us today where life was polarised, where the gap between the rich and poor was vast, and there in the middle was metro-man, London's middle class.

The extension of London's underground system during the 1920s and 1930s led to a mass migration from central London to newly formed, leafy suburbs. Living close to a tube station allowed the suburban dweller to be at work in the West End or the City within an hour. The Metropolitan Line with its faster trains extended suburbia to the Chilterns. John Betjeman, while understanding Londoners' aspirations to own a house in the suburbs, famously wrote, 'Come friendly bombs and fall on Slough, it isn't fit for humans now.' While this was funny, few agreed; the need for many to escape from London was overwhelming.

The London underground system had started life in the nineteenth century with the line connecting Stockwell to the City of London. By 1920 the tube system had been taken over by the London Electric Railway Company, which eventually became London Transport, and run by the inspirational Frank Pick. Initially, as publicity manager, he commissioned leading artists to design fabulous posters that helped publicise travel for recreational purposes, rather than just a method of getting to work. He was also responsible for the bull's eye logo, the tube's trademark symbol, which still appears on every underground platform today. Pick's influence extended far beyond visual design as the tube system continued to fan out from central London. Endless rows of neat houses followed each extension as speculative builders gambled heavily on the continued migration. From the southern outpost of Morden to Edgware in the north, small hamlets and ancient villages gave themselves up to an orgy of house building.

Although house prices had fallen during the war, living in London was either far too expensive or, alternatively, squalid and run down. A survey carried out in the mid-1940s found that people living in a previously relatively well-to-do area were fed up with their living conditions. There was chronic overcrowding. This lack of privacy and the general feeling of decay had residents longing for a move to an outer-London suburb. The attractions of a semi-rural life drew people from the professions: local government officials and commercial managers. They were joined by a workforce happy to find employment in the numerous factories which lined the main arterial routes out of London. It was still possible to buy a mock-Tudor semi with a small garden for under £1,000. For between £2,000 and £3,000 you could purchase a substantial four- or five-bedroomed detached house in a lovely setting in a desirable area. Suburbia also offered an impressive range of leisure facilities. Dozens of golf courses had been built and most communities had tennis clubs, the genteel setting for many a romance. Unfortunately, for some, the pleasures of suburban life, so aggressively promoted before the war, had lost much of their charm. Due to wartime shortages, many houses were now looking run down and in need of repair. The promised semi-rural setting had been eaten up under the tide of building. The time spent on the train going to work in the morning was the same, but now they were crowded, with few seats available. Expensive fares and strap-hanging were not an attractive combination.

Generally, the middle classes were feeling angry and aggrieved. Many had voted Labour in the 1945 election, but their perception was that the swing in favour of the working class had come at their expense. Despite the gains given to them by the welfare state, including free secondary schooling for their children and a free health service, they were feeling put upon and unloved. Their lifestyle had been downgraded. Most could no longer afford a car and holidays were often spent doing odd jobs or gardening at home. Food was still rationed and their clothes were old and shabby. To add to their woes, council estates were invading their neighbourhoods. It was estimated that 10 per cent of middle-class buying power had been transferred to the working class. They ignored that fact that the Labour government had created thousands of white-collar jobs to help run the expanded reach of government departments. In 1949 *Picture Post* published a feature, 'Is the Middle Class Doomed?' The middle class certainly agreed. They genuinely felt they represented the very best of Britain – hard-working, industrious, honest and bound by a deeply felt moral code. While looking enviously at the establishment, they thought the aristocracy were weak, lazy and condescending, while the working class were crude, dishonest and feckless. Where class was concerned, each looked at the other with suspicion and scarcely concealed contempt. My own parents' views reflected some of these prejudices. As they had totally opposite political opinions, I felt, overall, they offered my sister and I a fairly balanced view of life. As I remember it, they were too worried about what other people thought of them. 'Never wash your dirty linen in public' was a phrase often repeated.

A middle-class upbringing in the 1940s was comforting rather than comfortable. Good manners and politeness were the norm, although everyone was very judgemental. They were easily shocked and outraged by bad or dishonest behaviour. It was a time of simple pleasures. A visit to the cinema was a huge treat. Even listening to a favourite radio serial or just reading a good book was satisfying. How tedious it all sounds now but, although everyone seemed to moan endlessly, my sense is that most people were happier then. You could go out and leave your door unlocked without fear of being robbed. While organised crime still flourished in the West End, elsewhere in London you felt completely safe, with policemen still thick on the ground if they were needed.

In January 1948 the BBC *Light Programme* broadcast the first episode of *Mrs Dale's Diary*, which ran for almost twenty years. It featured the lives and tribulations of a middle-class family living in a fictional London suburb. The serial centred on Mary Dale, the wife of a GP. Her son, Bob, had recently been demobbed and she also had a teenage daughter, Gwen. By today's standards it was extremely uncontroversial, but it was interesting as the series began to gently explore and reflect the social problems from a comfortable middle-class perspective.

Perhaps even more divisive than class in post-war London was religion. While most people still regarded themselves as Christian, church-going was already in steep decline. Two devastating wars had soured many people's belief in God. Attendances for Church of England Sunday services were down by half a million since 1935. Now only 3 million were attending regularly. Attendances at Baptist and Presbyterian chapels were also diminishing and it was left to the Roman Catholics alone to add to their number of worshipers. This was attributed to Irish and foreign immigration. There were reckoned to be no more than 8,000 black or Asian citizens living in Britain during the 1930s. The first mosque in London was opened in 1926 in Southfields, but there were still few people from the Subcontinent living in London in the 1940s. Because there were so few black and brown faces to be seen, there was little outward sign of the colour prejudice that was to break into the open with the arrival of the *Windrush*. Although London's Jewish population was under 200,000, they were well-represented by the large number of synagogues, despite many being destroyed or damaged during the war.

So, as ever, London remained a city separated by politics, religion and class. The most obvious underlining of that class divide was to be found in London clubs. Not the dodgy nightclubs of Soho, or even the respectable working men's clubs dotted all over London, but the grand gentlemen's clubs where the old order and the establishment put the world to rights over a whisky and soda. These members-only clubs became popular in the nineteenth century and have been imitated throughout the world. The area around St James is still referred to as 'club-land'. Although some have now moved on to new premises, these clubs represent a haven from the restless energy coming from the streets outside. They offer a place to meet friends or people with similar interests in a conducive, if rather old-fashioned, setting. The food served may be plain, but well prepared, with many clubs offering accommodation for the out-of-town visitor. Most of the top establishment clubs had memberships which were strictly controlled. Once again, breeding rather than money or achievement opened these exclusive doors. The old boy network was still keeping the rest of us at bay, for a few more years at least. Only the green baize of billiard tables united the men born with power and influence with those playing in snooker halls across London. They were born to serve, but social changes were underway. It was no easier to spot than seeing ourselves age as we peer into the mirror each day. Perhaps imperceptible, but irreversible too.

14

1947: The Big Freeze

In 1947 the birth rate in Britain soared to record levels. The 'baby boomers' had arrived. A prime factor was couples being reunited after years of separation, but so also was the weather. Not passion brought on by hot, sultry nights but by relentless, inescapable cold. London had to endure the longest, coldest winter in living memory. A cold that still remains in the memory of those who lived through it. An all-encompassing cold that gnawed away at every bone and sinew. A cold that tormented your chilblains, attacked your chapped hands and entered your very soul.

New Year's Day had heralded the nationalisation of the British coal mines. Three weeks later, much of its production was stuck at the collieries as snow engulfed the country. Borne on an easterly wind, this was not just a flurry, or even a heavy fall soon to disappear as a thaw set in. This was serious snow of Siberian magnitude. For days the temperature remained below freezing. The cold cut through extra layers of clothing and made your eyes water. Across London pipes burst and hot water geysers froze. By the end of the month the big freeze had tightened its grip. In an attempt to save electricity London was again plunged into darkness as the street lights were turned off. Only traffic lights went eerily through their routine, but most roads were impassable anyway. Huge drifts brought everything to a standstill. Trains were trapped for hours. Food was even scarcer than usual. Meat and vegetables were trapped at the farms and imports stuck at the docks. Life was utterly miserable.

My mother didn't believe in easy options. She was not about to let a little snow interrupt my education. Not trusting me to make it to school on my own, she once again dragged this reluctant student out by the hand. The level of the snow was way above the sides of my wellington boots, causing blocks of ice to form on top of my feet. Soon they melted, leaving me to squelch the mile or so to school. We hardly saw a soul on our travels and almost no-one, even the teachers, had made it in. So, feeling morally vindicated, we struggled home again to a cold house and no electricity.

Still the snow came. Then a temporary thaw that was cut short by a deep frost. Now the roads and pavements were rutted and treacherous. Then another heavy fall of snow made even venturing outside hazardous. London, which for years had increasingly looked drab and cheerless, now retreated further under this continual winter onslaught. Foreign visitors seeking some cheer reported that even London's swankiest restaurants looked dark and squalid. Thousands of workers were laid off as electricity was denied to offices and factories. Unemployment soared to almost 2 million. Strangely, the West End stores were reported to be busy. They were. They were actually packed, but few people were buying. Many wandering the aisles were unemployed or simply seeking refuge from the all-encompassing cold. Steam rose from their clothes. There was a hum of bodies slowly thawing out. With soap very hard to find we had united in becoming a nation of 'the glorious unwashed'. Shop assistants struggled to write out bills for the few customers actually buying in the gloomy light. With the electricity off, candles and gas lamps created an impression of shopping in a previous century. Escalators on the underground were motionless. London was gripped in a freezing half-life.

For basic food, queues now stretched even longer. A delivery of potatoes to the local greengrocer had housewives waiting patiently. They stood stamping their feet like prisoners in a Siberian gulag. The cold was so unforgiving that many went to bed in the clothes they had worn all day. The Kew Observatory recorded not a glimmer of sunshine between 2 February and 22 February. Still the weather didn't relent. By the beginning of

March the Thames had frozen over. People skated and even rode bikes across in complete safety. Poor old Big Ben was silenced again as its machinery froze up. British industry and farming had been brought to its knees. The population was fed up. Many blamed the government. A popular view was that Churchill would have done something. What exactly he would have done was another matter.

Nothing lasts forever and by mid-March a thaw had set in. Unfortunately, it coincided with heavy rainfall. The soaking ground was unable to cope with the millions of gallons of muddy water that spilled out over the Thames valley. Flood defences were limited and many of the locks had been damaged in the war. The great flood brought misery for ten days, moving upstream to engulf both Windsor and Oxford. At least the students at Eton were spared as the school was situated on higher ground (where else?). Thousands were not so lucky, as their houses were ruined by the inexorable black tide. Surely soon there had to be some good news.

What some viewed as very good news was actually taking place in Paris. While Britain shivered under an Arctic blast, Christian Dior was warming women's hearts with the launch of his first collection as an independent designer, labelled the 'Corolle Line'. It instantly became known as 'The New Look'. In reality, it was not so much a new look, rather an exaggerated reworking of a style that had been popular in the late 1930s. It excited such a varied reaction because it represented a radical change from the wartime make-do-and-mend mentality. It offered rounded shoulders, a pinched-in waist and a very full skirt; billowing and stretched to the ankle, using as many as 15 yards of material. The killjoys were soon on the march, declaring that the New Look represented a reckless waste at a time when fabric was in short supply. This was countered by many from a war-weary, austerity-driven population who insisted that here, at last, was a symbol of a more outward-looking, prosperous future. It also pointed the way to pre-war femininity. Some women were suspicious – having gained greater independence during the war, they felt the New Look was a subtle attempt to put women back in their place as subservient to men. Most, though, didn't think that deeply. Here at last was a chance to look glamorous and they were not going to miss out. Not only glamorous, it was also elegant and sophisticated. It was no contest. Soon London stores were packed with women trying at last to throw off the mantle of war, and few men were complaining.

While Christian Dior was an exciting new talent for the fashion industry, the years immediately after the war saw a glut of hugely talented comics emerge in the very centre of London. The Windmill Theatre opened in 1932 and flourished under the astute management of Vivian Van Damm. It still attracted full houses because it remained one of the only venues in London where it was possible to gawp at nude girls on stage. Despite his ability for spotting new talent, it was surprising that few of his pre-war artistes achieved stardom on leaving the company. Charmian Innes (who had once been sacked by Van Damm for being overweight) did go on to appear in a succession of British films. Another success was comedian John Tilley, who was for a time a regular performer on the radio and who also appeared at the London Palladium. Unfortunately, his career was cut short by his tragic death in 1941. Why so few good-looking and talented girls who appeared at the Windmill never flourished professionally remains something of a mystery. Some fell for one of the constant stream of stage-door Johnnies and duly got married, but most simply enjoyed the camaraderie of the 'Windmill family' which, somehow, seemingly lessened their ambitions.

All this was about to change when a tide of incredible talent was unleashed on the British public, to soar to national and international fame. The first to arrive was Jimmy Edwards. During his active service in the RAF he had suffered severe facial injuries. This led to him growing his landmark handlebar moustache in an attempt to cover the extent of the damage. As graduate of St John's College, Cambridge, he became known as 'Professor' Jimmy Edwards. Appearing in front of an audience only interested in ogling the girls was a daunting experience. He uniquely grabbed their attention by insulting them, much as a schoolteacher would a classroom of naughty children. They loved him and he stayed on at the Windmill for eighteen months before falling out with Van Damm. During the rest of the 1940s, numbers of top-class comedians continued to cut their teeth at the Windmill. Tony Hancock reckoned that any comic who could survive for more than six weeks at the theatre was destined for success. The talent drawn to Great Windmill Street was astonishing. The crazily inventive Michael Bentine went on to be a founder member of the Goons, along with Harry Secombe and Peter Sellers. Secombe, like Alfred Marks (another Windmill performer), had an ambition to eventually become an opera singer, but that had to wait as the small group of comedians set about redefining British comedy.

The most talented, yet distinctly difficult, personality was Peter Sellers. It is not surprising that he went on to achieve international stardom. Agents and show producers started to visit the Windmill regularly. Dennis Main-Wilson, a producer for the BBC, saw the potential in the young comic. He promised Sellers that he would recommend him for a new radio programme being planned. Days passed with no contact forthcoming. That might have been the end of the opportunity, but Peter Sellers then made a phone call that galvanised his career. Imitating the voice of the well-known comedian Richard Murdoch, he rang the producer demanding to know 'why this Sellers fellow hasn't been given the chance to broadcast'. He then broke into impersonations of radio stars Kenneth Horne and Sam Costa in quick succession. 'What on earth?' Main-Wilson queried. Peter Sellers quickly explained himself, and for him the BBC was just the beginning.

There were other comedy partnerships who could trace their roots back to the Windmill. Bill Kerr was to team up with Tony Hancock later in *Hancock's Half Hour*, but Van Damm was not infallible. He gave a chance to a double act appearing as 'Bartholomew and Wiseman'. They were terrible. They bombed, enduring either slow handclapping or total silence. After three days Van Damm called them into his office and told the disappointed pair that they should leave at the end of the week. Eric Morecambe and Ernie Wise must have cut forlorn figures as they left the stage door. For them it was back to the drawing board. Bruce Forsyth, who had started work at the Windmill as a dancer, returned after the war honing his skills as another comedian who was to enjoy huge fame and fortune. Arthur English gave up his job as a painter and decorator after walking into the theatre for an unscheduled audition with Van Damm. He quickly came to represent the archetypal spiv with his loud suit, ridiculously long tie and a non-stop stream of Cockney patter. A likeable spiv, shooting out punch-lines at 300 words a minute, he was an instant hit. The prince of the wideboys had arrived. Still they came, this eruption of comic talent, learning their trade in front of the uniquely demanding audience. Tommy Cooper, Barry Cryer, Des O'Connor, George Martin, Arthur Haynes and Bill Maynard all moved onto huge success. So did other acts with seemingly less obvious appeal, like Leslie Welch, known as the 'Memory Man'. He was able to recall the minutest detail of sporting events. Even at the Windmill, he managed to keep the audience's mind off the girls for a few minutes. During his time at the theatre, it was reckoned he answered roughly 5,000 questions, only failing on very rare occasions.

In 1947, over in Islington, another legendary British comedian was also taking on a difficult audience for his first professional appearance. Collins' Music Hall on Islington Green was a notoriously rowdy venue. Since taking alcohol into the auditorium had been banned, artistes were at least spared having bottles being thrown at them, but acts had to make an instant impression or they were likely to be barracked unmercifully. Young Rocky Knight was enjoying a night at the theatre where greats like Marie Lloyd and Dan Leno had appeared. The last 'turn' before the interval was reckoned to be the most difficult spot. Half the audience were already making their way to the bar when a small, rather pathetic figure came on stage. Soon roars of laughter were erupting, drawing the audience back again. Norman Wisdom was to become the great British clown. Much of his appeal was similar to that employed by Charlie Chaplin – the down-trodden underdog who somehow overcomes authority. It didn't take long for Wisdom to be catapulted to the top of the bill.

Earlier in December 1946 the grandest and best-known London theatre reopened, having been badly damaged by a bomb in October 1940. The Theatre Royal, Drury Lane, needed a sure-fire hit for its re-launch and what better than a musical written by Noel Coward? For once the master failed to deliver. *Pacific 1860* was thought to be old-fashioned and out of touch with a public whose tastes had changed. Like the political pundits at election time, he has misread the mood. Languid charm was out, what London theatregoers wanted was colour and excitement, and they were just about to get it. Amid great anticipation *Oklahoma* opened at Drury Lane on 30 April 1947. There had been a clampdown on sales of the sheet music so no-one knew what to expect. Here was a show of fantastic energy with memorable songs and dance routines. The audience was ecstatic, the critics rapturous in their praise. The show was the pure escapism that Londoners craved. Howard Keel and the cast were called back for endless encores that finally subsided after forty-two minutes.

The excitement caused by *Oklahoma* faded into the background when in July the engagement of Princess Elizabeth to Prince Philip of Greece was announced. Now again there was to be a grand showpiece event for the public to look forward to. The eagle-eyed may have realised that the developing romance was progressing when the future queen was bridesmaid to her lady-in-waiting, the honourable Mrs Vicary Gibbs. After the wedding at St Margaret's church, Westminster, the reception was held in the River Room at the Savoy. This was the first time that the entire royal family had been seen together in a London hotel. Outside, the entrance was crowded with photographers, but only one of their number was allowed to photograph the reception. When the photographs were released one pictured the princess standing alongside a good-looking naval officer. It was their first public appearance together. A generally enthusiastic pro-royalty public approved and anxiously awaited developments. A poll in the *Sunday Pictorial* asked readers, 'Should Elizabeth Marry Philip?' 62 per cent were in favour, with 32 against. Not all were so impressed, however. Despite his excellent record during the war there were problems. Philip was extremely poor and his German background was underscored by his three sisters all being married to Germans. None of them were invited to the wedding. Never mind, he had been educated in Britain and spoke English without a hint of an accent, despite having been born in Greece, and he had become a naturalised British citizen. He looked like a film star and was no chinless wonder. He would do.

How to project the wedding was causing concern. An extravagant display of wealth was certain to attract criticism in a time of ongoing austerity, and yet a royal wedding demanded a certain pomp and ceremony. Over 2,000 guests were invited to the service at Westminster Abbey and London's hotels were full to bursting. The barman in the American Bar at the Savoy offered a 'wedding bells' cocktail and gala dinners were planned at all the leading hotels and restaurants throughout the West End. At Claridge's, royalty from across Europe were falling over each other. In her last public appearance before the wedding, Princess Elizabeth appeared at the Flower Ball held at the Savoy. Jean Nicol (admittedly something of a sycophant) reported that she 'had never seen her look prettier, her hair longer and softer than usual and her petal skin glowing like a pink pearl'.

No public holiday had been granted for the wedding, so the young princess was astonished to see huge crowds gathered round the palace as she looked down from a second-floor window. It was a grey, damp morning and people had slept outside on divan mattresses and in sleeping bags. The wedding morning is normally a stressful time for brides and so it proved for the princess. Her dress, designed by Norman Hartnell and worked on by no fewer than 350 women was stunning, but then disaster – the Russian tiara that had been worn by her grandmother at her wedding snapped. The court jeweller was summoned and a hasty temporary repair undertaken.

The procession of the bridesmaids, including Princess Margaret, set off to the abbey. So did Philip, fortified by a stiff drink. He was accompanied by his cousin, the Marquis of Milford Haven, who was his best man. The previous day, Philip had renounced his Greek and Danish titles and on the morning of the wedding had been appointed His Royal Highness, the Duke of Edinburgh. As the bride set off from the gates of Buckingham Palace with her father in the Irish state coach, the crowds roared their support. The BBC had fifty-five microphones positioned along the route, with television and newsreel cameras also recording the scene.

It was estimated that some 200 million people listened to the radio broadcast which was covered by commentators, including Wynford Vaughan-Thomas, Richard Dimbleby and Frank Gillard.

During the wedding service, the Archbishop of York became rather carried away by suggesting that the wedding was, in essence, little different than those carried out in many a humble village church. The major part of the service was conducted by the Archbishop of Canterbury, Geoffrey Bishop. A rather dry, but godly man. Unusually for a leading cleric, he was also a committed Freemason.

Over in the River Room at the Savoy, banks of chairs were arranged in front of a tiny, flickering television set for those who had been unable to secure a seat along the route. Waiters ducked and dived, carrying trays of coffees and cocktails, in an attempt not to obstruct the distorted pictures being transmitted from the abbey. The newly married couple travelled back to the palace in a glass coach. There were 150 guests for the wedding breakfast, who enjoyed a family-themed menu starting with Filet de Sole Mountbatten. Certainly no-one was able to accuse the couple of embarking on a lavish honeymoon. There were no luxury yachts or Caribbean beaches for them to look forward to. Instead, they travelled to Waterloo station in an open landau with hot water bottles at their feet. Maybe three's a crowd, but the princess's favourite corgi went too. The honeymoon was spent at Broadlands, the country estate of the Mountbatten family. Doubtless, like most of us at a similar time in our lives, they pondered what the future held in store for them. Later in the month, a curious public queued round St James to get a close up look at the bridal gown. It was on display together with over 2,000 gifts the couple had received from around the world.

The celebrations over, a collective gloom settled in. People had become disillusioned. Record numbers were making enquiries about emigrating. South Africa and Australia were favoured destinations. The middle classes felt particularly hard done by. Most felt that their standard of living had declined compared to pre-war days. The gap between them and the working class had closed, while the wealthy, despite increased taxation, appeared outwardly unaffected. H. V. Morton spoke for many when he said, 'England had become a society where things moved steadily towards Communism.' However put upon the middle classes were feeling, few surely could have objected to the school leaving age being raised to fifteen. Many were initially pleased when the Chancellor of the Exchequer, Hugh Dalton, was forced to resign after leaking details of his budget to a lobby journalist. He was succeeded by the 'holier than thou' Stafford Cripps, and Middle England realised that for them life was not about to get any easier.

The end of the Raj, with the partition of India in 1947, was another reminder that Britain's place in the world was being diluted. The Empire on which 'the sun never set' was beginning to unravel. Partition in Palestine was also underway. British military losses in the Holy Land had led to a new wave of anti-Semitism in Britain. This loss of power and control was having a strange effect on the nation's psyche. We had won the war and yet we were now seemingly in retreat. Many were experiencing a collective loss of confidence while the government continued with its radical reforms and off-loaded long held assets.

The country needed a boost, and London provided it as all eyes turned to Wembley.

15

1948: An Olympic Summer

My parents' outlandish neighbour, Miss Wakely, sat next to me on the settee, peering intently at the minute, flickering television screen. This was the first time I had ever watched television and it was proving to be a frustrating experience. Wembley was just a few miles away but the picture fluttered like a dying heartbeat and the screen went blank. Miss Wakely was probably in her fifties and I knew she was the butt of local gossip. I didn't care that she was strange. I really liked her. She fiddled with the indoor aerial and magicked the picture back to life. Now it was possible to make out lines of athletes acknowledging the cheers of the crowd. Miss Wakely poured me some homemade lemonade and insisted on my eating another piece of cake she had baked. She looked different, her hair shorn shorter than most men. She wore heavy tweed suits which were always complemented by a collar and tie. She was also the only woman I have ever met who smoked a pipe. None of this bothered me. She knew I was a sports fanatic and I was comfortable in her company. Now we could see the king in naval uniform, announcing the opening of the XIVth Olympiad of the modern era. Although television transmissions had started again in 1946, very few people owned one. For the next two weeks I was lucky to see much of the sporting drama unfold.

The road to London hosting the 1948 Olympics had been long and arduous. The 1940 games had been awarded to Tokyo before being withdrawn when Japan invaded China in 1937. Next, Helsinki was also thwarted when the Soviet Union invaded

Finland in November 1939. London was earmarked to host the 1944 games, but by then war raged across Europe. Finally, after a gap of twelve years, it was still left to cash-strapped London to somehow host the 1948 Summer Olympics.

The modern Olympic movement was the brainchild of Baron Pierre de Coubertin, a French aristocrat. He wanted to encourage competition between amateur athletes from different countries by promoting peace and understanding across cultures. He was convinced 'the most important thing in life is not to have conquered, but to have fought well'. His Olympic dream was 'to combine a balanced body, will and mind and to create a way of life based on joy formed from effort and respect for ethical principles'.

An organising committee for the London games was set up in 1946. The government, while anticipating welcome, hard currency being created by the games, was not about to risk much investment to finance the event. There was no money available for the building of new stadia or specialised venues. Herne Hill Velodrome in South London was designated for the cycling events while Haringey and Empress Hall in Earls Court were also thought suitable for basketball, weight-lifting and the martial arts. The Empire Stadium at Wembley was the obvious choice for the opening and closing ceremonies. It could also feature the football and equestrian events. There was still a problem with the staging of the athletics as the dog track was not suitable and would have to be replaced.

The twin-towered Empire Stadium at Wembley had been built in time for the British Empire Exhibition in 1924. It was an area that had been associated with sport and recreation for many years. Wembley Park was first created in the eighteenth century. In 1889 Sir Edward Watkin, attracted by the success of the Eiffel Tower in Paris, decided to build a British version. It would be bigger and better, the centrepiece of an entertainment venue containing restaurants, theatres and dance halls. The grand idea became known as 'Watkin's Folly'. The scheme soon ran into financial problems and a pared-down tower was planned to be surrounded by landscaped gardens and ornamental pools. The real success came in the laying out of football and cricket pitches, which drew in great crowds. These were helped by Wembley having exceptional rail access. This led to the 200-acre site being developed in 1924.

By 1948 the chairman and managing director of Wembley Stadium was Sir Arthur Elvin, a former scrap dealer. He won the contract to demolish the redundant Empire exhibition buildings, which he sold on for a sizeable profit. Following the exhibition, he managed to acquire Wembley Stadium after its owners had gone into liquidation. He paid £127,000 for the stadium, mostly with borrowed money. Bizarrely, the former owners promptly bought it back from Elvin again, showing him a profit. This was in the form of shares rather than cash, which gave him the largest stake in the new company and allowed him to become chairman. In 1934 he went on to develop the Wembley Arena next door to the stadium. His most profitable use of the Wembley Stadium was the introduction of greyhound racing. Attendances often reached 50,000 and it provided Elvin with his major source of income, but in preparation for the Olympics he tore up the dog track and laid the Olympic running surface at his own expense. His rags-to-riches rise was honoured in 1947 when he was knighted by King George VI for his huge efforts in helping stage the forthcoming London Olympics.

While Elvin was a self-made man, the chairman of the Olympic committee was drawn from one of Britain's aristocratic families. Lord David Burghley had a genuine athletics pedigree. He competed in the 110 metre hurdles in Paris in 1924 and then went on to be the first Briton to break fifteen seconds in the event. In 1927 he set a British record for the 220 yards, which lasted twenty-three years. The following year he won a gold medal in the Amsterdam Olympics in the 400 metre hurdles. This obviously was no ordinary lord. Becoming a Tory MP and being Governor of Bermuda might have been seen as consigning him back into the role of an establishment blimp. He never really fitted that role. True, he lived in a colossal, stately home in Stamford, surrounded by hundreds of acres and an army of servants, but he had the gift of great personal charm and persuasion, which was so important in his capacity as chairman of the Olympic committee. He succeeded in convincing the government that the

Olympics would be hugely beneficial for the country, both in prestige and financially. Burghley said, 'We have a reputation for hospitality, good sportsmanship, tolerance and kindliness, so let us each and everyone do our utmost to show our visitors that this reputation is well founded.' While no doubt accepting that the government was more interested in the estimated £1 million hard currency likely to be generated, he was convinced that more revenue could be raised by commercial sponsorship, which was still in its infancy. Any company spending over £250 was entitled to use the Olympic five-ring logo in their advertising. By having Gilbey's gin, Martell brandy and Craven A cigarettes as leading sponsors, today's administrators would surely have been reaching for the smelling salts, but there were no such concerns in 1948. Many leading athletes continued to smoke. Guinness, another sponsor, did claim 'Guinness is good for you', while Coca Cola had been sponsoring the Olympics since 1928. Other sponsors, like Ovaltine, Quaker Oats and Sloan's liniment, would probably still have passed muster, even today.

The BBC was also asked to contribute. £1,000 was to cover both radio and television rights. While owning a television set was still a rarity, with only about 100,000 in circulation, almost every household had a wireless set. The BBC network now broadcast to over forty countries worldwide. The Olympics coverage was going to be the largest outdoor event they had ever covered. Four hours a day of live TV coverage was planned. For radio, there were to be 250 commentators backed by a further 400 engineers and administrative staff. It was a huge undertaking.

A major worry as the opening date approached related to accommodation. There was to be no Olympic village with hotel-styled sleeping facilities and themed restaurants. Athletes, coaches and managers were all to be housed at minimum cost. One of the few highlights of the Berlin games had been the lavish facilities. Four new stadia were surrounded by 150 cottages, each fitted out to cosset the competitors. The 1936 games had been as much about propaganda as sport. A sinister, flag-waving, goose-stepping travesty and an insult to the Olympic ideal. London was going to be different. The austerity gripping Britain was about to give the Olympics its innocence back. After much debate, thirty housing centres were earmarked. These were deemed to be 'reasonable but not extravagant'. They included Army camps, nurses' hostels and schools. Each nation was to be housed together (although the sexes strictly segregated). This was back-to-school time with everyone sleeping in dormitories. Bed linen was supplied but, bizarrely, competitors were requested to bring their own towels. The Ministry of Works supplied the hostels and camps with furniture and crockery. A few billiard and table-tennis tables were seconded to provide some recreation.

Food was always going to be a problem in a time when rationing was still such a restricting factor. British athletes were already complaining about the basic ration, which only amounted to about 2,500 calories a day. Once selected, they were allowed to increase this intake by 50 per cent, while just wearing an Olympic blazer often led to preferential treatment in restaurants. Caterers supplying British athletes were allowed 25s a day for each competitor to cover three meals. Foreign teams were allowed to bring 25 lbs of food for each competitor. The Chinese team, housed at Willesden county school, had their food supplied by Leon's Chop Suey restaurant in Wardour Street. The Indian team went very upmarket with their curry being prepared by Veeraswamy's. Although 300 tons of provisions were imported to feed the competitors, the Americans were horrified by the rations allotted to them. They complained about both quality and quantity. They were right, British food in the 1940s was horrible. Margaret Patten described is as 'all winter greens and root vegetables, and hamburgers made of grated potato and oatmeal with just a little meat'. Another food guru, Elizabeth David, reported on visiting a hotel restaurant, 'Still there is no excuse, none at all for such unspeakably dismal meals.'

The work to improve the facilities at Wembley stadium, including the laying of the new cinder running track, was completed within a couple of months. This included the surfacing of Olympics Way leading to the stadium, undertaken by German prisoners of war. Kiosks and shops selling souvenirs were built, together with huts which were to be used as dressing rooms. They included showers and mini plunge pools for the competitors to cool off after their exertions. There had been complaints that there was little decoration in London to indicate the games were about to start. As if on cue, posters and flags began to appear in the West End. Three weeks before 'the off', the Minister of Transport officially opened Olympic Way, but the build-up in public anticipation was muted. It was easy to bring in huge crowds to watch greyhound racing, but would Londoners turn up to watch athletics? Elvin issued an apology to the greyhound fans for depriving them of their favourite sport. The doom-mongers insisted sales for the games were disastrous. Tickets from abroad were certainly less than anticipated. By the beginning of July only half the revenue required to cover costs had been registered. The committee issued a statement informing the public that demand for tickets was steady and they accelerated in the week leading up to the opening. In fact, it was the opening ceremony that was giving the most concern. To avoid the embarrassment of swathes of empty seats and terracing, standing tickets were issued free to school children, students and nurses.

Thursday 29 July was the day of the opening ceremony, and what a day. London threw off its cloak of post-war drabness as it shimmered under a cloudless sky and a burning sun. Londoners in the 1940s were uncomfortable in heat-wave conditions, particularly the men in an age before casual sportswear was generally available. The women and young girls were fine in their cotton frocks, but the men struggled as they put newspapers or a knotted handkerchief on their heads in an attempt to keep cool in what was the hottest day for over thirty years. Still the thermometer rose to a steaming 33.8°C. Sweating people, numbering 80,000, surged towards the entrance, longing for the shade of the stands. First aid stations were overrun as ladies swooned and tough-looking men collapsed. Inside the stadium, the crowd watched the Brigade of Guards Band march, swathed in thick red tunics and bearskins, defying the heat. Those with seats sat on wooden benches, munching their sandwiches. Queues for ice cream and soft drinks stretched into the distance. A souvenir official programme was on sale for a hefty 5s, while the daily version cost 1s.

The royal party, including the glamorous Princess Margaret, was enthusiastically greeted by a cheering crowd. The king was then introduced to the members of the International Olympic Committee. It is extraordinary how many self-seekers and people with dubious pasts manage to obtain high sporting office. This lot included former fascist collaborators and political extremists. They stood proudly, puffed up with their own importance and sweating profusely under their morning coats and top hats. They were soon forgotten as the parade of athletes started, while the temperature continued to rise. The band struck up 'The March of the Gladiators' and the parade was headed, as tradition demanded, by the Greek team. The Irish team had been causing some concern for the authorities since their arrival, with a contingent of over 100, including officials. They had received no financial backing from their government. They even had to borrow money for their travel expenses. They were already grumpy and out of sorts when they finally arrived after a disrupted journey. Then a spat occurred that was in danger of developing into an international incident. Due to lack of funds, the team had only a limited number of uniforms, but more importantly their manager was insisting that they should march under an Ireland banner and not Eire as the authorities had planned. After heated discussion Eire was agreed upon, but a letter of complaint was sent to the international organising committee. Eire, they insisted, was Gaelic, but as other countries were being referred to in English, why, they asked, were they being singled out? Why not España, or Italia?

Tempers were frayed in the British team as well. Last to appear in the parade, they were left smouldering in the heat with few places to seek the shade. Although the team was given free uniforms, many were ill fitting and far too heavy for the tropical weather. No matter, while not the smartest, at least they marched with a military precision (most of them had been in the services during the war). The crowd rose in unison to give the team a noisy and emotional welcome. This was a chance to show a fervour not normally associated with the British. It was a mass outpouring of national pride that Britain had endured, survived and was now looking forward. It was as if they wanted the world to witness this too. Many were surprised at the sense of pride they felt.

At four o'clock Lord Burghley invited the king to declare the games open. Without a single stutter the king said, 'I proclaim open the Olympic games of London, celebrating the fourteenth Olympiad of the modern era.' Trumpeters sounded a fanfare and a huge Olympic flag was hoisted. It was the same flag that had been used at each Olympics since 1920 in Antwerp. Thousands of pigeons were released and from outside the stadium came the sound of a twenty-one-gun salute. Then a tall, blond figure appeared at the tunnel entrance. With theatrical timing he paused before holding the Olympic torch aloft to another burst of impromptu applause.

A few miles away at Stoke Mandeville hospital, the inspired neurologist Ludwig Guttmann was organising a sporting event for severely injured ex-servicemen. It was the forerunner of the Paralympics, which gave hope and dignity to a group who formerly had been sidelined and ignored.

The heatwave continued and intensified for the first day of competition. Over the next two weeks, Olympic and world records would be smashed. The games also introduced the public to some extraordinary characters, two of whom appeared on that steamy Friday. The first medals awarded were for the women's discus, and the winner was not a lumpy Russian nor a bulging Bulgarian, but a slender Frenchwoman of unusual talent. Micheline Ostermeyer was tall, willowy and attractive. She was 5 feet 11 inches in height and her main athletic event was the high jump. Having only taken up the discus a couple of months prior to the Olympics, she was only entered by having come third in the French national championships. It was with her last throw that she won the Olympic title, although it was 20 feet under the record set in Berlin by the Nazi blonde Gisela Mauermayer. How the lithe Frenchwoman managed to beat all the beefy specialists in the event remains a mystery, but no-one was more surprised than Micheline. Astonishingly, athletics came second in her list of priorities. Micheline Ostermeyer had graduated from the Conservatoire de Paris with honours and hoped to become a concert pianist. This ambition had to be put on hold as she amazed the world again by winning the women's shot put. It was the first time the event had been held at the Olympics and the last time a truly feminine figure triumphed. She was by now acclaimed as a national heroine, and with her best event still to come a third gold seemed possible. This event also proved to be historic, although the long-legged Micheline could only bag the bronze meal. The gold was won by Alice Coachman of the United States, who narrowly beat Britain's Dorothy Tyler. Although they both cleared the same height, Coachman achieved this at her first attempt. It was a disappointment for Britain and France, but Alice Coachman became the first black woman to win an Olympic gold medal. It was only subsequent events at Wembley that prevented Micheline Ostermeyer becoming 'the face' of the 1948 Olympics. Later, her musical career took wing, as for years she toured the world as a concert pianist, but she always maintained that 'sport taught me to relax; the piano gave me strong biceps and a sense of motion and rhythm'.

On the first day of competition, a new legendary figure burst onto the world scene. Emil Zátopek was a young Czech army lieutenant who, like Micheline Ostermeyer, was physically an unlikely candidate for Olympic success. Neither good-looking nor long-legged, he was bald and puny, appearing much older than his twenty-six years. There were thirty entrants for the gruelling 10,000 metres race. By the start at six o'clock it was still hot and humid. Astonishingly, some of the runners had been advised not to drink the day before the race, confining their intake to a little liquid honey. The need to drink in order to replace liquid in the body while running in searing heat was not understood at the time. Pounding round the cinder track under the fierce sun soon had several runners dropping out from dehydration and heat exhaustion. They should have realised the dangers, as earlier in the afternoon some of those competing in the high jump had collapsed.

Zátopek appeared close to collapse himself. Every step appeared to mangle him through a pain barrier, which was difficult to watch. His tongue lolled from the side of his mouth and his face was contorted into a frightening grimace. His head nodded from side to side as if every step was to be his last. Despite the contortions and seeming agony he was putting himself through, by the tenth lap the Czech was in the lead. He was introducing a technique later to be refined by the Russian Vladimir Kuts. While maintaining a steady lap speed of seventy-one seconds, Zátopek would alternate between an injection of speed followed by a slower pace. This enabled the other runners to catch him up, at which stage he accelerated again. It confused them and broke their resolve. The world record-holder Viljo Heino and his Finnish teammate Evert Heinström were crushed. Heino was one of seventeen to collapse during this race, and still the iron man from Czechoslovakia was surging towards a new Olympic record. The crowd went mad as he started lapping the other standing competitors. Only two were saved that ignominy as Zátopek went on to win by 300 metres. Even then the drama was not over, as the timekeeper rang the bell for the last lap one circuit early. Luckily Zátopek had kept his own count and carried on, but others too exhausted to care didn't. It caused a real rumpus over the minor placings, but the crowd didn't mind, they had just witnessed the arrival of a new superstar.

Three days later the weather had changed and the 5,000 metres final was held on a rain-soaked track. Zátopek had been in a hard-fought heat, but was still favourite to win. Tiredness obviously took its toll as the Belgian runner, Gaston Reiff, made a break for glory with four laps to go. At the bell, Reiff led Willem Slijkhuis of Holland by 20 yards with Zátopek another 30 yards adrift. Zátopek now called on all of his reserves. With his head rolling as if it was about to become detached, he dredged a final surge which gradually developed into a genuine sprint. The crowd chanted his name as if at a political rally. They suffered with him as he forced his racked body forward. He passed the Dutchman and set off in pursuit of Reiff. He revved up his speed yet again. Mud- and cinder-splattered, he was catching the Belgian with every stride. No-one remained in their seats, shouting, screaming, Záto-pek, Záto-pek. Reiff, at last sensing the danger, lengthened his stride, winning by 0.2 of a second. Pure theatre, real drama – and there was much more to come.

On the second day of competition, the sun still bore down from a cloudless sky, heralded as the race for the fastest man on earth. It is over in the blink of an eye and yet it is a contest that still excites and intrigues today. In Berlin, much to Hitler's fury, the title had gone to Jesse Owens, who won four gold medals, including the 100 metres. Ironically, Owens was ignored by his own president on his return to a country bedevilled by segregation and prejudice. 7s 6d was enough to secure a good seat at Wembley to watch men who had been inspired by Owens. These included three Americans, including the favourite Mel Patton, the thirty-year-old Barney Ewell and Harrison Dillard. Also fancied was the Trinidad-born British sprinter McDonald Bailey. They had all fought their way through a series of tough heats and a capacity crowd of over 80,000 waited expectantly as the athletes went to their blocks. Harrison Dillard was the world record-holder for the 110-metre hurdles, who had unexpectedly not made the US hurdles team by failing in the Olympic trials. He had made it into the sprint selection as third choice, but in the final he led from the gun. The runners crossed the line in a blur and for the first time the result was verified by a photo-finish camera. After a tense wait, Dillard was pronounced the winner over his fast-finishing compatriot Barney Ewell. Another shock was that the Scottish sprinter Alastair McCorquodale finished fourth, relegating the more fancied McDonald Bailey to last place.

No event emphasised the spirit of the Olympics more than the marathon. A race of 26 miles and 385 yards, it was the distance covered by Pheidippides, a Greek messenger who ran from the Battle of Marathon to Athens. By 7 August, the British weather had offered the athletes a full menu ranging from burning heat to tropical deluges. Luckily, the day was relatively cool, but still humid for the forty-one runners who set off by completing a lap of the Wembley stadium before heading north towards Kingsbury. I stood with a couple of friends as the runners headed towards Borehamwood and Radlett. We cheered them all – the leaders and the stragglers. Some almost floated across the tarmac, while others gave an impersonation of the tortured Emil Zátopek. It was a testing course over hilly countryside and by the time the runners returned to Stanmore on the final stretch towards Wembley, many were suffering.

The most fancied British runner was the national cross-country champion, Jack Holden, but he developed severe blisters and retired towards the midway point. We had no idea as the runners made their way past us that the scene was being set for one of the most sensational finishes in Olympic history. As Holden faltered,

Étienne Gailly of Belgium took up the running. Despite it being his first marathon, Gailly had opened up a gap of over forty seconds by the 25-kilometre mark. During the next 10 kilometres he was overtaken by the Korean runner Choi Yun-chil, who had established a lead of twenty-eight seconds at the 35-kilometre post. Making a move was an Argentinian fireman, Delfo Cabrera. Now it was Choi's turn to crack, and approaching Olympic Way Gailly was again in the lead but looking exhausted. He was being chased by two runners, one of whom was Tom Richards, a thirty-eight-year-old Welshman living in Tooting. With just half a mile to go Gailly led Cabrera by 50 yards, with Richards a distant third. Entering the stadium, the disorientated Belgian staggered the wrong way onto the track in a clockwise direction. Alerted to his mistake, he turned, finally setting off in the right direction. The finishing line looked a lifetime away. He had nothing left to give. He didn't care, he just wanted it to be all over. Drunkenly, he tottered forward. It was terrible to watch, only instinct driving him on. It was a repeat of the 1908 London marathon, involving Dorando Pietri, who collapsed in sight of the finishing line. The Belgian appeared to be in a daze as first Cabrera and then Richards passed him. He staggered and stumbled, urged on by the crowd to finally claim the bronze medal and his place as one of the all-time plucky, unlucky Olympic losers.

There was no doubting the heroine of the London games. Her achievements were so great that in 1999 she was declared 'female athlete of the century' by the International Association of Athletes Federation. Francina 'Fanny' Blankers-Koen was already thirty years old by the start of the London Olympics. She was also a housewife and mother of two young children. Surely, she was too old to ward off eager young competitors from around the world. The Olympic rules decreed that she could only enter three individual track and field events. She decided to concentrate on the sprints – the 80-metre hurdles, the 100 and 200 metres, while joining her Dutch teammates in the 4x100-metre relay. Astonishingly, she chose not to compete in either the long or high jumps, in both of which she held the current world records.

Although there were over 4,000 competitors covering the various events, less than 10 per cent were women. Even in

1948 it was considered somehow unseemly for women to exert themselves unduly. They were even denied entry into disciplines where they were known to excel, like equestrianism. They were only allowed to enter in nine athletics events. Quite why these should include the heaving of a discus or the shot put was strange. There were problems and suspicions relating to women's athletics. Two sprinters in the 1946 European Championships had subsequently been found to be men; however, nobody doubted Fanny's femininity. She was tall, with incredibly long legs and flowing blonde hair. She eased through the heats and semi-final of the 100-metre dash. By Monday 3 August the heatwave had given way to torrential rain which was still bucketing down as the final approached. Despite the puddles, it was really no contest. Fanny's long legs took her ahead from the start. Her style was strange to modern eyes, leaning back as she approached the tape, beating the British sprinter, Dorothy Manley, by a full 3 yards. The following day she was back on the track to compete in the 80-metre hurdles. The weather had deteriorated further to swamp conditions. Her major threat for this event came from a glamorous nineteen-year-old British girl, Maureen Gardner. Each won their heats and avoided each other in the semi-finals where Gardner only managed third place after hitting a hurdle. No matter, the British press was convinced that Maureen was about to become the nation's 'golden girl'. The British team manager made a mistake by saying in public that he thought Fanny was too old. It is always dangerous to dishonour a champion. For once, Fanny had a very poor start, but she kept cool and by the halfway mark was level with Maureen Gardner. Being so close, they both faltered slightly, but throwing herself at the tape, Blankers-Koen seemed to have just edged it. The result of the photo finish appeared to take an age, but Fanny was announced the winner and again a British athlete had to settle for silver. Both shared the time of 11.2 seconds, a new Olympic record.

Fanny had been competing for six days and she felt tired, depressed and was missing her children. It took a deal of persuasion for her to agree to compete in the 200 metres. She set a new Olympic record in her heat, having obviously rediscovered her appetite for competition. The rain continued to deluge – the track was muddy and covered in puddles for the final. Fanny was unstoppable. She decimated the field, winning by an astonishing 7 yards, which still remains the largest winning margin in the event today. Once again, a British runner, Audrey Williamson, came second. It appeared that British girls were destined only to be the bridesmaid and never the blushing bride.

Fanny joined three good friends to form Holland's 4x100-metre relay team. They won their heat but were not favourites to win the final. Taking the anchor leg, Blankers-Koen watched helplessly as the Dutch squad fell well behind the strong Australian team. By the time she took over the baton the Dutch had slipped to fourth place. Wearing her baggy orange shorts, Fanny set off in what appeared to be a hopeless pursuit. She reckoned she ran as she had never done before. She was inspired, eating up the ground, her hair flowing in the breeze. The crowd were on their feet, not even cheering for their own country, but for a woman who was changing the face of women's athletics and, more importantly, of a woman's place in a fast-changing world. Not too old, not too weak, a mother. Here was proof that in life anything is possible. With just a few yards to the tape, Fanny went into the lead and earned herself a fourth gold medal. Typically, she was not just pleased for herself, but for her less-talented friends and teammates. Modesty and huge talent are a rare combination.

America dominated the track and field events. Perhaps their most notable victory was obtained by a seventeen-year-old from California. The decathlon is the most demanding of any event and the winner can rightfully be acclaimed the best all-round athlete in the world. Bob Mathias became the youngest male athlete to win gold, although he was lucky because Heino Lipp from Estonia was not allowed to enter as Estonia was now annexed by the Soviet Union. A week after the Olympics, Lipp recorded a points total in his home country that would have easily won him the gold, but the American teenager remained a hero in the States.

Of course there was a huge range of events taking place away from Wembley. Britain recorded their best success at the Herne

Hill Velodrome, winning a medal in each event, eventually bagging three silvers and two bronzes. Gymnasts and archers, boxers and weightlifters, all strained for success. From Bisley to Torquay, and venues dotted around London, some of the world's finest athletes competed in a games that still honoured the amateur tradition. Back at Wembley, even the football competition was contested by those who played for fun. England was coached by Matt Busby, but even he was unable to weave his magic with the willing band of part-timers. The final was won by Sweden, who beat the Yugoslavians 3–1 in the final.

Since 1912 in Stockholm, the arts had also competed for Olympic recognition. Baron de Coubertin had hoped that the modern Olympic games would be an outlet for artistic expression as well as sport. Categories included music, painting, sculpture and literature. It soon became obvious that the entries in London were going to be limited. Works had to have been completed since 1944 and many well-known artists and musicians were concerned for their reputations should their entry not win. Sir Alfred Munnings, never shy of publicity, entered two dozen works, none of which were eligible, having been painted before the cut-off date. Other well-known artists did submit entries and the gold medal was awarded to the prolific artist and Royal Academician Alfred Reginald Thomson. While medals were awarded in other categories, including the gold for 'Olympic Symphony' by Polish composer Zbigniew Turski, overall the standard of entries was disappointing. For future Olympics, it was decided that entries could be made, but that London was to be the last where medals were awarded.

After two weeks, during which records had tumbled and extreme weather had added to the excitement, another capacity crowd waited in anticipation of the final event. Here was an indication that outdated practices still existed in sport. The equestrian events were not only restricted to men, but only to those who were commissioned officers. This had massive implications for the Swedish winners of the team dressage event held earlier at Aldershot. It was discovered that Gehnäll Persson was a mere sergeant. Months later he was disqualified and Swedish team gold was awarded to France. None of this concerned the crowd at Wembley, which was to stage the hugely popular showjumping events. Britain was fancied to do well in both the team and individual sections, but it was the Mexicans who caused a major upset by winning gold in both. To the crowd's delight, Britain did claim the bronze in the Prix des Nations (the team event). The course was so difficult that only three of the fourteen teams managed to finish. One British competitor, Colonel Harry Llewellyn, riding his famous horse Foxhunter, would shortly raise the profile of showjumping so that it subsequently became popular prime-time viewing on television for years to come.

With the thrills and spills of the showjumping over, there was a sense of sadness as the arena was cleared for the final ceremony. Despite the rousing music of the Brigade of Guards, it was a low-key event. The Olympic flag was lowered and the flame extinguished. London could reflect with satisfaction on having organised a successful Olympic games despite all the difficulties. It was the innocent games, the last before professionalism ruthlessly elbowed its way in. A games that, like London itself, was on a cusp, waiting to see what was going to happen next.

16

Major Changes: The NHS and the Arrival of the *Windrush*

Each Monday morning, just as George Elrick was introducing the first record on *Housewives' Choice*, our front doorbell would ring. My mother would always have a tray with tea and biscuits ready for our visitor. Mr Foster was the representative of Cook and Shutler, our local grocery. This was convenience shopping 1940s style. He was always smartly dressed, whatever the weather, although his bicycle clips rather compromised his overall neat-and-tidy look. This was no fast-talking, confident salesman. I thought him too deferential, even obsequious. He sat at the dining room table with my mother, his order book open. She had made a list of her known requirements and he wrote them down slowly, thanking her for every packet of tea and few ounces of bacon. He had a strange habit of licking the point of his pencil as the order began to fill the page of his duplicate pad (I often wondered if he eventually died of lead poisoning). With the list now seemingly complete, he would gently make suggestions of other products which might have been overlooked. This genteel form of shopping was concluded at a leisurely pace before Mr Foster cycled off to his next customer. The following day the order would be delivered to our house by a young boy riding a three-wheeled bicycle, with a large pannier situated behind the saddle to carry the provisions.

This was 1948 and witness to a dying form of pre-war shopping which was to prove unsustainable. Individual service was about to be overwhelmed by one of the three major events that were about to change Londoners' lives during the year. Enter a retail revolution – the supermarket. Not Tesco or Sainsbury – they were waiting in the wings. Take a bow, the London Co-operative Society. Self-service shopping had existed in the United States since the early thirties. Its migration to Europe had been postponed by the war, except in neutral Sweden. A pilot scheme had been tried by the Co-op in their Romford store back in 1942, but it was thwarted by lack of suitable shop fixtures. So it was early in 1948 that the Co-operative Society introduced the people of Manor Park to the wonders of self-service. They were quickly followed by Premier Supermarkets, who opened their first self-service store in Streatham. Marks & Spencer were always among the first to transfer American enterprise to the home market, and they converted the food section of their Wood Green store to self-service early in 1948.

At first the London housewife was nervous about the new innovation. Previously, handling goods led to a suspicion of shoplifting. It didn't take long for them to get the hang of picking goods from the shelves and placing them in the wire baskets provided. It was easy, but tempting as well. Best of all, it cut down on queuing. Premier Supermarkets recorded an incredible tenfold increase in sales. Others entering the modern retail world reported more modest gains, only doubling or trebling their previous turnover. Pile it high and sell it cheap had arrived and the independent grocer was left stranded. Most were unable or unwilling to invest in completely refitting their shops. Like so much of British industry at the time, they failed to react to change. Hopefully, they reasoned, if ignored, the new format would fail and disappear. Within months Mr Foster stopped calling on my mother. The shop struggled on for a few more years before closing.

Britain's doctors were also suspicious of change, but they were submerged by government policy rather than market forces. The National Health Service was the flagship at the heart of the ambitious and radical legislation introduced by the Labour government since their election in 1945. The economist William Beveridge had laid down some of these aspirations in his 1942 report. He identified 'five giant evils' which needed to be eliminated. They were 'squalor, ignorance, want, idleness and disease'. Some of these are still with us today and probably always will be, but tackling public health was to be Labour's greatest legacy. Prior to the introduction of the NHS, many people put off going to the doctor, thus harbouring problems that could have been helped by early treatment. I saw my own parents weighing up the necessity of calling out the doctor for a cost of 7s 6d. Money for most people was tight.

The implementation of the NHS was in the hands of the cherubic-looking, lisping, Welsh firebrand Nye Bevan. He was determined to ensure that Britain would be the first Western country to introduce free medical care for all, based on need rather that the ability to pay. First, he had to overcome the deep-rooted opposition of many doctors. We all find change difficult, particularly if it is being imposed on us. A former Secretary of the British Medical Association upped the rhetoric by insisting that what Bevan was proposing was 'uncommonly like the first step towards national socialism as practised in Germany'. Surely rather wide of the mark when addressing a left-wing socialist. Bevan's plan had the great advantage of clear-cut simplicity. All hospital services were to be brought together in a single system. There would be fourteen regional hospital boards and they would be overseen by local management committees. Teaching hospitals were to be directly responsible to the Ministry of Health, thus serving the nation and not just the locality. Dentistry and eye tests were also to be free, with referral notes from GPs being required by opticians. The doctors and consultants remained unhappy. It was time for some 'horse trading', a skill that Bevan employed effectively. Bullying mixed with charm drew an agreement from the medics. Concessions were granted to the consultants. They were allowed to retain some of their hospital pay beds and the ability to practise privately. He won the GPs round by promising they could be paid by the number of patients they treated rather than just a straight salary. In return, they conceded their right to buy and sell their practices. Always one to have the last word, Bevan reckoned he had 'stuffed the consultants' mouths with gold'.

5 July 1948 was known as 'Enabling Day'. Overnight, the NHS had become one of the world's largest employers and a

massive, bloated bureaucracy. Within weeks, well over 90 per cent of the population had registered with a GP. A huge pent-up demand for treatment saw bulging waiting rooms at surgeries. Hospitals struggled to cope with the increased demand, while chemists were overwhelmed with requests for prescriptions. It was as if the entire population had been carrying on with a huge range of complaints and aches and pains. Raging toothaches too, apparently, as waiting lists for dental treatment stretched into weeks, sometimes months. At a contribution of 4s 11d per week, it amounted to almost 5 per cent of an average income, but was still judged to be good value by most.

It didn't take long for serious worries to develop over the costs of implementing the service. There was evidence of a cavalier approach of prescribing on demand by some doctors. Within a year, millions of free spectacles had been prescribed; even the follicularly-challenged could apply for a free wig. It was as if we had become a nation of hypochondriacs. The government had budgeted for a cost of £140 million for the first year of the NHS. The actual figure weighed in at over £200 million. Alarm bells were ringing, but it seemed the doctors and administrators were not listening. They were spending with all the abandon of a winner on the football pools. The following year, the budget was set at a staggering £350 million. The Chancellor of the Exchequer demanded cuts to the hospital-building programme. Most of the existing hospitals dated back to the Victorian era and hardly represented this brave new world envisaged by Bevan. He fought savagely against other proposed cuts. He knew he had the support of most of the population. The NHS was the high point of post-war idealism. Even today, a free health service at the point of use remains sacrosanct. It is as British as roast beef or fish and chips. It will take a brave or, more likely, foolish politician who seeks to take this right away.

On 22 June 1948 an ex-German troop carrier docked at Tilbury. A month earlier it had set sail from Kingston, Jamaica with some 500 West Indian men and one female stowaway. They were to be the first of a wave of immigrants from Britain's former colonies and Empire. In time, they were going to help change the character of life in London and other major cities throughout the country. At the end of the war it was estimated that there were no more than 30,000 non-whites living in Britain and this figure had not increased in the interim. Immigrants had arrived in the country, mostly from Europe, and had been assimilated without any major problems. Many had gone to work on the land, while others arranged employment work in existing family businesses. Although some of the *Windrush* passengers were servicemen returning to their units, the prospects of hundreds of West Indians arriving with no jobs to go to caused alarm in government circles. A spokesman for the Colonial Office warned that a disorganised rush of West Indian immigrants would be a disaster. Labour minister George Isaacs added his weight, stating that 'the arrival of these substantial numbers of men ... are bound to result in considerable difficulty and disappointment'. Sensing trouble, the Ministry of Labour even tried to delay the arrival of the *Windrush*. Colonial Secretary Arthur Creech-Jones realised that the men were entitled to come to Britain. With a misplaced confidence that appears to be a requisite of British politicians, he predicted, 'I do not think that a similar mass movement will take place again.' He remained sanguine, assuring anyone who would listen that the men 'wouldn't last one winter in England'. A spokesman for the Ministry of Labour perpetuated that myth. Caribbean workers would be 'unsuitable for outdoor work in winter due to their susceptibility to colds and more serious chest and lung ailments'. His real thoughts (shared by many) came when he concluded 'many of the coloured men are unreliable and lazy'.

So they arrived, these 500 or so trailblazers for the thousands to follow. They came dressed as they imagined a typical Englishman would look, wearing smart suits and trilby hats. In fairness, this initial group was welcomed by well-meaning clergy and church-going locals. Jobs were sought for them while they were housed in a wartime deep shelter in Clapham by the London County Council. Later, many were re-housed in Brixton, which became one of London's first centres for the West Indian community.

Iris Chapple had lived in Brixton all her life and was ten years old when the first West Indians arrived. She and her mother had survived the war despite being bombed out twice. Brixton was already home to many nationalities, which added to the vibrancy of the community. Her mother rented a room to a Hungarian refugee whose cooking made the young girl realise that food could be wonderfully tasty rather than just filling. Something to be enjoyed rather than the usual overdone meat and watery sprouts. She was invited to taste delicious goulash. She loved the smell of paprika wafting its way through the house. It was the smell of foreign food that first alerted Iris to the arrival of the West Indians. Tantalising smells and sensational sounds. Music like she had never heard before. She had been dancing since she was five and showing real talent and a natural sense of rhythm. Most of the West Indians were living then in Somerleyton Road and Craven Road. On a warm summer evening, the young Iris would stand and listen to the music booming out. She found the new arrivals were really friendly, but already the white population were resentful. Neighbours warned her about mixing with these black men. Soon KBW (Keep Britain White) graffiti started appearing on walls and shop fronts as more immigrants continued arriving. The white population even muttered about the exotic fruit and vegetables appearing on the market stalls – mangoes and peppers. They hated the smell of West Indian cooking and the endless rhythm of their music. To her parents' neighbours, it was hell. Hackneyed stereotypes were being invented. Tales of sexual excess and drug taking were levelled at the newcomers. Certainly, because so few West Indian women arrived early in the migration, the young men were not slow in looking for female company. Their success, albeit limited with local girls, ratcheted up the racial tension. The use of marijuana and heavy drinking probably helped the young men who were doubtless homesick, but also caused further alienation from their white neighbours. Although some cross-ethnic friendships were forged, the scene was being set for an ongoing racial tension. With accommodation in London so difficult to find, huge resentment soon built up. Because of the shortages, the West Indians welcomed successive newcomers into their homes, leading to severe overcrowding. This in turn led to white neighbours vacating their properties, which were then also inhabited by immigrants. The relaxed attitude shown to the African Americans during the war was a distant memory as neo-Nazi groups began to be heard across London. Crooked landlords realised there was money to be made. This was the beginning of difficult times for successive waves of immigrants. Hostility was to spiral over the coming decades before Britain groped its way towards a multi-racial society.

Racial integration was unlikely to appeal to a man who had been married in the house of German propaganda minister Joseph Goebbels. It had been a small, private ceremony, also attended by Adolf Hitler. It was natural that the far right in British politics would look to Oswald Mosley for leadership after the war. Instead, in 1946, he purchased a 1,000-acre estate in Wiltshire. Crowood was an eighteenth-century manor house and he settled into the life of a 'gentleman farmer'. He also wrote a couple of books; the first, *My Answer*, set out to justify his previous actions while promoting himself as a resolute British patriot. He followed this in 1947 with *The Alternative*, in which he set out his ideas, which were to form the basis for his Union Movement. He wished to see Europe speaking with one voice on the major areas of defence, foreign policy and economics, while leaving other, less important, sectors to be carried out by local governments. These rather lofty aims provided a cover for his ongoing hatred of the Jews. By 1948 he was again organising provocative marches in the East End, where he continued to enjoy some support. Still a relatively young man, Mosley continued to believe in his destiny, supported by his wife Diana.

Writing to her sister, Nancy, Diana described going to a May Day meeting in the East End: 'It wasn't a great success because the police kept everyone away, friend and foe alike.' A march had been arranged in defiance of a ban and Diana, together with other supporters, found herself cut off. 'We always seemed to be almost in a terrifying procession of young and very strong-looking Jews who were chanting "Down with Mosley" ... I kept fearing we would be recognised and overwhelmed.' Their luck held that day, but the Union Movement was racked by internal disputes and gaining little support outside of a hard core of racists. Deaths of British troops in Palestine created more tension, but Mosley was now in danger of becoming a laughing stock as opposed to a threat. Britain was just not fertile ground for flag-waving, ranting politics. Disappointed at not being recognised as an inspired visionary, the Mosleys went off to live in Ireland. Later they moved to France, forming a friendship with the Duke and Duchess of Windsor. Two disillusioned couples with time on their hands to ponder where it all went wrong.

Back in London, the incumbent royals were doing rather better. Princess Elizabeth was performing the vital function of any royal dynasty by producing a son and heir. Crowds assembled outside Buckingham Palace were informed by a policeman, 'It's a boy', although they had to wait for the christening to learn that he was to be called Charles. Bells were rung at St Paul's and Westminster Abbey, while the fountains in Trafalgar Square were illuminated with blue lights. A royal birth was always good for public morale, but the press had already decided that Princess Margaret was likely to provide stories with a little more spice. Unfortunately for them, protocol restricted their reporting and it was left to the Continental press to cover her increasingly colourful love life. As an eighteen-year-old, she already attracted a stream of eligible young men. Blue-eyed and petite, she tended to wear very high heels and heavy make-up. She was described as being 'high spirited to the verge of indiscretion'. Her wish to appear informal, yet demanding due deference, created her an enigma, and she continued to fascinate observers for the rest of her life.

It was not just the royal household who sought to regulate what information was to be circulated to the general public. The BBC was being at its most protective when it produced its guide for writers and producers, known as the 'Green Book'. It sought to eliminate coarseness and vulgarity from all its programmes. Humour, 1948 style, had to be 'clean and untainted directly by association with vulgarity and suggestiveness'. This was quite at odds with the history of the British music hall, which had been the main source of public humour prior to radio. The list of restrictions neutered most areas of traditional comedy. No jokes about infidelity, honeymoon couples, effeminate men, prostitution, religion, politics or physical peculiarities. Not even the mildest form of swearing, such as 'ruddy', 'my God', or even 'damn' was allowed. 'Auntie' BBC had decided to project a totally unrealistic world. Comedians like Max Miller, who relied on good, wholesome vulgarity, were cast aside. It was left to a clever young Frankie Howerd to get round the restrictions by the use of innuendo. This buttoned-down BBC approach was also used to a lesser extent in British films. We were a nation being fed a diet of life that defied reality.

As the year progressed, conditions for most improved, but only imperceptibly. Bread rationing ended in July and there was an easing of clothes rationing. Less coupons were now required, allowing major items like suits and overcoats to be purchased. The West End stores were now full of 'The New Look' fashions. Another breakthrough came with footwear being taken off ration in September. Despite these concessions, London was still only running at half-cock. The Regent Street Association was anxious to brighten up the West End for Christmas, but was forbidden to light the Christmas trees that lined the street. Instead, Londoners headed to the first motor show to be held since the war. This was window shopping on a vast scale. Well over half a million visited Earls Court over ten days. They crowded round the gleaming new models from Ford, Vauxhall, Rover and Jaguar. They queued to sit in models and makes that have now disappeared from the showrooms, like Hillman, Humber, Wolseley and Sunbeam Talbot. There were salesmen with nothing to sell, as most of the industry's production was being compulsorily reserved for export. The *Daily Express* dubbed the event 'The biggest please do not touch exhibition of all time'. Of course, the public did touch. They caressed these sleek saloons with the longing and ardour of a hopeful lover. Maybe unobtainable for now, but offering a glimpse of opportunity for the future.

17

Looking Forward

Khaki uniforms, bell-bottomed trousers and air-force blue were still seen throughout London long after the war ended. From the beginning of 1949 even more military uniforms appeared with the introduction for the first time of peacetime conscription. The National Service Act of 1948 required all young men from seventeen to twenty-one years old to serve in the armed forces for a period of up to two years. Only those working in the mines, on the land or serving in the Merchant Navy were exempt. Suddenly, all of London's major railway stations and crowded tube trains were clogged with young squaddies sporting severe haircuts and struggling with bulging kit bags. Britain's continuing overseas commitments made conscription a necessity. As well as protecting our interests abroad, it was felt that a little military discipline would be good for a generation of young men thought by many to be feckless and lacking in a work ethic.

For a few weeks, basic training threw youngsters from totally different social backgrounds together. It was here that class and education again emphasised the gap that continued to exist in British society. Commissions were granted almost exclusively to those with a public school education. Even those with exceptional qualifications were likely to be denied entry into the officer class if they had a heavy regional accent. National Service in the late forties offered a perfect mirror for British society. One where opportunity was often denied to those with genuine talent, given instead to those with the right connections. The old boy network was in full flow and suspicion of those from outside your social class remained as ingrained as ever.

A new, influential group which didn't fit comfortably into any of the class groups were those who had made fortunes during the war. Hard-working, savvy entrepreneurs and super-spivs were now appearing in increasing numbers at London's swankiest hotels and restaurants. Establishment figures looked on in horror as these nouveau riche were fawned over by staff who had previously exclusively devoted their attention to them. The wartime food restrictions on the price restaurants could charge remained in place, widening the clientele base still further. A set price of 5s would still secure a meal at restaurants such as La Belle Meuniere in Charlotte Street or at Rules (London's oldest restaurant), but subject to a house charge of up to 2s 6d plus a 10 per cent surcharge. For those wanting a night out, dinner with dancing at the Trocadero in Shaftesbury Avenue was on offer at 9s 6d, while round the corner at the Piccadilly Hotel, it would set you back 11s plus a 10 per cent surcharge.

At these prices it was possible for a middle-class couple from the suburbs to enjoy an occasional night out 'in town'. Certainly, the 1940s housewife deserved it as hers was a life dedicated solely to endless house chores, plus looking after her husband and family. The day began by cooking breakfast and seeing her husband off to work and the children to school. Monday mornings were devoted to laundry duties. Forget washing machines, wash-day was hard labour. While she waited for the water in the metal copper to heat, the dirty washing was divided into whites and coloureds. The whites, which went in first, would have been scoured with soap. Each bubbling wash was then poked with a wooden stick until it was reckoned to be clean. Each wash load was then rinsed in the sink before being hung up to dry. With a small family the task was likely to take all morning. The ironing would then be squeezed in sometime during the week, but the workload was non-stop. Each day was a continuous round of hoovering, dusting and cleaning. Then there were beds to be made, fireplaces to be cleared and re-laid. Daily shopping was arduous, with endless queues. There was no one-destination shopping, instead the housewife would have to trudge round a variety of specialist shops, lugging increasingly heavy shopping bags. Alternatively, she could pile her provisions into a wicker pannier on her 'sit up and beg' bicycle. Whichever, her list of jobs was endless and tiring and our 1940s housewife would then be expected to change in time to greet her 'hubby' home, looking fresh and glamorous so he could regale her with the tribulations of his day. So London's suburban housewife was due an occasional night out. A trip to a theatre was often favourite with perhaps a late night supper at Josef's in Soho Square or maybe Albert's in Beak Street. For the more adventurous, a visit to one of London's reputable 'bottle parties'. Here, at places like the Astor or the Coconut Grove, for a contribution of about 17s 6d it was possible to party until four o'clock in the morning. Obviously, food and wine also had to be paid for. Some men chose to entertain a hostess rather than their wife. Then, perhaps feeling a tinge of conscience, it was off to a Turkish bath to unwind. Jermyn Street or Northumberland Avenue were generally thought to be the most agreeable.

Still London continued to look drab and tacky. Much of Oxford Street was given over to garish amusement arcades with pinball machines and tawdry sideshows. There was some good news with the ending of clothes rationing in March 1949. Although the West End stores showed a healthy sales increase in women's wear, the lack of available material for manufacturers led to shortages. Money was also still tight for most householders. The fashion gap was filled to a great extent by home dressmaking. Whole departments were given over to dress patterns, with Butterick being the market leader. Ancient Singer sewing machines were kept busy as an army of do-it-yourself dressmakers attempted to knock up the latest fashions.

Shortage of money extended across society. In 1947 it was reckoned that there were only thirty-seven people living in the UK with an income of over £10,000 after tax. The attempt to reduce inequality by the tax system was strangely accompanied by a general fear of communism. This was highlighted when partners at John Lewis stores were required to sign an agreement stating they were not members of the Communist Party, nor had any sympathy with their doctrines.

So gradually the streets of London started to witness fashion-conscious young women appear after years of 'make do and mend'. No matter that many of the creations had been run up at home. An appreciative student was recorded as saying, 'It is pleasant to see as the young women discarding their square fashions are wearing garments that let everyone see they have a curve here and there.' Good news indeed.

Good news is invariably followed by bad in Britain. Sweets were taken off ration in April 1949, but the rationing was cruelly reintroduced four months later due to excessive demand. Then London dockers came out on strike. Much of the ships' cargo was meat and other perishable food. The government sent the troops in and the bitter dispute lasted for almost three weeks. During July and August, Sir Stafford Cripps, the Chancellor of the Exchequer, languished in a Swiss sanatorium. There had been months of bitter discussion about the merits of devaluation against the US dollar. With Britain's reserves running down, Cripps warned that without action there would be a complete collapse of the pound. Hardly endorsing the urgency of the situation, the chancellor, along with Foreign Minister Ernest Bevin, set sail for the States. Bevin was also ill and had been advised not to fly. The sickly pair had been authorised to agree with the Americans the extent to which the pound was to be devalued.

At a meeting at the British Embassy in Washington, a rate of $2.80 was agreed against the pound. This was, effectively, a 30 per cent devaluation against the previous rate of $4.03 and was a decision that was going to affect everyone in Britain. It had wider, instant implications, leaving tourists abroad stranded as foreign banks refused to accept pounds. The announcement caught the public off-guard and many didn't understand the full implications; it substantially increased the price of imports, while making our exports cheaper. Cripps explained, in a broadcast, that not devaluing would have led to huge unemployment and a drastic reduction in social services.

Strangely, it was the artistic community that highlighted some of the changes worrying the wider population. Changes in society brought about by a raft of government policies, culminating in the devaluation of the pound, were seen as bewildering by older, reactionary figures. Two events in 1949 magnified the void that existed between those welcoming and others resisting change towards a more modern society. It was Sir Alfred Munnings, the president of the Royal Academy, who caused something of a sensation when speaking at their annual banquet. It was his passing shot before stepping down. He had been president since 1944, the same year that he received his knighthood. Munnings was the arch-traditionalist. He hated the changes taking place in the country, particularly the continued march towards greater modernisation. Despite his humble beginnings, his unique talent for painting horses in stately settings had led to constant commissions from the great and good.

He was a difficult man, witnessed by his first wife's attempt to commit suicide while on their honeymoon (she succeeded later). He had a reputation for being bluff to the point of rudeness. Encouraged by his friend Winston Churchill, and emboldened further by a mixture of sherry and champagne, he rose unsteadily to address the distinguished guests. His speech was covered by BBC radio so the broadcast was heard by millions of listeners. Although at times almost incoherent, his message was clear. He said, 'I find myself president of a body of men who, shall we say, are shilly-shallying. They feel there is something in this so called modern art.' He blundered on to say he would rather have a damn bad failure of a picture than all the affected juggling. 'If you paint a tree, for God's sake, try and make it look like a tree!' He had previously described work by Picasso as 'queer distortions'. As Munnings sat down there were cries in support, but also derisive laughter. The switchboard at the BBC was overwhelmed with calls from the public, mostly supporting Munnings' view. Not so from the more informed and influential, who pilloried him as an out-of-touch reactionary. A memorial plaque in St Paul's Cathedral for the artist erected ten years later reads:

O friend, how lovely are the things
The English things you help us to preserve

Back in 1949 there was an influential body of opinion which didn't want to just preserve loveliness. These people sought to stretch boundaries. Not just in art galleries, but on the stage too. It was another figure who was thought to be conservative, if not completely reactionary, who polarised public opinion further when he presented a controversial play by the American Tennessee Williams. *A Streetcar Named Desire* had opened the previous year in New York to packed houses. A posse of English managers pursued the producer, Irene Mayer Selznick, in an attempt to secure the London production. Irene Selznick was born into Hollywood 'royalty'. Her father was Louis B. Mayer, a founder of MGM Studios, and her husband, David Selznick, had produced the epic film *Gone With the Wind*. Irene was shrewd and not about to be rushed into a decision. She made enquiries and was assured that Binkie Beaumont was the man she needed. She was also warned to beware of his charm as he was a ruthless negotiator. He met her from the airport and, despite the warning, she had already been won over by the time his Rolls-Royce pulled up outside Claridge's, where he wined and dined her and a long-lasting friendship was formed.

Although Binkie's reputation had been built on a diet of light comedies and classics, he didn't flinch from a play that he knew would cause great controversy and offence. The male lead of Stanley Kowalski had introduced the world to the animal magnetism of an unknown Marlon Brando in New York. A perfect match for the hard-drinking salesman and poker player, who was given to beating up his pregnant wife, Stella. The uncouth ogre brought a rawness that had not been seen previously on a London stage. Binkie was convinced that the part of Blanche could have been written for Vivien Leigh, but there were snags. The author, Tennessee Williams, and Selznick wanted the play to be directed by Elia Kazan, who had been responsible for the Broadway production, but Vivien Leigh would not appear unless Laurence Olivier was given the job. This agreed, the opening had to be delayed for the couple to honour tour commitments in Australia. The choice for the male lead was also compromised as there were few American actors resident in Britain with a valid Equity card. Eventually, the part was awarded to Bonar Colleano, who was to die in 1958 at the age of thirty-four in a tragic road accident. The combination of the Oliviers and advanced publicity, which emphasised the sexual content of the play, led to record advance bookings. A week before the opening, over 10,000 applications had been received for the first-night performance. Most were disappointed as the Aldwych theatre only had 1,200 seats. Certainly the audience loved the play and Vivien Leigh appeared for fourteen curtain calls. Later, the leading members of the cast went to a party at Binkie Beaumont's apartment to await the press notices. They were mixed with the tabloid headlines screaming 'obscene pornography', 'disgusting', 'squalid, vicious, degrading', 'a trip down a sewage tunnel'. Binkie was delighted. He knew the British public well. Bookings stretched into the months ahead. The *Sunday Press* weighed in with the *Sunday Pictorial*, moralising that the play was 'a garbage heap, a crude bellowing of sex ... the reptile house at the zoo'. On went the invective and up went the bookings. A London cleric described the play as having 'a pathological obsession with sex' and being 'a mark of every dying civilisation from Sodom to Gomorrah'. The most telling comment came from Lady Ravensdale, the chairwoman of the Public Morality Council. She managed to mix high-moral outrage with laughable snobbery when she declared, 'Our senses are being dragged down by the lowest possible denominator. The play is thoroughly indecent and we should be ashamed that our children and servants are allowed to sit in the theatre and see it.'

Like Sir Alfred Munnings, Lady Ravensdale was in denial. Picasso and Tennessee Williams were just two of an increasing army of talent pointing the way forward. The BBC continued to protect the public from anything remotely salacious, as did the film censor. So for a time, realism was being parried away. Escapism and gentle comedy was prescribed by those in authority, who thought they knew what was suitable for public consumption. Paternalistic maybe, but it spawned a number of classic British films. The West London suburb of Ealing had been a centre for British film-making since the formation of Associated Talking Pictures back in 1929. During the next two decades, the studio built a reputation for producing comedy films starring the likes of Gracie Fields and George Formby. The quality improved after the war with *Hue and Cry* in 1947 and two years later Ealing Studios released three films in quick succession, which cemented their reputation for a uniquely British genre. Well made and beautifully acted, *Kind Hearts and Coronets*, *Whisky Galore* and *Passport to Pimlico* offered a gentle, civilised reflection on British life. Full of eccentrics, rather goofy young men and innocent young women. This is how the Britain of the late 1940s chose to project itself, but was it true?

In 1949 the first detailed British sexual survey was undertaken by a mass observation group of social anthropologists. They interviewed over 2,000 people chosen at random. The results were considered so shocking that the findings of the report were suppressed for over fifty years. The image of the English rose, all twin-set and pearls, was about to be revealed as a sham. The results relating to men were also shocking, but possibly more predictable. A nation appeared trapped in guilt and inadequacy. Ill at ease, bound by convention and an inability to discuss their worries openly.

Unlike the Kinsey report (known in the popular press as the 'K Bomb') undertaken the previous year in the United States, Britain's 'Little Kinsey' included women in their investigation and it was probably their response that had the authorities running for cover. Obviously, the war had changed attitudes and opportunities for sexual activity. Young men stationed abroad, away from the restraints of parents and families, sampled the delights of many a foreign brothel. Back home, their sisters and girlfriends were frequently bowled over by the attraction of GIs or men in uniform generally. Outwardly, most continued to agree that sex should be confined to the marital bed, but the report suggested that many were only paying lip service to the idea. Certainly, young women had to exercise much greater care before the availability of the pill. A combination of ignorance and many men's cavalier attitude to contraception led to numerous unwanted pregnancies. The report blew apart the façade of a prim and proper Britain.

A key finding revealed that 25 per cent of men had been with a prostitute. The true figure was probably far higher. It was reckoned that this was due to men not wanting to submit their wives to their wilder fantasies. For their part, women reported that their husbands submitted them to sex at its most basic level, devoid of love or tenderness. Many felt trapped in loveless marriages, with sex seen just as an unwelcome duty. An extramarital affair was something 20 per cent of women admitted to having had. Sensationally, the same percentage had been in a sexual relationship with a female partner. Men had to be extremely careful in admitting any gay activity as male homosexuality was still against the law, but again one in five volunteered the information. The result of the survey suggested a population confused and embarrassed by sex and their own sexuality. It was normal for women to deny having had sex prior to marriage, but not for men. Was it hypocrisy or just common sense that perpetuated an outdated moral code? Whichever, London was reckoned to have more prostitutes than any other European city.

There had been an exodus of some 70,000 British girls who elected to marry GIs and go and make their home in the States. Some, predictably, lived to regret their decision. It was estimated that 10 per cent of these marriages ended in divorce. Jean Sporle, living in Hammersmith, remembers two neighbours returning home totally disillusioned. Their expectations had been too high. One woman told Jean that, stupidly, she had left London expecting Hollywood-style living, but was actually subjected to a life of squalor in New York. Exaggerated promises of a millionaire lifestyle had left another Hammersmith girl feeling cheated, lonely and homesick. Luckily, others found a warm welcome and long-term happiness. I remember a daughter of a neighbour returning home with her husband. Within a couple of years she had acquired an American accent, a fur coat and her own Chevrolet tucked away in their garage back in New Hampshire. How we envied her.

So the most tumultuous decade in London's colourful history was drawing to a close. Much had changed over those years, but it remained a London so different from today. No computers or mobile phones. No young people sitting on the tube listening to their MP3 players. Instead, rows of heads bowed as if in prayer, reading. It was not unusual for commuters to plough through twenty titles a year. If not books, newspaper sales were at record levels. The *Daily Mirror* sold 4 million copies a day and on Sundays that figure was doubled by the *News of the World*. London also had its own evening papers, the *Standard News* and *Star*. There were few black or brown faces, but legions of cloth caps and genuine Cockney accents. There were no Starbucks, but Lyons tea shops. Fridges and televisions were a rarity and washing machines unheard of. Tall, bulky policemen pounding their beat were always visible. There was little hooliganism or street violence. On the surface it was a place of conformity, but still edgy and ever-changing, never letting you totally relax.

In 1949, for the first time since the war, Christmas trees lining Regent Street were illuminated. Celebrations were more festive. A few managed to buy a turkey and chickens were plentiful. By New Year's Eve, Londoners were ready to party. The liveliest and most outrageous event was the Chelsea Arts fancy dress ball. Londoners had lived through possibly the most momentous decade in its long and turbulent history. It had lost some of its sense of community fostered during the war years. Old divisions had reappeared. Yes, London was still drab and grimy, but there were the first faint signs of a better future. For the moment, there was no 'big brother', 'double think' or 'newspeak', the frightening world outlined in George Orwell's novel *1984*, published earlier in June. London is the great survivor, taking whatever the centuries throw at it. London is exciting and excitable, turbulent and unpredictable, constantly reinventing itself. It also has a darker side that runs just beneath the surface. It took an Irishman, William Butler Yeats, to capture this when he wrote, 'This melancholy London – I sometimes imagine that the souls of the lost are compelled through its streets perpetually. One feels them passing like a whiff of air.'

Stand for a moment on Shaftesbury Avenue outside what was the US Rainbow Club and half-close your eyes. It doesn't take a great deal of imagination to cut out the noise of modern-day life and to transport yourself back seventy years. You sense the cluster of GIs and pretty girls all around, and in the background the music of Glenn Miller. The ghosts of London past are always there, if you look for them.

Acknowledgements

My particular thanks to the following, whose recollections made this book possible:

Jean Picton, Rocky Knight, Jean Sporle, Iris Chapple, Sylvia Cooney, Raymond Cooney, Jean Clarke, Iris Rose Robinson, Robin Burns, Brenda Burns, Ann Spiers, Brian Abbott, Jack Pleasant, Terry Norton, June Hewitt, Pat Desbruslais, Michael Switzer, Patricia Weber, Peggy Weber.

Roger Fry for his constant help and encouragement.
Joan Beretta for transcribing my illegible writing and her knowledge of photographic history.

Also:

Judy Faraday, archivist, the John Lewis Partnership
Susan Scott, archivist, The Savoy Hotel
Staff at the Ritz, Grosvenor House and Dorchester hotels
Staff at the Museum of London
Staff at the Jewish Museum, London
Staff at the Westminster City Archives
Rob Marriott, archivist, Wetherbys
The Artur Lloyd website

Photographic Acknowledgements

The author is grateful to the following for permission to reproduce the illustrations used in this book:

Amberley Publishing
Judy Faraday, archivist, the John Lewis Partnership
Susan Scott, archivist, the Savoy Hotel
Mary Evans Picture Library
Getty Images
J & C McCutcheon Collection
Susan Angel
Jane Kerner
Gary L. Moncur
Windmill Theatre Company Ltd
Peggy Weber

Select Bibliography

Bishop, Patrick, *Fighter Boys* (Harper Collins, 2008).

Breese, Charlotte, *Hutch* (Bloomsbury, 1999).

De Courcy, Anne, *The Viceroy's Daughter* (Webbenfield & Nicholson, 2000).

Donovan, Paul, *The Radio Companion* (Harper Collins, 1991).

Foster, Andy, *Radio Comedy 1938–68* (Virgin, 1996).

Gardiner, Juliet, *Wartime Britain* (Headline, 2004).

Hampton, Janie, *The Austerity Olympics* (Arum Press, 2008).

Hobhouse, Hermione, *Regent Street* (Philmore, 2008).

Hopkins, Harry, *The New Look* (Secker & Warburg, 1964).

Huggett, Richard, *Binkie Beaumont* (Hodder & Stoughton, 1989).

Jackson, Alan A., *London's Metroland* (Capital History, 2006).

Laver, James, *Costume & Fashion* (Thames & Hudson, 1969).

Linnane, Fergus, *London, The Wicked City* (Robson Books, 2003).

Lovell, Mary, *The Mitford Girls* (Little Brown, 2001).

Lycett Green, Candida, *John Betjeman Letters 1926–51* (Methuen, 1994).

Marr, Andrew, *A History Of Modern Britain* (Pan Books, 2008).

Matanle, Ivor, *World War II* (Colour Library Books, 1989).

Montgomery-Massingberd, Hugh, *The Ritz* (Arum Press, 1980).

Morley, Charlotte, *The Mitfords* (Fourth Estate, 2007).

Morton, James, *Gangland* (Little Brown, 1991).

Nicol, Jean, *Meet Me At The Savoy* (Museum Press, 1952).

Porter, Roy, *London, A Social History* (Hamish Hamilton, 1994).

Soames, Mary, *Speaking For Themselves* (Doubleday, 1998).

Summers, Judith, *Soho* (Bloomsbury, 1989).

Sweet, Matthew, *The West End Front* (Faber & Faber, 2011).

Thames, Richard, *Sporting London* (Historical Press, 2005).

Thomas, Donald, *An Underworld At War* (John Murray, 2004).

Waugh, Evelyn, *The Diaries of Evelyn Waugh* (Penguin Books, 1982).

Wallechinsky, David, *The Olympics* (Arum Press, 2000).

Ziegler, Philip, *London At War* (Pimlico, 2002).

Index

Also available from Amberley Publishing

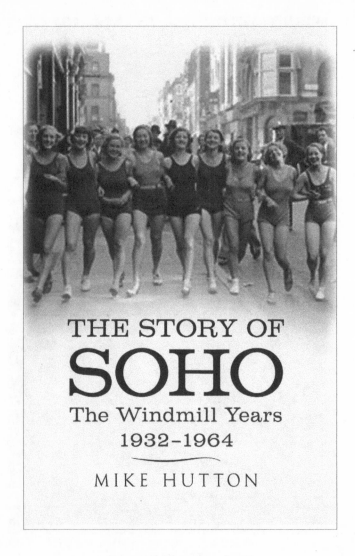

THE STORY OF
SOHO
The Windmill Years
1932–1964

MIKE HUTTON

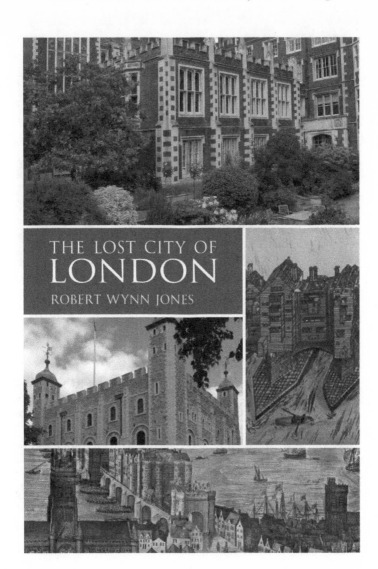

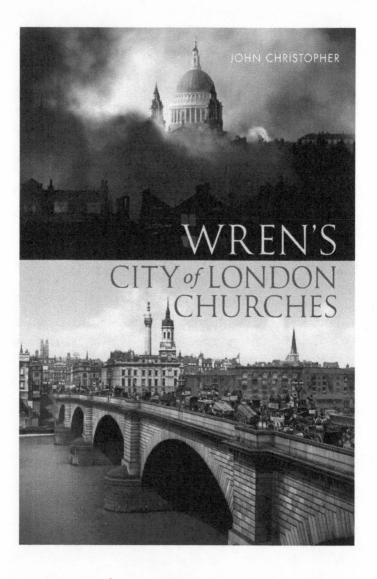